FAIR TRADE AND A GLOBAL COMMODITY

Coffee in Costa Rica

PETER LUETCHFORD

Pluto Press

LONDON • ANN ARBOR, MI

First published 2008
by PLUTO PRESS
345 Archway Road, London N6 5AA
and 839 Greene Street,
Ann Arbor, MI 48106

www.plutobooks.com

British Library Cataloguing in Publication Data
A catalogue record for this book is available from
the British Library

Hardback
ISBN-13   978 0 7453 2699 3
ISBN-10   0 7453 2699 4

Paperback
ISBN-13   978 0 7453 2698 6
ISBN-10   0 7453 2698 6

Library of Congress Cataloging in Publication Data applied for

This book in printed on paper suitable for recycling and made
from fully managed and sustained forest sources. Logging, pulping
and manufacturing processes are expected to conform to the
environmental regulations of the country of origin.

10   9   8   7   6   5   4   3   2   1

Designed and produced for Pluto Press by
Chase Publishing Services Ltd, Fortescue, Sidmouth EX10 9QG, England
Typeset from disk by Stanford DTP Services, Northampton, England
Printed and bound in the European Union by
CPI Antony Rowe Ltd, Chippenham and Eastbourne, England

FAIR TRADE AND A GLOBAL COMMODITY

WITHDRAWN

Anthropology, Culture and Society

Series Editor:
Dr Jon P. Mitchell, University of Sussex

RECENT TITLES

CONTENTS

To Helen, Alex, and Nathan, who came with me,
and Eva and Isabel who arrived later.

ACKNOWLEDGEMENTS

During the writing of this book I have accumulated debts too many to mention, some intellectual and some personal. First and foremost it would not have been possible to write without the people of El Dos, Costa Rica. Their generosity in adopting my family into their lives was a humbling experience that we will never forget. I am similarly indebted to all the cooperative staff and managers in the Coocafé group. In particular, Juan Carlos Alvarez Ulate opened many doors and is an inspiration in his work. The spirit of openness and transparency of the Costa Rican people we came to know has led me to use real names, only obscuring identities when I feel discretion is necessary. Many who touched our lives deeply appear between the pages, and this book is my small testament to them.

Intellectually, my greatest debt is to my supervisors and mentors at the University of Sussex. Richard Wilson believed in me and supported my project from the start. Jeff Pratt has guided me through difficult times with sensitivity and compassion. His support has been unwavering, and his wisdom during our shared intellectual journey is an inspiration – he has become a true friend. Over the years numerous other people have contributed to the genesis of the book. I especially wish to thank James Carrier, James Fairhead, Jon Mitchell, Sutti Ortiz, Geert de Neve, David Lewis, David Mosse, Jock Stirrat and Pete Stewart for the encouragement, guidance and help they have given me in various guises and at different times. Comments on and gentle criticism of some of the material has been made at seminars, conferences and workshops at Sussex, the LSE, Goldsmiths and Oxford Brookes. Fieldwork was made possible by a generous grant from the Wenner-Gren Foundation for Anthropological Research, and the British Academy and the Nuffield Foundation generously offered funding for a return visit.

Finally, my family have helped and supported me in different ways and at different times. Mark Luetchford deserves special mention for planting the seed in the first place, and for remaining a great friend and brother. His energy, enthusiasm, optimism and commitment is awe-inspiring and infectious. Helen had the courage to pursue the Costa Rican adventure, and without her this book would never have seen the light of day. She, along with my children, has taught me more about life and love than words can tell. This book is dedicated to them.

ACRONYMS AND PROPER NAMES

Asociación de Desarollo Integral:	Integrated Development Association
Asociación Latinoamericana de Pequeños Caficultores:	Latin American Small Coffee Farmers Association
ATO:	Alternative Trade Organisation
BNCR:	National Bank of Costa Rica
BANCOOP:	Cooperative Bank
CAE:	Agro-economic Consultancy
CCMC	Central American Consortium for Cooperative Marketing
Coocafé:	Coffee Cooperative Consortium of Guanacaste and Montes de Oro
Coopeldos:	Coffee and Multiple Services Cooperative of El Dos de Tilarán
Fedecoop:	Federation of Coffee Cooperatives
FODESAF:	Family Development Fund
Icafé:	Institute of Coffee
IMAS:	Institute of Social Security
Infocoop:	Institute for the Promotion of Cooperatives
MAG:	Ministry of Agriculture and Livestock
PLN:	National Liberation Party
R.L.:	*Responsibilidad Limitada* (Limited Responsibility)
VIVIENDA:	National Government Sponsored Housing Programme

GLOSSARY OF SPANISH TERMS

a medias:	a sharecropping system whereby half the product from the land goes to the landowner and half to the landless labourer
adelanto:	the first payment, or 'advance' made by the processor on delivery of coffee
aguas mieles:	the contaminated water that remains after wet-processing of coffee
argullo:	cartel or 'trust'
asociado:	cooperative member
ayote:	a root vegetable
beneficio:	coffee-processing plant
brete:	shackles or fetters
broza:	the fruit pulp that remains after removal of the coffee bean
en cereza:	coffee still in the fruit or cherry
café oro:	processed coffee before it is toasted
cafetal:	coffee grove
cafetalero:	coffee farmer
cajuela:	box used to measure picked coffee in the field = 20 litres
campesino:	rural person who makes a living from agriculture
caña:	sugarcane
canasta:	basket (into which coffee is picked)
chamol:	a root vegetable
colones:	Costa Rican unit of currency ($1 was worth about 520 *colones* in 2007)
criba:	a revolving cage used to separate different qualities of coffee during processing
despulpador:	processing machine that removes the fruit from the coffee bean
en firme:	illegal practice of buying coffee outright upon delivery
evangelico:	Protestant evangelist
fanega:	standard measure for coffee at the processing stage = 400 litres

finca:	(small) farm
frijoles:	red beans, a staple
fuerza:	force or strength
gancho:	hook used to hold down branches while picking coffee
jornalero:	day labourer
jugar(se):	play (juggle); used with reference to economic endeavour
junta	assembly or council
liquidación final:	final payment and gate price of coffee
lotería:	lottery; used with reference to the market
lucha:	struggle
manzana:	most common measurement for land area = 7,000 square metres
mercado alternativo:	alternative market; the usual name for fair trade at the production end of the market
monte:	wilderness, wilds, uncultivated land
nica:	Nicaraguan
parcela:	plot of land
patrón:	employer
peón:	labourer employed on a regular basis by a *patrón*
pilón:	A shallow basin designed for hand-washing clothes
por el gasto:	food grown for home consumption
pulpería:	general grocer
reajuste:	instalment in payment for coffee
recibidor:	collection point for coffee
rendimiento:	weight in kilos of green coffee extracted from one *fanega* of unprocessed coffee
si Dios quiere:	God willing
tantear (los precios):	act of moving between buyers in order to get an optimum price
tico:	Costa Rican
tiquisque:	a root vegetable
tope:	festival involving tests of horse-riding skill

INTRODUCTION
APPROACHING FAIR TRADE:
COFFEE IN COSTA RICA

'From the culture of small producers' proclaims the message on the tin of fair-trade coffee on my desk. Underneath the words a group of women and men in colourful dress stand in a sea of hessian sacks we presume contain coffee. The scene is obviously Latin American, though there is a mix of races, cultures and styles. The men wear Western shirts and long trousers; one sports a cowboy hat, another a baseball cap. The women are more traditionally dressed, and their clothes and their faces suggest a blend of the indigenous and the European: a *mestizo* culture. The picture illustrates the words, evoking an unknown world of coffee production; we cannot tell exactly where the people come from but we assume they are small farmers. They smile and look content, secure and comfortable. The photo alongside the logo contrasts with mainstream generic brands and is meant to reassure.

The stark, white background makes the message stand out, but the figures float free of context and much is left to the imagination. Ultimately, the picture and the words are a sign, a symbol, a promise, which is what allows the packaging to succeed. But we are left with a nagging doubt, a desire to know more about the people who grow our coffee and the conditions under which it is produced, and we are concerned that the deals that bring such an intoxicating, flavoursome stimulant into our daily lives might be exploitative. This wish to connect to and 'know' the producers in a world and a market that sets them apart inspires increasing numbers of people to buy ethically branded goods. But can the products be trusted, and do we really 'know'? The purpose of this book is to help meet that desire for knowledge by providing some of the missing context to the highly emotive subject of fair-trade coffee.

When I began to work on Latin America, coffee economies and fair trade some ten years ago, the idea of ethical commercial exchanges, in which consumers are invited to pay a premium to guarantee prices to producers, was in its infancy. The fair-trade concept had emerged after the Second World War and had maintained a niche into the 1980s (Grimes 2005; Tallontire 2000). Emerging from the political fringes, it was popular among activists and favoured by development groups, but had yet to gain the popularity and exposure it now enjoys. Today, web searches return millions of hits – you can read testimonies from farmers, are persuaded by campaigns and publicity, and may buy merchandise online. Total sales of fair-trade goods in Britain have escalated from a reported £16.7 million in 1998, to £195 million in 2005.[1] But in the early 1990s there were little data available, and scholarly engagement with the subject was in its infancy. Information came from advocates of an alternative trading system, which gave a view from the North (Barratt Brown 1990; Coote 1992), or visiting representatives of farmers needing new trade outlets, who came to speak to activist groups. Consumption at that time was inspired more by politics than the quality of coffees such as Africafé or those promoted by the Nicaragua Solidarity Campaign, which were, by common consensus, almost undrinkable.[2] Nevertheless, such products were important precursors to the current vogue for alternative goods, since they showed that some consumers wished to politicise shopping.

The sea change in Britain began in the early 1990s with a conscious effort by a consortium of NGOs to enter the mainstream coffee market.[3] By 1993, their product, Cafédirect, had jostled its way onto the shelves of national supermarket chains, a timely achievement given the collapse of the International Coffee Agreement in 1989. As a pact between producer countries, this agreement had regulated the supply of coffee, curbed overproduction, and kept prices reasonably stable. With its demise, activists pointed to the sad plight faced by producers in an unregulated market; prices fell disastrously for a sustained period, with only a brief respite in the late 1990s. As has been graphically illustrated by the Oxfam campaign that implies a bitter brew by showing a cracked and leaking cup and a drinker looking distastefully into her mug, producers receive a very small part of the amount consumers pay for their daily cup of coffee (Gresser and Tickle 2002).[4] Popularising the issue put fair trade on the mainstream development map; for the first time it became more than a minority political campaign. But increasing visibility and success in the North generates its own tensions, reflected in debates among NGOs about 'mainstreaming'. The political legacy of oppositional politics remains, but there is also the capacity for business to incorporate fair trade into commercial strategies in order to extract more profit. A key question is the degree to which fair trade is compromised by success and dragged into the economic imperatives of exchange. To what extent are fair-trade goods distinct from corporate brands, given the propensity for the latter to claim the moral high ground and incorporate fair trade into their marketing strategies?[5]

There seems little doubt that shoppers want to show concern and solidarity with growers through acts of generosity. A central feature of the fair-trade project is the desire to draw producer and consumer together; this is why it puts real people on its packaging, and it is what the brand name Cafédirect is intended to evoke. In ethical consumption the aim is to break down and demystify the distance between parties in the exchange and accentuate the relation between them. One approach would then consider issues of 'connectivity' and shared meanings, with implications of intimacy or trust, operating through producer groups and alternative trading organisations, whose motives go beyond the purely commercial desire for profit.[6] The aim is to follow Harvey's call to 'lift the veil' on the conditions under which the things we consume are produced, and take seriously our material and moral connections to other people (Harvey 1990; Hudson and Hudson 2003; Lind and Barham 2004). Foodstuffs, it would seem, and exotic ones in particular, are remarkable vehicles for that desire. They often transcend great distance to enter the most intimate moments of our sensory lives (McMichael 2000). The combination of proximity and distance lends to foods a capacity to encompass and satisfy a broad range of aspirations (Pratt 2006). For example, part of the attraction of fair trade lies in its ability to evoke 'cultural others' and yet draw upon traditions of localised food and family-based subsistence activities that exemplify the production-consumption link in our mind's eye (Carrier 1995; Friedmann 1999). This allows it to draw popular support and appeal to consumers from across the political spectrum.

Conversely, there is a more pessimistic strain that identifies a tendency for alternatives to be appropriated by capitalist enterprise. It has been recognised since at least the days of Marx that the labour process and the origin of goods are obscured in modern production regimes. Indeed, the ability of capital to monopolise and then package the qualities of goods is a key component of the ability to generate profit (Harvey 2001). The implication is that an unresolved paradox lies in alternative trading relationships, which is exacerbated by commercial success. The contradiction lies in the desire to build and maintain an alternative economic space by revealing the conditions of production and forging connections between producers and consumers, and the enormous capacity of capitalist enterprise to monopolise those conditions by keeping producers and consumers at arm's length and profit from the distinctive qualities imparted to goods at the point of origin. Work on fair trade has to varying degrees, whether consciously or not, engaged with such conundrums.[7] Some scholars seem to reproduce an optimistic populism by pointing to the creation of production-consumption links, the extension of trust across space, and the construction of an alternative to mainstream markets. Others draw on wider ideas about governance and regulation in the food industry (Lowe, Marsden and Whatmore 1994), from whence it is a small step to deconstruct the whole fair-trade edifice and show how it is subsumed to capital and market rationality.[8]

Despite diverging opinions on the transformative potential of fair trade, most studies to date focus on institutions and the formal relationships between organisations. Data are often generated from 'grey' literature, websites or interviews with managers and other executives. Producer groups are frequently understood from the perspective of preferential trade agreements, so that organisations come to exist only as 'fair-trade cooperatives', a misconstrued term that also appears in the media. In this way local, regional and national histories and struggles are elided from accounts. Another outcome of this institutional focus is a lack of engagement with or understanding of the complexities of the political economy of coffee growing. As a result farmers are often placed in a catch-all category of small producers or smallholders, so scholars tend to reproduce popular conceptions of coffee economies. There is little or no recognition of the enormous difference in livelihoods and options facing a farmer with a hectare or less, and a neighbour with five or even ten hectares of coffee, let alone large landowners who grow a little coffee as one agricultural option.[9] More disturbing still is the failure to acknowledge the invisible reserve army of landless poor, women, children and migrants who harvest coffee yet often lead the most precarious and marginal existence of all.

A second notable feature of the literature to date has been the lack of sustained attempt to explore fair trade as a specifically cultural concept, at least as this is understood within anthropology. Rather than taking culture to be a matter of conventions,[10] it is important to understand the commitments and meanings that people express and adhere to in their everyday lives. From there it is possible to relate fair trade to wider ethical ideas and the existing and longstanding literature on moral economies. Taking an ethnographic approach puts people, location and history into the account while at the same time opening up a discussion on the moral 'problem' of trade.

MEETING THE PRODUCERS

In August 1998 I flew to Costa Rica with my young family, driven by curiosity about coffee production and the ethical and political ideas that fair trade draws upon. After a few days we travelled north to the blustery town of Tilarán in the northwest highlands. It was a relaxing, friendly place with a little market, a range of small shops selling basic goods, a taxi rank, street hawkers, a municipal park, administrative offices and schools. There was even a coffee cooperative, but not a coffee bush to be seen. Tilarán felt like an outpost; beyond lay the countryside, a land of rolling agricultural hills, with pastures and coffee plantations, interspersed with patches of woodland and larger areas of forest. I spoke to the hotel manager. His brother was a coffee grower and a key member of a producer cooperative called Coopeldos, which the receptionist described as 'the best coffee cooperative in the world'. His sister had a house to rent in a place also called El Dos. We hired an off-road taxi for the afternoon and paid a visit. The house felt neglected, but we had a close neighbour, and it was near the village shop, the telephone and the bus stop. We bought some basic secondhand appliances in town, loaded up a hired truck, and bounced out of Tilarán down 25 miles of rutted dirt track, towards our new home.

So, within a week of our arrival, my family moved into the somewhat damp bottom half of a house in rural Costa Rica. The settlement we came to is one of many dispersed across the countryside, with houses and farms strung out along a complex network of tracks. Outside our back door was a tropical garden full of exotic fruit, unknown animals, weird insects and colourful birds. Despite vague warnings about snakes and other dangers, this became the children's playground. Close by was forest, into which parrots flew in colourful clouds and where booming *mono congo* monkeys called at first light. To the left, in the shade of avocado trees that dropped their fruit on passers-by in alarming fashion, were rows of coffee bushes. To the right lay outhouses, a cattle shed and green pasture with grazing black and white cows, which made it strangely reminiscent of the England we had left behind.

We stayed in the village for a year; it became the only place the youngest of us remembered as home. We travelled out more than the locals; we went to visit other cooperatives and to San José to arrange visas, but like other villagers we put on better clothes for the bus trip to town and became mesmerised on our visits to the capital by the flashy displays in the alien, consumer-driven world of the downtown shopping malls. With the locals we rose early and lived the daylight hours, scrubbed our clothes by hand in a *pilón*, picked coffee in the warm but driving rain, and wandered the hillsides with our adopted dog, visiting neighbours and more distant farms and making new friends and acquaintances. I learnt about coffee from farmers and picked it till my fingers became wrinkled and raw. The cooperative staff taught me how they process the beans, and the manager told me about marketing, business strategies and the cooperative's history. Above all, I talked to local people about their lives and ideas, visiting them in their homes and in the fields, and I soon adapted my European *castellano* Spanish to the Central American accent and local vocabulary. Having a family made for easy acceptance though my conversations, and social interactions, in keeping with local practice, gravitated largely towards other men.

Many of the people I spoke to at great length were elderly. There was Carlos, who lived in a house surrounded by coffee trees, set back from a track not 100 yards from where he was born more than 70 years ago. Retired now after a long life of work, he revelled in relaxation and discussion. He told me about his early life as a coffee farmer, an ox-driver, the string of packhorses he had used to hawk goods to market, and his disastrous attempts at cattle-ranching. He spoke of life before electricity and motor vehicles, of the days when his life was dedicated to brewing maize beer, before his conversion to evangelical Christianity. Even older was Amadeo, who had arrived barefoot in the 1920s, had gone on to build up a successful cattle business, but also grew coffee. He was most commonly found sitting on the veranda of his house, amazed at the tourist traffic threading its way to the nature reserve at Monteverde, but always ready to converse and tell stories about his life and the old days.

Other elderly residents had to get by on the meagre state pension, supplemented by whatever they could turn their hand to. There was Juan Pedro, always scraping around for work and money, who lived with his wife, daughter and grandson in a very bare and basic two-room house he had built on a small patch of unproductive donated land. Washing always hung outside his place, rain or shine, and the yard was decorated with old tins, plastic bags and rusting pieces of metal. More productive was the little garden opposite in which Felix grew a vast array of fruit and vegetables, as well as coffee that he processed and roasted at home. He kept chickens, and cows that he fed with grass collected from the roadside and transported by wheelbarrow back home. This earned him the sobriquet 'Mr Wheelbarrow', but the dairy products he produced gave vital income to feed his family. Carlomagno was equally keen on kitchen gardening but did it on a more extensive scale on the edge of the small coffee plantation that he still worked diligently, despite being in his sixties. Then there was Chico, a Nicaraguan who had been around as long as anyone could remember and was so old people made jokes about it. He lived down by a gurgling river in an old shack with an earth floor and invited us to visit to collect oranges from his trees, which he refused to sell although he accepted our 'donations'. Despite his crooked hand and bent back he was incredibly tough and continued to work long hours in the fields. We often met him shuffling along in the countryside as he moved from one job to another.

Two things struck me particularly about the lives of the people of the Tilarán Highlands. First was the resourcefulness of people in making a livelihood. Many people there have more than one income stream, often working in different types of agriculture and combining this with other ways of earning money. For example, women have jobs in the cooperative offices or clean the houses of better-off families, cut hair or run small businesses, while husbands grow coffee and supplement this by producing fruit and vegetables, repairing appliances or doing waged agricultural work. If a family owns more land they are more likely to produce milk, or keep cattle for beef. But landless people have nothing to sell but their labour power. They can be reasonably successful, as Miguel was in his work as a carpenter, but most landless people generate income from a limited range of economic pursuits – coffee picking, milking and clearing land; outside of the harvest season, work can be hard to find. In this way the image, both in our minds and projected on packaging showing small landowning farmers producing only coffee, which is also a central theme in Costa Rican national identity, is revealed as a simplification. To describe these different roles I use the terms grower, farmer and producer to refer to landowners, and labourer, worker, *peón* or *jornalero* to refer to the landless. Pickers and harvesters are generally, though not always, without land. *Campesinos*, on the other hand, may equally own land, or not.

The second striking feature is the way people's lives are framed by social and moral context, particularly the family and the household. So although I have spoken of individuals it would be more correct to consider their activities as embedded in social relationships. As we shall see, extended families commonly work together on projects. What is more, if a person has no land, they often need to rely on wealthier, landowning neighbours to give them work. When this involves cooperation within and between families who own land there is an easier correspondence with the vision of a society of small producers evoked on the label of my tin of fair-trade coffee. But when agreements are between landowners and workers the relationship is framed by patronage and inequality; it can still be couched in terms of moral responsibility and social duty,[11] but it is more difficult to reconcile with the notion of fair trade for independent producers.

OVERVIEW OF THIS BOOK

To consider fair trade as a serious project for establishing ethical relations in the economy this book follows two avenues. The first arises from the material on Costa Rica, based upon extended anthropological fieldwork and the knowledge gained about coffee production and trade at the producer end. The purpose is to explore how growers and cooperative managers understand and engage with fair trade, and ground the deals in social practices, moral ideas and commitments at the local and regional level. At first sight this might seem to compromise the more global aspirations of fair trade, but the deeper underlying purpose of establishing economic relations between producer and consumer as a moral relation and demystifying the distance between them remains. The second ambition emerges out of this; it draws on a long tradition in social and political thought on ethics and economics to show how the concept of fair trade is culturally embedded within enduring moral thinking about the economy. The distance between the worlds of production and consumption might never have been greater than in today's global economy, but the desire to know and make connections between those worlds has not been lost.

The book follows a strain of Western thought which pursues a desire to connect producers to their product. For Marcel Mauss (2002 [1925]) the spirit of the gift impels the product to return to the producer, creating social relationships as it does so. But Mauss also had socialist commitments and worked on behalf of consumer cooperatives to set up more direct links in the economy (Graeber 2001). Marx, on the other hand, begins at the other end; for him our engagement with markets and commodities is pathological because it ruptures producers' relationships with the things they produce, as well as the social ties that are the consequence of productive activity. In this view it is only by working to transform nature that we transform and so realise ourselves as truly, socially, human.

Reading backwards, the privileged connection we wish for producers with their products attracts us to peasant forms of provisioning in which family households are romantically assumed to work their own land, to produce what they consume, and consume what they produce. The idealised household exists in our imagination as an autonomous space outside the impersonal market, in which needs and wants are satisfied from nature and through the mutually supportive and reciprocal activities of family members. When this vision is compromised, because households cannot always produce all that they need, the model allows for exchanges between persons and households, not for profit, but so the house can reproduce itself by accessing things for use through known, personalised, local exchanges. This agrarian vision appears across the political spectrum positioning agricultural production as the privileged domain of economic activity.

The capitalist market presents the flip side of the coin. Here, the separation between producers and their product is near complete. Intermediaries in this scenario can be viewed as agents of exploitation because they step in to profit from the distance between producer and consumer. Our experiences of the world then come to be lived not through our productive activities in transforming nature, but as alienation; alienation from the things we produce, in our relationships with ourselves, with other people, and in our intercourse with the natural world. Because activities based upon relationships then become troubled, the economy becomes a place of uncertainty, danger and exploitation. This essentially Marxian view does not have to be taken as universal; rather it is here understood as a Western cultural model, and it is used to interrogate the manifold attractions of fair trade.

In Northern industrial societies such ideas can but be viewed through a glass darkly, or glimpsed in alternative economic forms such as those proposed by fair trade. Even here the tendency is to worry about, and even give precedence to and so empower, the capacity for capitalism and the mainstream to appropriate and subvert. The case of Costa Rica presented in the pages that follow is somewhat different. As an idealised moral type, the model of the economy outlined above appears here in a starker, purer, light. If one surmises, as Gudeman and Rivera (1990) have done, that economic ideas and practices were transposed from the European context by settlers who came to farm in the new-found world, then by drawing on their ideas on the economy we can better understand our own concerns and, by extension, issues and agendas that have preoccupied economic anthropologists.

The first part of the book focuses on coffee cooperatives and the commodity market for coffee. In Costa Rica cooperatives are an answer to the problem of intermediaries, who trouble the small coffee producer at the centre of national identity. Cooperatives are therefore impelled by practical and moral concerns to maximise returns to producers and excise exploitation. Although fair trade aims to help in this mission, complications arise because it deals in a commodity, and because it operates in the arena of the market.

Chapter 1 presents the history of the Costa Rican coffee economy and charts both the establishment of the social democratic system of government and the rise of the cooperative movement. Following this, I look specifically at those cooperatives that engage with fair-trade deals, reveal the commitments expressed and strategies engaged upon by cooperative managers, and document their experiences of the fair-trade relationship. Although the evidence is that fair trade has played a significant role in helping these organisations achieve their ambitions, there are also difficulties and inconsistencies that need to be taken seriously. Some key tensions are those between cooperative managers' commitments to farmers and the scope to use fair trade to that end; managers' experiences of the fair-trade relationship; problems of participation in a limited market; and anomalies between the demand for quality and the mission to help needy beneficiaries.

The next chapter examines the case of the producer cooperative operating in the village: Coopeldos. The focus is initially upon the history of the organisation and its explicit role in modernising coffee production and processing, and instilling development at the local level. Again, it is recognised that fair trade has a part to play in this process. From there, I consider the sometimes turbulent relations between the cooperative and its members, and locate this within the history of national struggles between producers and processors in Costa Rica. We learn that the demands and issues that farmers have long projected mirror those expressed by exponents of fair trade.

The following three chapters examine coffee production itself. An analysis of the political economy of coffee growing lifts the lid on the simplistic representation of small farmers working for themselves on their own land and growing coffee as a mono-crop. Obviously the realities of agriculture and political economy are far more complex than this in a wider setting; but it is a point that needs to be made and can best be done by close scrutiny of a specific, localised case. The second important point is that farmers and rural people do not consider the market and trade as an arena of life in which fairness is expected. Borrowing from local idioms I show how farmers consider commercial agriculture as an activity circumscribed by risk. Uncertainties emerge from the market, from the labour process and from nature.

Chapters 3, 4 and 5 focus on different sources of risk; I look at how actors strategise in order to cope, depending upon the resources they can bring to bear and the options they possess. To view market agriculture as an arena of risk that requires strategies, as farmers and workers partly do, implies the application of a particular kind of means-ends maximising logic, commonly construed as market rationality. A side-effect of bringing this to view is to lose sight of social and moral inflections in the economy. What is more, because agriculture for the market separates producer from product and transforms the quality of things produced by work into quantities measured in money, it is an alienating activity. In as much as social relations in production are measured in quantities of output and return they become estranged relations. And so far as nature is seen as a source of maximising profit, so the human relationship with the environment becomes strained and unsustainable. Commercial agriculture, viewed as a mix of strategic engagement to negotiate risk, of coercion, and of exploitation, makes the whole notion of fair trade problematic.

So, if fairness is not to be experienced in trade, where can it be found? To answer that question the remaining chapters document the moral evaluations and commitments of farmers and rural people, which are also part of a sustained commentary on economic morality in Western culture. Here we find a reading of the economy in which humans' relations to themselves, to other people, and to nature, take an idealised and contrary form to the money economy.

Chapter 6 pursues the local history of the settlement of El Dos by 'pioneer' farmers who opened up the 'wild' interior in the early twentieth century. Ideas about political and economic rights and duties are embedded in Catholic social doctrine; the importance of and right to own and work land; the earth as provided by God for human sustenance; agricultural work as the source of all value; the household, the family and the farm as central to social life. All these are key themes voiced by local people, but they are also boldly stated in papal encyclicals and pastoral letters written by Central American bishops. In Chapter 7 the values attached to the family and the farm are shown to be extended to local-level associations and self-help groups, which step in to fill the void left by what is commonly understood to be an incompetent and corrupt state apparatus. The operations of local groups, as well as social relations more generally, are activated, inspired and regulated in everyday life by a series of morally laden local terms, such as humility and egoism. These concepts frame relationships and are used to attempt to constrain others' profit-seeking and risk-taking within the money economy.

Chapter 8 brings together ethical and political components by exploring the dissent expressed by farmers towards market interme-diaries of all kinds, including, at times and from certain quarters, their cooperative. I propose that this relates back to the idea that working the earth produces value; intermediaries, who do not engage in manual labour and live from buying and selling, are seen to not properly work and to appropriate value from those who do. This idea underpins the rural people's moral evaluations of the economy. For example, to produce what one consumes and to live directly from the land as an individual or a family becomes an ideal and idealised activity in as much as no one mediates and profits from the value-creating activity of agricultural work.

In the Conclusion these observations, informed by fieldwork in Costa Rica, are linked to moral commentaries on the economy in Western culture. The key theme, which may relate to Romanticism (Kahn 1995), is the reaction to the experience of capitalism. In political economy people concerned with fair trade reject the excessive appropriation by intermediaries of value derived from nature through work. More tellingly, there is a cultural objection to the separation of producers from consumers, production from consumption and the worker from the value that labour creates. By following in the long tradition of attempting to make social and moral links in the economy, fair trade becomes more than a political struggle over the distribution of value down the coffee chain or a charity campaign to help people by 'gifting' them a fair price; it is also a cultural response to an increasingly impersonal market economy.

1 CREATING COOPERATIVES: THE WELFARE STATE, COFFEE AND FAIR TRADE IN COSTA RICA

To situate fair trade in Costa Rica requires knowledge of the social and historical background. This chapter begins that task. It examines regional and national context, the political and social traditions of the country, and provides a short history of the Costa Rican coffee industry. We learn how a group of self-styled marginal cooperatives composed of small farmers emerged to engage with Northern alternative-trade organisations. The political orientations, motivations and experiences of the coffee cooperatives are central to locating fair trade in Costa Rica.

A useful starting point for the study of cooperatives, their politics and trade, which is the subject of this and the following chapter, is the commodity form. I define commodity as an item that has both a use value and an exchange value. For those on the left, influenced by Marx, value derives from the labour that goes into creating an object. In the case of coffee, therefore, value is created by the physical work of growing and processing it. Capitalists can make profits only because they own industrial machinery for processing and because they control the supply from producer to consumer through ownership of exporting companies. Commodity exchange then becomes exploitative; surplus is extracted from the value produced in labour by paying workers less than the value they create.

Although Marx was concerned primarily with industrial labour in factories, his approach informs much of the political agitation for 'trade justice'. It has also been adopted and adapted by value-chain analyses of the coffee industry in discussions about the power of companies, often multinationals, to extract profit by exploiting the productive power of independent family farmers working their own land. Significant value is now generated in the coffee chain by advertising qualities, such as place of origin (a specific country, a certain altitude or a single estate) or the conditions of production (small farms, sustainable practices, organic or wildlife-friendly) and turning them into a quantity, measured in money. For Daviron and Ponte (2005) the trick is then for farmers to 'upgrade' in the chain by appropriating the value generated by the qualities imbued in their product.

Analysing the coffee industry in terms of the capacity to convert 'qualities' into 'quantities' in commercial exchanges tells us much about how transnational markets operate, and the next two chapters explore similar processes at the national level that Daviron and Ponte, among others, discuss in a global context. However, in this book this approach forms part of a larger cultural argument about the way value is realised through certain creative activities and forms of livelihood, which gives a frame of reference outside and in opposition to the market. Clearly evoked and drawn upon by rural Costa Ricans, this politics of value is also part of a Western cultural repertoire that provides a basis for judgments about trade and ethics.

Costa Rican coffee cooperatives are part of the conversation about value appropriation because they are inspired by the need to help farmers impoverished by the capitalist system. It is important to note that the cooperatives are reformist rather than radical. Their ambit is to improve the negotiating power of small landowners in the market, a pressing issue in a country in which small coffee farmers play a key role in the national historical imagination. From this perspective, farmers may control the means of production up to the farm gate, but from then on industrialists corner the commodity market by governing processing and export facilities. The solution offered by cooperatives is for farmers to share ownership of the industrial and commercial sides of the business, and so circumvent private control.

In discussing their efforts to secure a better deal for the cooperative membership, the managers tell a twin tale. They speak of the need for efficiency and modernisation, ideas that are now somewhat out of fashion in development circles (Escobar 1995; Ferguson 1990; Apffel-Marglin and Marglin 1990), but are intrinsic to industrial models of agriculture (Pratt 1994). Coupled to tales of growth and success are expressions of moral commitment to social values; cooperation, participation, sustainability and struggle by the disadvantaged in the face of unfavourable conditions and an unforgiving market. The roots of these dual concerns are to be found in a political conjuncture that can be traced back to the middle of the twentieth century, a time when a rising Costa Rican middle class seized power and put into operation a model of development based upon state intervention and aimed at fostering improvements and efficiency, but with an eye to social reform and welfare. The producer cooperatives of small farmers carry with them the legacy of this approach.

These messages – one moral and social, the other rational and instrumental – at times contradict one another. There are points of conflict in the cooperatives' activities between their collective

and the volcanic mountain chains extending to the northwest.[17] The settlers in these marginal areas began to grow coffee and raise cattle. They are important here as they later founded cooperatives that today supply fair trade markets. For this to come to pass required a series of national events that pushed aside the old coffee order, and saw the rise of a development model that combined state intervention, social welfare, with measures to support cooperatives.

SOCIAL UNREST AND REFORM

The first half of the twentieth century was a period of turmoil and change in Costa Rican political and social life.[18] It was marked by a steady decline in the power of the *cafetaleros*, that small group of wealthy and politically influential families who had controlled the processing and export sides of the coffee industry throughout the nineteenth century. As a challenge to this group, an urban, modernising and rising intellectual bourgeoisie, with their own agroindustrial agendas, began to inject progressive and democratic ideas into the political process. With the introduction of suffrage in 1913, and secret ballots in the late 1920s, the stage was set for a new political order in Costa Rica.

Change was precipitated by economic depression and the rise of the Communist party. The Costa Rican branch of the party was founded in 1931; they quickly gained support amongst the rural and urban poor, particularly in the banana enclave, where conditions were dire and labourers were left without rights.[19] The party attracted followers and gained influence throughout the 1930s. Communist deputies were elected to congress, and in 1934 a strike by 10,000 banana workers rocked the establishment (Winson 1989:42). More pertinent, and documented in the next chapter, was increasing tension between coffee producers and processors, demands for reform and trade justice by growers, and state intervention in the coffee industry.

In 1940 the conservative Calderón Guardia came to power with the support of the Republican party. Calderón had a Catholic background, and had come under the influence of the Catholic sociologist Cardinal Mercier during time spent in Belgium; he declared that his government would adhere to Christian social ideas (Calderón 1942, cited in Palmer and Molina 2004:136; Williams 1989:109). A series of papal letters, or encyclicals, had previously laid the foundations for Catholic social doctrine, and these ideas had then been pursued and developed by Mercier and the National Union of Social Studies.[20] Proposing a 'third way' between unbridled capitalism and radical left-wing politics, they advocated state reforms to help the poor, emphasised social harmony over class conflict, and stressed the sanctity of the family, individual freedom and the necessity for social justice. This had a profound influence on both the Costa Rican church and on political life; in 1943 the *'Rerum Novarum* Labour Organisation' was formed (Miller 1996; Williams 1989). To implement the Catholic model Calderón and the reform-minded head of the church, Monsignor Sanabria, entered into an unlikely pact with the leader of the Communist party, Manuel Mora. They ironed out their differences and together proposed reforms. These encompassed specific guarantees, including a bill of rights, a social security system and a labour code, as well as the principles of the protection of family life, work as a social imperative and support for cooperatives (Paige 1997:143; Williams 1989:109). Social Christian doctrine, by permitting a rapprochement with the Communist party, had laid the foundations for the much-lauded Costa Rican welfare state, and for a development model based upon state intervention and cooperatives.

By the end of the Calderón era politics had descended into intrigue and accusations of corruption, and by the 1948 elections the political process was in disarray. When the election results were nullified, an armed insurrection, led by José Figueres, broke out; Figueres was arguably the most influential figure in twentieth-century Costa Rican national life. After several weeks the government forces were defeated and Figueres set up an interim assembly or *junta*[21] with the support of the Social Democrats. Figueres and his followers were reformists; they adhered to the social democratic principles of the centre and looked to the urban middle-class and small and medium-sized landowners as their natural constituency. Both these groups had an interest in eroding the grip of the coffee elite, but were also opposed to the more radical politics of the left. Despite paying lip service to the principle of democracy, the *junta* were ruthless in the execution of their plan; communists were persecuted and imprisoned and the Communist party banned.

Support for Figueres and his politics had never been unconditional amongst coffee growers; suspicious of state intervention, unhappy with excessive and wasteful bureaucracy and resentful of taxes, they had long espoused a spirit of independence and maintained a somewhat conservative outlook. Often anti-communist, some growers also organised opposition to the social reforms of the 1940s. Whereas small and medium-sized producers had once sworn common cause with agricultural workers (*peones*), some now campaigned against the imposition of a minimum wage for labourers in the coffee industry (Acuña Ortega 1987:145; Bowman 2004:179; National Association of Coffee Producers 2004 [1922]:125). For their part, the *junta* identified with many of the ideals of the small and medium-sized producers. Democracy, social harmony, welfare and the importance of economic independence were values leading politicians, farmers and the Catholic Church held in common.

Figueres and his followers had ambitious plans for a welfare state and a comprehensive cooperative movement, ideas that they started to implement as their party, the *Partido Liberación Nacional* (PLN), came to prominence in national political life.[22] Under the guidance of leading intellectuals, Figueres moved Costa Rica towards policies of state intervention. This aimed to encourage development and generate wealth, but also maintain and extend the social reforms introduced in the Calderón era (Winson 1989:59). The most significant tools were a programme of nationalisation of key industries, and state-sponsored development projects. Of specific interest is the policy directed towards the coffee industry, which included provision of credit and technical assistance, and measures to support the establishment of cooperatives (Paige 1997:253–254). Given the importance of coffee to the national economy it is hardly surprising that the state tapped into the industry as a source of revenue. To fund the welfare state, a coffee export tax was introduced, exporters were forced to sell their foreign currency to the Central Bank, and an *ad valorem* tax on processing was levied (Winson 1989:78–85).[23] The raising of these revenues coincided with political struggles between producers and processors, in which the state played the role of interested mediator.

The *junta* quickly nationalised the banking system to direct funds and finance projects and created a state electricity company (ICE) to develop power output and a national grid. Putting the infrastructure and incentives to promote cooperatives in place was less swiftly accomplished. Nevertheless, the idea that economic life should be based upon beneficial cooperation between autonomous individuals accords with both the liberal democratic model and Catholic social doctrine. Commitment to equality, democracy, self-help and individual responsibility, underpinned by a concern with social welfare, are central to national identity, and are values that crystallise in the figure of the independent smallholding yeoman farmer.

COFFEE COOPERATIVES: THE PILLAR OF THE ECONOMY

Successive governments have provided support for cooperatives via the Institute for Promotion of Cooperatives (Infocoop) and the Department of Cooperatives within the National Bank, through tax concessions and preferential rates for primary goods, through laws regulating cooperative organisations, and by imparting cooperative principles in civic education.[24] Today there are more than 300 cooperatives in the country (el Cooperador 1998:1) and as many as 30 per cent of the economically active population, and a third of agricultural producers, belong to cooperative organisations (Edelman

1999:59). In the coffee sector in the 1960s and 1970s there were as many as 35 producer cooperatives, but by the mid-1990s only 25 remained. Today they process about 40 per cent of national output (Peters and Samper 2001:147).

In the coffee industry cooperatives are associated with the empowerment of small and medium-sized farmers (Winson 1989:108). They provide processing facilities (*beneficios*) and market outlets for members (*asociados*), who pay a fee to join, after which they are expected to deliver their crop to the cooperative for processing and subsequent sale. In this way farmers can hope to bypass private companies, secure a stake in the industrial and marketing phases and receive a greater part of the profits.[25] Cooperatives also play an active role in administering credit, supplying affordable agricultural inputs, and offering technical support in farming. The establishment of a national federation of coffee cooperatives (Fedecoop) in 1962 considerably advanced these services. By promoting coffee cooperatives the state sought to achieve the goal of improving social welfare, while introducing rational, technical and more efficient agriculture to small farmers. The aims and aspirations of the sector are well captured by a Fedecoop pamphlet: 'The Cooperative Effort: pillar of the economy, peace and national democracy'.

While the cooperative principles remain enshrined in legislation, the primacy of the cooperative model as a foundation for economic development has come to be challenged, and in recent years special privileges and tax breaks have been rescinded.[26] Structural adjustment enforced in the early 1980s required reductions in public spending and withdrawal of state support for the agricultural sector. As a result credit has become less available, technical assistance has been cut and producer debt has increased. Direct action against these policies by organisations of basic grain producers, supported by coffee growers from the Central Plateau and vegetable farmers, has been well documented (Edelman 1990, 1999; Vunderink 1990). Meanwhile, coffee producers and cooperatives in peripheral areas have fought shy of joining political mobilisations and sought out alternative avenues to cope with changing conditions.

No part of the coffee industry has remained immune from trade liberalisation, but neither has it suffered to the extent that other sectors of the economy have. The Costa Rican government was at the forefront of the campaign to renegotiate the International Coffee Agreement, which precipitated its collapse in 1989 and the end of the system of international regulation of supply through quotas. In part this was because rising production meant Costa Rica was forced to sell a large part of its coffee to countries outside the agreement, and even traded coffee for Eastern European buses and power stations (Paige 1997:260). A second motive for escaping the confines of the agreement was the high quality of Costa Rican coffee, imparted by favourable growing conditions. Whereas the mass market for generic brands has been in long-term decline, in the face of stiff competition from manufacturers of soft drinks, the gourmet and speciality market is expanding (Jiménez 1995; Neilson 2004; Paige 1997; Roseberry 1996). Costa Rica is well placed to exploit the move towards niche markets. Fair trade is symptomatic of this trend, and, whether by accident or design, the collapse of the International Coffee Agreement was immediately preceded by events that allowed a group of Costa Rican cooperatives to put themselves at the forefront of sales to fair-trade outlets.

REGIONAL DEVELOPMENT: THE CAE AND COOCAFE

A key moment in the story of fair trade in Costa Rica was the establishment of the Agro-Economic Consultancy (CAE) in 1985, under the auspices of a German NGO, the Friedrich Ebert Foundation. This event takes on symbolic importance in accounts of the history of the Costa Rican cooperatives involved in fair trade. The CAE was set up to introduce technical and business professionalism to the organisations, and it took steps that affected the activities, relationships and status of the cooperatives locally, nationally and internationally.

The CAE aimed to establish 'a regional project for economic development which would serve to support decentralisation and to encourage associative production structures in the rural sector' (Orozco 1992:20, my translation). In Costa Rica this stipulation effectively meant cooperatives. Also central to the CAE's specifications was a requirement to work with small, disadvantaged farmers; the goal was 'to make the life of *campesinos* and their families, who have always been the most marginalised in our country, more bearable and decent, by generating employment and better incomes, with more just and egalitarian participation in decision making at both the economic and political level' (Orozco 1992:22, my translation). The farmers of Highland Guanacaste, in the northwest of the country met these requirements. In the words of one manager, Guanacaste was 'at that time one of the most economically underdeveloped parts of the country'. The historical legacy of a policy to sell land cheaply to prominent individuals had led to the concentration of vast tracts of the lowlands in the hands of a few families (Gudmundson 1983), but this did not preclude the existence of large numbers of smallholding peasants in highland areas around the town of Tilarán and upland Nicoya. It was this class of peasant-proprietor that the project aimed to help.

Establishing offices in Cañas, Guanacaste, the CAE identified suitable coffee cooperatives to work with: Coopecerroazul, Coope Pilangosta and the now defunct Coope Cenizosa on the Nicoya Peninsular, and Coopetila, Coopeldos and Coope Montes de Oro in the Tilarán Highlands. These cooperatives met the criteria for assistance; they were situated in peripheral areas with poor infrastructure, and were composed of small farmers. The CAE arranged meetings between the managers of the organisations. The representatives of the groups already knew each other from the annual assembly of Fedecoop, but had failed to draw up a common agenda, as their interests were always subsumed under those of the larger cooperatives dominating the federation. Meeting as a group for the first time, the cooperative personnel realised they faced similar impediments. Firstly, they had problems accumulating capital, and so credit was hard to secure; without capital they were perceived as high-risk and were charged crippling rates of interest on loans. Secondly, they had difficulty maintaining the quality and quantity of production due to outdated and inefficient processing machinery and the approach to production of their members, who had failed to adopt the modern techniques that had transformed the industry in other parts of the country. Thirdly, all had problems marketing their product; the prices they attained for members were consistently below the national average. Finally, those running the organisations were drawn from the ranks of coffee producers and were respected locally, but were unqualified in business and unprepared for putting into operation the programme envisaged by the CAE. This required professional administrators.

Between 1985 and 1987 the CAE instigated policies to transform the cooperatives from 'traditional' into 'modern' organisations, with a professional bureaucracy and trained staff, equal to the task of competing in the modern coffee industry. An assessment of the strengths and weaknesses of each cooperative was carried out. Management training provided the basis for transforming the cooperatives at an organisational level. At the same time agricultural field officers were appointed to improve techniques of production, but with an eye to sustainability and conservation. They would also play a promotional role and attract new members, and were given the title 'technical promoter' (*técnico promotor*). Regular meetings between management, agricultural technicians and administrative staff at the CAE offices set in motion a common agenda. This forum eventually led to the formation of a second-level consortium made up of the six cooperatives, named Coocafé. Cooperatives that had laboured under marginal conditions as disparate organisations now had a common institution to evaluate the challenges they faced and seek common solutions. The consortium also hoped to wield political influence; as Juan Carlos, the manager at Coopeldos pointed out during one interview, 'it is not the same to attend a meeting as a representative of the 500 members of one cooperative as it is to go with the support of the 3,000 members of Coocafé'.

Coocafé is now a conglomerate of nine cooperatives, with its headquarters near the capital city, in Alajuela. Over the years four other groups have joined the group: Coope Sarapiqui, Coopesanta Elena, Coopabuena and Coope Llano Bonito. These cooperatives generally meet the conditions for membership; with the exception of Coope Llano Bonito they are situated away from the principal coffee-producing areas, and very few of the members have the 10 hectares deemed the minimum required for a family to make a living from coffee (Cubero 1998:2).[27]

Yet these cooperatives have other positive qualities. They are either historically linked by personal and professional ties, or are seen to fulfil specific needs. Coopesanta Elena is situated close to Monteverde National Park and so complements ecological advantages and has direct access to a lucrative tourist market. Coope Llano Bonito is at altitude, in the prime coffee-producing area of Tarrazú, and able to provide a high quality 'hard bean' that enhances demand for the Coocafé coffee blend.[28] Two of the new members, Coopabuena and Coope Llano Bonito, were also independently added to the register of fair-trade suppliers maintained by the Fairtrade Labelling Organisations International (FLO), while Coopesanta Elena has separate preferential agreements with North American coffee businesses. By absorbing these cooperatives Coocafé has become the export agency for all Costa Rican fair-trade coffee. A final advantage of expansion is the greater income generated by the inclusion of other groups. Each cooperative that joins must invest into Coocaf a sum based on average yearly production. This contributes to the financial strength and overall stability of the group.

The expansion of Coocafé has been remarkable. In the early days these small cooperatives consistently failed to exercise influence. Today they have representatives in a wide range of organisations. By participating in regulative, financial and campaigning groups, Coocafé accesses sources of information and finance which would otherwise be unavailable. Some of these are regulatory and financial bodies, including the national coffee institute (Icafé), the institute for the promotion of cooperatives (Infocoop), the cooperative bank (Bancoop), the Central American Consortium for Cooperative Marketing (CCMC), and the Costa Rican Agency for Export Certification. Other organisations, such as the Association of Latin American Coffee Producers (known as *Frente de Cafetaleros Solidarios de América Latina*), are more overtly political.

Coocafé has also developed the means to commercialise their product. Since the gaining of an export licence and the establishment of a marketing department, the complicated arrangements for the shipment of consignments of coffee and the administration of invoicing and certification are handled by the Coocafé team. The aim is for all the cooperatives to commercialise their product exclusively through Coocafé. The organisation does not itself buy or sell coffee, but acts as a channel for affiliates, and whether the commodity goes to alternative trade organisations or through conventional outlets, the export operation facilitates control of marketing and sales. In the year 1997–98 Coocafé increased the volume of exports through its export department by 101 per cent, to reach 35,091 sacks, while the value of these exports, according to Coocafé figures, jumped from 636 million to 1,405 million *colones*.[29]

Managers attribute the financial success of Coocafé to the successful integration of political and financial processes, and the rationalisation of administration. Close relations between the personnel of affiliated cooperatives and staff at headquarters is key; they have frequent telephone contact, attend weekly gatherings of the Coocafé administrative council, and the managers of the individual cooperatives determine financial and political policy at monthly meetings. The results of the work of this close-knit group of business people can be measured in fiscal terms. After five years of operation the capital assets of Coocafé had reached 50 million *colones*, but since 1992 the figure has increased by the same amount year on year. By the end of 1998, capital assets stood at 383 million *colones*, or almost £1 million at the time.[30] It is the sustained financial success that is impressive, not the total, which remains modest in business terms. This may be taken as evidence of the claim by management that they know how to perform in a prudent and businesslike manner.

MORAL MOTIVATIONS, SOCIAL COMMITMENTS AND COLLECTIVE IDENTITIES

The managers present a professional image of technical efficiency, but unlike in modern business the ideals and commitments of the cooperative movement are social and moral, rather than financial. The central tenet of Coocafé policy is service to a collective of small farmers struggling against the odds to find space in the market. Decisions are made at various levels, but always with reference to the needs and opinions of the members of the cooperatives, or the interests of others in the group. In this way, and in keeping with Costa Rican tradition, political processes are deemed democratic and transparent; for example, my own attendance at business meetings was unproblematic.

Putting into practice the ideas outlined in the CAE brief has required 'vision' and 'untiring struggle'. The first director of the CAE, Berthold Leimbach, is taken as representative of these qualities. He is described as the 'tireless instigator' and 'the great director' of the project.[31] The achievements of the modernisers at Coocafé is represented as 'harvesting success' (*cosechando logros*), but under a rubric of 'cooperation' and 'solidarity', the work of individuals being geared towards improvement and service for the benefit of the small coffee farmer. Harnessing individual creativity and putting it to work at the service of the many, in the name of progress, comes across clearly in the words of the manager of Coocafé in his tenth anniversary address:

> Ten years have passed since a group of men and women with a future vision came together with the purpose of resolving, with valour and solid and practical plans, the problems of the small and marginal coffee producer. Ten years have gone by since a seed of hope was sown on behalf of a life of dignity and sustainability for the small Costa Rican coffee farmer. A seed which sprouted with vigour grew strongly, and today has borne fruit in terms of competitiveness and solidarity in legitimate defence of the interests of the small and medium coffee producer of our country.[32]

According to the managers the desire to help others comes from personal formative experiences, often linked to cooperative values, but also located in national history. They refer to the close association between the smallholding peasant farmer and the classless rural society central to national identity. Thus Carlos Vargas, who was head of Coocafé until 2004, points to the fact that despite its name the country should really have been called 'Costa Pobre' (poor, rather than Rica, or rich) since the common background is of well-distributed land, with small and 'humble' landowning farmers living in shared poverty, which breeds 'solidarity' and requires people to work together in adversity. Cooperatives are one clear manifestation of this idea.

Alvaro Gomez, the manager at Coope Sarapiqui, like many of his colleagues, believes his motivation to help coffee farmers is inherited; it comes, he says, 'from his father, his grandfather, and his uncles', all lifelong members of the cooperative. People, he points out, are either *cooperativista*,[33] or they are not: it is a 'question of origins'. In accounting for their commitment, managers also often refer to a family background characterised by economic scarcity. Carlos Vargas spoke of the challenges his parents faced raising twelve children, but added that such a large family encourages sharing. Similarly, Juan Carlos talked of the sacrifice his parents made, of periods of 'financial crisis' and their 'great struggle' to put himself and his four brothers and sisters through college and university. Both men are sons of coffee producers and see the experience of growing up in relatively poor economic conditions as highly formative. In short, the managers share and make explicit a common identity with producers, and most of them are themselves coffee farmers and deliver unprocessed coffee 'cherries' to the cooperatives they manage.[34] This, they say, allows them to empathise with producers, and 'share in their trials and tribulations'.

Despite being raised in marginal areas of the country and in difficult economic circumstances, the managers have had the opportunity to gain professional qualifications. Their work on behalf of small farmers is inspired by their own experience and social background; it gives them a 'personal goal' to take up the challenge and use their advantages and skills to help others, through service to the cooperative and the communities in which they work. They combine the qualities of professionalism and efficiency with an ethic of service and adherence to cooperative values. The growth of Coocafé is presented as testament to their success.

TRANSNATIONAL CONNECTIONS AND FAIR TRADE

One key advantage Coocafé has had is access to the markets offered by alternative trade organisations in the North, principally in western Europe, but increasingly in North America. The arrival of fair trade in Costa Rica predates the CAE and Coocafé, and can be traced to the early 1980s and the activities of the Dutch NGO, SOS Wereldhandel.[35] In 1982 a representative of this organisation arrived in the country looking for a suitable producer group with which to develop a relationship based upon preferential terms of trade. Members of Fedecoop took him to visit the remote cooperative at Cerro Azul on the Nicoya Peninsular, a meeting that is now seen as historically significant as it marks the beginning of fair trade in Costa Rica. Throughout the 1980s commerce between SOS Wereldhandel and Coope Cerro Azul remained constant at a modest 750 sacks per year. With the establishment of Coocafé, and the common agenda this entailed, the other cooperatives in the group were conceded access to the preferential trade; a 'generous act', which required a 'lack of egotism' on the part of Coope Cerro Azul. In this way, and at an opportune moment, the other producer cooperatives in Coocafé were able to link into the fair-trade concept.

What are the consequences of this? A positive assessment of the role fair trade has played in the life of the small farmers, the cooperative, and Coocafé itself, came across clearly in an interview with Alvaro Gomez of Coope Sarapiqui. He describes fair trade as a 'windfall' or 'gift' (*una ganga*) in the period following the failure of the International Coffee Agreement (ICO) in 1989. Prices on the international market fell to below $100 in the wake of the collapsed agreement, prompting a five-year crisis in the coffee industry. Many farmers cut down or abandoned their groves. At the same time the economic policy of structural adjustment meant withdrawal of state support; cooperatives and producer groups had to compete on equal terms with private business and many cooperatives went bankrupt.

The minimum price of $121 with the $5 premium meant cooperatives received $126 for 46kg from an expanding fair-trade market, which helped immunise them against the worst ravages of declining prices and the shock of neoliberal policies. Some 70 per cent of the money paid over and above the market price is directed to the producer, while the bulk of the remainder is retained by the cooperative and held as a development fund (*fondo de desarrollo*) under the auspices of Coocafé.[36] This helps the consortium endure crisis, but allows the individual cooperatives access to financial resources. As a result, and due to high sales in alternative trade markets, these cooperatives were able to consolidate their position and develop at a time when many others involved in coffee production and trade faced ruin. The financial rewards during the market lull were matched by social benefits. Because of the minimum price, farmers were able to continue to grow coffee, maintain investment in production, and take out loans without fear of negative consequences. They were protected from market instability and able to remain on the land. In this respect fair trade is seen to counteract the national tendency towards concentration in property ownership, and population drift from the rural to the urban sector; it is portrayed as a mechanism that has maintained small producers and rural communities in difficult times. During periods of low prices fair trade is seen to help provide stability and reliable incomes to farmers engaged in production for unstable global markets.

As Alvaro then explained, a rather more problematic situation emerges when prices rise beyond the $121 minimum price, which provides a clearer indication of the place of fair-trade deals in business strategies. The system of a minimum price was developed during a market low, and is intended to compensate for this situation. The $5 premium was introduced to differentiate the alternative and the conventional markets when prices rise above $121 and the minimum no longer has meaning. The aim is to keep fair trade an attractive proposition. However, because managers are aware that even when prices are high, they will at some future date inevitably fall below the $121 threshold, they feel obliged to provide regular consignments for fair-trade customers, and so must reserve supplies. This prevents them from taking advantage of good prices on the open market, and deals may have to be foregone in order to maintain supplies to fair-trade customers. Agreements to supply coffee to ethical consumers, and the consequent advantage of a sustained minimum price, have to be balanced against the lack of freedom to speculate that this entails.

The benefits of fair trade in a falling market, and the relative disadvantage in a bullish one, can be illustrated by the competition and strategising which takes place over participation of individual cooperatives in the Coocafé group in alternative trade agreements. This can lead to conflict, such as the 'minor disagreement' that occurred between Coopeldos and Coopesanta Elena during the present crisis on the coffee markets. The dispute arose because Coopesanta Elena had secured a good slice of the fair-trade market, achieved superior prices, and so attracted producers away from nearby Coopeldos.[37] A discussion during a meeting of the Coocafé Administrative Council in June 1999 aimed to resolve such difficulties. This meant laying down the terms that determine the proportion of coffees from the various cooperatives going into the exported product, called the HB Coocafé mix. A primary concern is to control quality and ensure the marketability of the coffee; since the cooperatives are situated in different zones, and are at a variety of altitudes, the coffees they produce vary in quality. Beyond that, the Administrative Council was seeking a method acceptable to all managers for determining the level of participation in fair trade, not an easy task when managers want to engage as fully as possible in fair trade when the price in conventional markets is low, but opt out when prices soar. By 2003 they had settled upon a system that weighted participation according to three measures: the scale of production of each cooperative (45 per cent), which clearly favours the larger cooperatives' loyalty in selling coffee through Coocafé (20 per cent); and a fixed quota of participation for each cooperative to demonstrate 'solidarity' (35 per cent). Added to this is an agreed ceiling on participation for each cooperative of 55 per cent, although for many of the cooperatives the actual quota now hovers around 30 per cent.

The manoeuvring that occurs around participation shows how fair trade is incorporated into professional sales strategies and suggests a hiatus between the commercial and the ethical component. This is the paradox generated by the fact that fair trade sets itself up as an alternative but must both operate and compete within the mainstream (Lewis 1998; Luetchford 2006; Renard 1999, 2003). The ethic of the managers is directed towards developing strategies to maximise prices they can pass on to farmers, rather than exhibiting any higher-level commitment to alternative market channels. Managers therefore balance their sales to alternative trade organisations against the advantages of the open market at any one point, and attempt to juggle their participation accordingly, although the process is tempered by social and moral considerations and negotiated between the various cooperatives in Coocafé.

But alternative trade organisations in the North are envisaged as operating according to similar business criteria. The clearest way to see this is through the issue of quality. The oversupply of coffee which has resulted in prices falling to a historic low (Daviron and Ponte 2005; Gresser and Tickle 2002) means that buyers can afford to choose only the top quality beans, while inferior grades remain unsold. As the current crisis continues, and with ever greater numbers of producer groups bidding for participation in fair-trade markets, so the alternative trade organisations are said to be more demanding in terms of quality. This is understandable; to be a commercial success they must market a quality product, but the producer groups which face the greatest obstacles are not those producing high-quality coffee; rather it is those in more marginal areas that are likely to suffer in declining markets. So the mission to help poor, marginal farmers is compromised by commercial considerations as alternative trade organisations balance the interests of producers and consumers with business success.

WHEN TWO MODELS CLASH: RELATIONS BETWEEN COFFEE COOPERATIVES AND FAIR-TRADE ORGANISATIONS

It might be tempting to attribute the success of Coocafé to fair trade, but Juan Carlos, the manager of Coopeldos, denies this. In his view involvement in fair trade is one *result* of development at the local and regional level. The modernising process, the establishment of bureaucratic structures, the setting up of common agendas and networking have, he feels, opened up the possibility for expansion and progress and generated access to alternative trade. This is only to recognise the agency of brokers involved in administering cooperatives at the local and regional level. For them fair trade is an opportunity, an 'alternative market' (*mercado alternativo*) that they have managed to access on behalf of their members.[38] Their achievements cannot and should not be seen as a 'gift' from fair-trade organisations or as attributable to the benevolence of consumers.

Such has been the success of Coocafé that their right to partake in the *mercado alternativo* has been challenged by certain parties in Europe.[39] Coocafé, so one argument goes, no longer needs the preferential trade terms on offer. Managers deny this, and vigorously defend the right to participate. They point out that to exclude them from fair trade would be a punishment for their own success. Their achievement is possible because they operate in an environment of political stability, unlike their war-torn neighbours, and to bar them from fair trade would, in effect, be a punishment for their country's democratic and peaceful traditions. Further grounds for the right to be part of fair trade relates to business acumen. Costa Rica cannot compete in terms of marginality and poverty with, for example, their Nicaraguan neighbours, but they provide efficiency in despatching consignments with the kind of quality product needed to improve the image of fair-trade goods in the North. According to this argument Coocafé constitutes a model demonstrating the potential of the alternative trade system, and they have offered their services to other cooperative groups who may wish to emulate their success.[40]

During fieldwork some informants voiced a more trenchant criticism of those who would exclude them, and there is a general disquiet about the organisation of fair trade. This does not refer to the principles underlying the notion of more ethical approaches to trade relations or the financial side of the operation. Rather, it focuses on two key areas: the limited scale of the alternative market and its slow rate of growth; and the nature of the relationship between producer groups and fair-trade organisations in the North.

We can put the effect of fair trade into perspective by looking at production figures and gate prices paid for coffee at the Coopeldos cooperative over the years, and comparing them to the nearest rival processing plant (Table 2, p. 187). The figures appear encouraging for the cooperative and for fair trade; Coopeldos consistently outperforms the Turín plant and the fair-trade premiums kick in when gate prices are low. Nevertheless, this cannot be seen as representative of a general picture, even nationally. In particular, it should be borne in mind that Turín is a small and inefficient plant and Coopeldos faces limited competition, a situation not enjoyed by cooperatives in other parts of the country. In any case, for the year 1999–2000, and with prices at rock bottom, Coopeldos sold only 27 per cent of its coffee through alternative trade outlets, which allowed an increase in payments of just over 9 per cent to the producer.[41] According to Carlos Vargas at Coocafé, the primary effect of fair trade today is 'psychological', rather than financial; it encourages producers to continue working and boosts morale. On a national scale, however, it has less importance; as Alvaro Gomez from Coope Sarapiqui pointed out, sales to alternative markets vary between 1 and 5 per cent, depending on the country; 'this is not sufficient to keep up people's morale', and at current prices the coffee industry in Costa Rica is not viable, since 'producers are not receiving what they should for their coffee'. In Costa Rica, as in Europe and North America, fair trade remains a niche market.

This is not to deny that fair trade is 'good', even 'excellent', and managers are generally quick to praise the principle if not the practice of fair trade. Its limited effect is said to be due to a failure to evolve. Some managers believe that fair-trade products are priced out of the market, and that they can be as cheap as conventional brands and still pay minimum prices. To justify this, reference is made to the removal of intermediaries, and a more direct link between producer and consumer. The claim that organisations in Europe have failed to 'project' and 'plan', combined with the 'unending queue' of producer groups joining the system, has meant fair-trade sales by many cooperatives in Coocafé have halved in recent years, despite the much-publicised boom in sales in the North.

Further criticism concerns the 'unwillingness to listen to producers'. Meetings between the producers' representatives and alternative trade organisations are characterised as forums in which the European partners dictate terms and conditions, and merely divulge information. It is claimed that only more junior staff from the European organisations attend the meetings and that higher managers make merely cursory visits, a sign that the opinions of the producers and their representatives are given little importance. This contrasts with their own cooperative assemblies in which open debate and an exchange of opinions is encouraged, and at which policies are determined by votes cast by members. So, while relations with some northern organisations are positively valued, links with other parties in Europe are not satisfactory; they, it is said, want to deal only with poor and acquiescent coffee farmers, who do not question decisions taken abroad. Some Europeans, said one local person, 'do not like to listen to the opinions of people in the Third World, and regard them as natives in loincloths'. Others allude to the church background to fair trade. Another interviewee claimed that some fair-trade managers in Europe see themselves as 'shepherds' and the producers as 'their flock', who should follow, be submissive and not take initiatives or ask questions. At the same time, it is admitted that the delegates from the South are often 'passive', and are afraid to question and challenge their European partners for fear that they might lose access to fair-trade outlets.

Here we discern parallels between colonial anthropology and the workings and discourse of aid and development agencies, with 'hidden' and 'public' transcripts (Scott 1992). What emerges is part of a 'neo-colonial tradition of political control through philanthropy – a celebrated missionary position' (Bhabha 1994:242). It seems that even within the moral imperative of fair trade, power relations are not easily abolished, and ethically inspired initiatives can be experienced as subjection and become a 'project of rule' (Li 2001).

CONCLUSIONS

The above story shows how preferential deals are incorporated into the historical and social context of producer organisations. The background against which the history is written shows the ability of dominant interests to extract surplus from the value-producing activities of small farmers. To counteract such power, and head off radical unrest, a Costa Rican reformist movement emerged to struggle on behalf of and represent the interests of coffee producers. As well as seeking to regulate the industry and curb the extractive power of the elite, the reforms entailed the active promotion of cooperatives. By processing and marketing on behalf of farmers, in organisations owned by them, cooperatives hoped to return a greater percentage of the profit from coffee to those who produce it.

In constructing the account I have distinguished between two sides of development activity; one morally concerned with promoting social welfare, the other geared towards putting in place necessary and efficient mechanisms to achieve that end. I locate the origin of these two streams in the social-democratic principles that arose in Costa Rican political and economic life in the middle of the twentieth century. For Coocafé managers there is little contradiction between an approach based upon expediency and morally informed aims: technical solutions are the means by which to respond to social problems; instrumental reason is subordinate to moral ends; and the technical and bureaucratic emerge out of and are inseparable from social and moral context (Murphy 1993:45).[42]

The argument that one of the principal effects of fair trade in Costa Rica is that it has helped the cooperatives involved build strong institutions is persuasive (Ronchi 2002). But to the extent that the data comes from management, cooperative documents and other interested parties, it is a partial, 'official' view of national and global relations. This chapter has revealed the benefits extracted by cooperatives from the fair-trade niche market, and at the same time has shown that there are points of contestation and conflicts of interest in the regional and transnational operation of the system. Differences between Northern alternative trade groups and Southern cooperatives are the first in a series of disjunctures between the parties. The next chapter explores these themes at the local level; the success of one cooperative becomes a topic of lively debate about the social and moral implications of economic activities, which is again part of the wider history of national political processes in the country.

2 SOWING PROGRESS AND CONTESTING DEVELOPMENT IN THE TILARÁN HIGHLANDS

The coffee growers' cooperative of El Dos de Tilarán, known as Coopeldos, is in the Tilarán Highlands of northwest Costa Rica. It is strategically located at the bottom of a deep valley, on the banks of the fast-flowing Río Cañas. The water from the river is essential for the wet-coffee processing plant (or *beneficio*) central to the cooperative's activities; it drives the power turbines and is used to ferment the fruit that surrounds the coffee bean, and force it through the processing system. For convenience other cooperative facilities are on the same site. There is a *recibidor*, or collection point where members can deliver their crop; furnaces for drying the processed coffee; massive steel silos, warehousing and machinery to prepare orders and shipment; a general store; and a shop offering agricultural supplies. The administrative offices are next to the retail outlets; from here the technicians, secretaries, accountants and management liaise with producers and oversee processing and marketing activities.

From the surrounding countryside unpaved roads lead down to Coopeldos. In the green season, wet and tropically verdant, they frequently and rapidly become barely passable quagmires. Nevertheless, the tracks must be negotiated since heavy rains occur during the coffee harvest. Farmers use a variety of means – pick-up trucks, motorbikes, packhorses, or, on occasion, typical Costa Rican ox carts – to make frequent, often daily, journeys down the steep-sided valleys to deliver their coffee for processing. During the summer months the rains ease, the hills turn brown and parched and winds whip in from the east, throwing up eddies and dust storms from the surface of the tracks. At this time the cooperative provides a different focus. From the settlements people come to shop for food and agricultural supplies, to meet and chat, to arrange loans or pay off debts, to consult management and staff, and to attend meetings and courses arranged to help farmers improve agricultural practice and share experiences. Over the years Coopeldos has been an outlet for coffee growers who need to process and sell their crop, as well as an employer, a provider of services, a forum for project discussion and implementation, and an avenue to engage with government agencies and NGOs.

The cooperative has many of the characteristics of a class-based social movement. It can be seen as creating an alternative space for the expression of cultural identity for a marginalised, smallholding peasantry, to be drawn upon in political mobilisations and utilised in economic strategies to renegotiate spheres of exploitation for coffee farmers seeking higher prices (Sklair 1995:497). Indeed this is the view that management and many members project, though there are other non-conformist voices to consider.

The initial focus of this chapter is the history of the cooperative; the events leading up to its establishment, and different phases in its development. Coopeldos is generally acknowledged to be the most successful of the cooperatives in the Coocafé group; for this reason the hotel receptionist in the town of Tilarán proudly described it as the 'best coffee cooperative in Latin America'. Such comments are pregnant with meaning; they bring together coffee, cooperatives and the small producers so central to national identity, and vindicate the reformist movement, the social welfare project and the drive to modernisation that has been a cornerstone of Costa Rican politics since at least the 1950s.

But like many examples held up as a success, Coopeldos is also the focus for conflicting views and agendas (Edelman 1999; Burdick 1992). To address this contestation I explore relations between the cooperative and its membership base of producers, locating it within the wider history of political struggles between processors and producers in the coffee industry. The settlements these parties arrived at were overseen by government, are inscribed in legal statute and have led to an enduring though somewhat uneasy peace. One cannot comprehend the concept of fair trade in Costa Rica without looking at these struggles and resolutions; neither can one understand the different and often contradictory views of the cooperative expressed by producers without this political context.

This chapter connects to the last point in its focus on the commodity form, farmers' experiences of exploitation and political mobilisations with respect to exchange relations in commodity markets. Cooperative managers, like fair-trade activists, object to multinationals, big exporters, the grip of elite families on the industry and the ability of these parties to extract undue surplus from small farmers. They justify their role as representatives of small farmers' interests and point to the services they provide. What do producers say? Many endorse the positive view of the cooperative provided by management. But the subtext expressed by some is an echo of the view presented by farmers in political mobilisations of the 1930s and

1950s. It is critical of bureaucracy and focuses on processors who fix prices and live from and hence exploit agricultural work. The focus in this chapter is on the critique of these social arrangements, which at times extends to the cooperative. In later chapters I will explore its justification.

A HISTORY OF COOPELDOS

The first wet-processing industrial coffee machinery (*beneficio*) in the Tilarán Highlands was installed after the Second World War by José Valenciano, a local landowner and farmer. A nascent coffee economy emerged with the settlement of the highlands in the early part of the twentieth century, and initially took the form of a cottage industry, supplying local markets. Individual growers hawked their dry-processed coffee to general grocers for direct resale to the consumer, and in this way the product entered a limited, regional economy. The dry process is an uncertain and protracted affair in the wet tropical highland climate, as it requires prolonged exposure to the sun. The superior and more efficient wet method meant that coffee could be dealt with in sufficient quantities and attain the quality demanded by commercial buyers and exporters in Costa Rica's Central Plateau.[43] With the installation of the *beneficio*, coffee farmers in the El Dos area could aspire to supplying the lucrative export market and European consumers, the traditional destination of high-quality Costa Rican arabica beans.

At his death, José Valenciano left no immediate heir, and although another prominent landowning family of coffee growers had established a second processing plant and temporarily took over at El Dos, growers were dissatisfied with the terms and conditions offered. As a result, some local farmers abandoned coffee production altogether; the problems encountered in selling their crop, the difficulties of transport, and the level of prices, particularly compared to rates in the premium coffee-growing areas, all conspired against them. Other farmers began to consider alternative arrangements for the processing and sale of their crop.

Given the incentives and institutional support for cooperative ventures it comes as no surprise that the farmers of El Dos considered a coffee cooperative. The idea was taken up at a series of informal meetings and attracted a small but enthusiastic following of men credited with having the 'vision' to put the plan into practice. Contact was made with the Cooperative Department at the National Bank of Costa Rica (BNCR) and the Federation of Coffee Cooperatives (Fedecoop). These institutions encouraged the farmers and pledged the necessary help. Significantly, included was a loan of 100,000

Costa Rican *colones* to purchase the processing plant. Meanwhile, the Institute for the Promotion of Cooperatives (Infocoop) made the judicial arrangements necessary to convert the putative organisation into a legal entity. These events culminated in the foundation of the El Dos coffee cooperative in May 1971, with an initial capital of 12,000 *colones* and 79 members (*asociados*).

The above acts and events are enshrined in the memories of the founder members (*fundadores*), inscribed in commemorative editions of magazines, and celebrated by a plaque listing the first Administrative Council displayed on the wall of the cooperative building. The establishment of Coopeldos is recognised as a pivotal moment in the history of the highlands. One narrative honours the founders of the cooperative. As a member of the first Administrative Council stated: 'for my part ... I feel very happy when I see the progress of the cooperative, God has helped us and blessed all those pioneers who began from nothing' (my translation). The cooperative may have had small and tentative beginnings, but in this version current success vindicates the struggle of the original founders.

While the beginnings of Coopeldos are celebrated, the early years are either optimistically described as a time of consolidation, or more pessimistically and retrospectively assessed as a stagnant and tradition-bound phase in cooperative history. Certainly the first members initially had difficulty persuading others to join them, since many doubted the capacity of the cooperative to cover expenses and pay for the coffee they processed. According to founder Carlos Vega, these early suspicions were partly justified as the cooperative was slow to take off, but with the help of loans from various quarters, including the National Bank, they did manage to pay the producers for the first harvest and were able to sell the crop on, through the coffee cooperative federation (Fedecoop).

The next crucial period in the history of Coopeldos came in the mid-1980s, when a process of expansion began. This watershed is not, however, entirely corroborated by data on the growth in membership. The number of *asociados* has increased steadily since the organisation was founded, with the most significant numerical rise occurring in the 1990s, during which time some 200 new members joined the enterprise (Table 3, p. 183). Nevertheless, processing output does support the popular conception of the 1980s as a key time in the organisation's history. Output remained stable until 1985, doubled in 1986, reached 8,000 *fanegas* by the end of the decade, and increased exponentially by 1,000 or 2,000 *fanegas* from then.[44] These results contrast markedly with the *beneficio* at Turín, its nearest competitor (Table 4, p. 184).

SOWING PROGRESS: LOCAL DEVELOPMENT, ENTERPRISE
AND GROWTH

Today Coopeldos is an institution imbued with an idea of progress
and a modernist outlook. The cooperative has pushed for material
improvements in infrastructure, facilitated through extensive organisational links to government departments and NGOs, both national
and international, and so it coordinates and contributes to a broad
range of local services. It is widely recognised by residents as the
principal 'motor for development' in the immediate vicinity, and
lives up to cooperative principles and its motto: *sembramos progreso*
(we sow progress), a message that is advertised on hoardings scattered
across the countryside.

The bus that winds its way along the dirt tracks to Santa Elena
twice a day, and often takes backpackers to the Monteverde Reserve,
is a visible sign of economic encroachment. So too are the hired
4WDs carrying better-heeled tourists through the village; some even
occasionally stop to buy a cold drink but most appear unaware of or
uninterested in the cooperative. The bus does not pass that way, and
the visitors make little or no contribution to the local economy.[45]
The tourists and the wealth they represent may provide a measure
for certain local aspirations, but the inhabitants of El Dos must look
elsewhere for development. This is what makes the idea of 'sowing
progress' telling; it is a modernising message, but at the same time it
is a metaphor with its roots in agriculture and the earth, which are
considered a less transient source of wealth than tourism.

The mission statement emblazoned on banners and prominently
displayed at functions such as the annual assembly summarises the
cooperative's goals:

Coopeldos has as its aim the socioeconomic wellbeing of its members, as
well as general development in its area of operation, through continual
improvement in the productive and industrial process, according to the needs
of our *asociados*, and via the appropriate use of human, economic, technical
and environmental resources (my translation).

The cooperative has had considerable success in achieving these
aims. The 'traditional and conservative' outlook attributed to the
cooperative in the early years serves to mark the beginning of a new
era. The cooperative model demands equality and participation of
members in decision-making structures and forms a moral template
for managers and administrators in their efforts to generate income
and wellbeing for members. In the post-1985 period, it was hoped
that the adoption of intensive agricultural techniques, ushered
in by the CAE would raise farm incomes, which in turn would
generate capital. By providing training and adopting state-of-the-
art business and accounting procedures a more efficient organisation

was envisaged. The aim was to improve quality, increase production and foster successful commercial strategies.

The yardstick against which any improvements could be measured was already in place, as many producers and processors in more centrally located parts of the country had already instigated similar changes. Economic depression in the 1930s, the interruption in markets as a result of the Second World War, and declining soil fertility all led to a national crisis in the coffee industry. In response, a series of government-sponsored initiatives were introduced in the postwar period to streamline production, administrative procedures and promote rural development (Hall 1991:152–166; Winson 1989). A national campaign was established to renovate existing groves by using modern hybrids, open up new areas for cultivation and encourage the application of fertilisers, which were provided at subsidised prices. At the same time the Institute for the Defence of Coffee, later to become the *Instituto de Café* or Icafé, took control of the industry. A fundamental role in the process of revitalisation was played by cooperatives, which were given preferential terms for credit and made exempt from taxes on profits and agricultural inputs (Cazanga 1989; Hall 1991:163; Paige 1997:258). So successful were the campaigns that production levels, which had been the lowest in Latin America, were transformed into some of the highest in the world (Cazanga 1989:71; Edelman 1999:59; Paige 1997:258; Winson 1989:98, 110).

Coopeldos was, by all accounts, slow to take full advantage of these programmes; it was not until the mid-1980s that intensive agriculture, designed to raise production, was introduced into the El Dos area. At this time *catimor* hybrid varieties, principally *caturra* and *catuai*, began to replace the variety known by farmers as *borbón*. These new bushes are resistant to disease, heavy croppers, are more compact and so allow higher density planting, and begin fruiting at a younger age. In tandem with the introduction of new varieties came an increase in inputs; chemical fertilisers ensure the bushes perform year on year, especially as more demands are made on the soil by intensive planting. To apply the technical model of agriculture a series of trained agronomists have been employed by the cooperative. Their role is to visit producers, run courses, and liaise with other experts, particularly those employed by the Ministry of Agriculture and Livestock (MAG) and Icafé.

Coupled with increasing technification was the drive to expand the area under coffee cultivation. The cooperative has over the years provided credit for starting new groves and been a channel for funds from a variety of sources; loans sometimes come through banks and sometimes via development agencies, such as the Usaid-Fedecoop programme. More recently the administration has managed to access credit to buy two large cattle farms, and has provided funding for individuals to purchase small plots and sow them with coffee. This measure is designed to increase the turnover of the cooperative and give it greater economies of scale, no trivial matter when smaller, less efficient processors have been forced out of business in recent years. A second intention of converting a large farm into many small plots is that in principle at least it reverses the general trend towards land concentration in Costa Rica.

Quality is key to the expansion of the coffee industry in the area of El Dos. At the processing plant the coffee is inspected as it arrives from the fields and is classified as 'excellent', 'poor', 'green' or 'fermented'. Efficiency also entails prompt processing and modernisation of the plant itself. Money for improvements and investment in the necessary machinery comes from a variety of sources; loans and grants for governmental and non-governmental organisations; the 4 per cent social capital paid by members; and the development fund that has accumulated from the cooperative share in fair-trade premiums. The success of the programme can be measured by the granting of the international quality norm, ISO 9002, to the Coopeldos plant, by all accounts the first coffee cooperative in Latin America to gain this accolade.

The link between quality and efficiency in the mill is fundamental; in effect the processing system not only extracts the green beans (*café oro*) from raw cherries (*en cereza*) ready for sale; it also separates the coffee into first, second and third-grade products. This is achieved by floating off defective fruit in tanks, by adjusting the hulling machines (*despulpadores*) to different settings, which divides the harder and more bitter unripe cherries from the softer red ones, and by passing the beans through cages (*cribas*), which separate them according to size. The mechanised sorting of the coffee continues through to the drying and bagging-up phase. Processing is a long and complex dividing system, in which increasingly fine distinctions are made. Quality is therefore not only dependent upon climatic conditions and the altitude of the farm; it requires an efficient and finely tuned plant and expert staff.

Increasing turnover has added to the institutional strength of the business and has allowed the cooperative to secure finance from national banks and to guarantee personal loans for members. The state-run Organisation for the Promotion of Cooperatives (Infocoop) provides credit for agricultural reform, which includes land-distribution programmes, technical assistance and support with planning. Other grants and loans have been made available for specific purposes; for example, the Chinese government and Infocoop have both provided credit to increase the area under coffee cultivation. In the seven-year period from 1992 to 1998 the credit managed by the cooperative rose from 14 million to 200 million *colones*. However, as the sums rise, so do the risks; some producers take out credit and find themselves unable to repay debts, despite relatively favourable rates of interest in the Costa Rican context. At the time of fieldwork the cooperative held more than 100 accounts they had been forced to close because members had defaulted on repayment.

In addition to production-focused concerns, and in accordance with its mission statement, the cooperative carries out a range of social programmes. It invests money in local schools and makes scholarships available to individual students, principally through the foundation *Hijos del Campo* (Children from the Countryside). Other grants fund the building and maintenance of roads, administered through local voluntary organisers (*fiscales de caminos*). At the annual assembly in February 1999 the members voted to continue to donate 5 *colones* for each box (*cajuela*) of their harvested coffee to this purpose.[46] An equal sum was apportioned to support old-people's homes in the area. Further financial aid goes to the many local development associations and self-help organisations active in the villages. The cooperative also plays an important administrative role in providing the bureaucratic channels for residents to apply for government programmes and grants, such as Vivienda, which, despite reports of corruption at the highest level, has allowed many Costa Ricans to build secure housing. In a similar vein, and conscious of the lack of building plots in the El Dos area, the cooperative has set aside suitable sites for house construction.

Environmental policy is another increasingly emphasised area of activity. Since the 1980s Costa Rica has moved towards a model of sustainable development and marketed itself with great success as a 'green republic' and ecotourist destination (Evans 1999). In keeping with this policy, the government has passed legislation to limit the impact of industrial processes on the countryside, the media broadcasts propaganda that preaches environmental responsibility to citizens, farmers and others have become aware of the effects of their productive activities on their environment and themselves, markets have opened up for organic coffee, and grants have become available for environmental projects. In short, sustainability, environmentalism and good practice have also become good business. Nevertheless, as I argue in a later chapter, the 'greening of discourse' noted by Edelman (1999:21) should not be seen as mere opportunism, nor should it be seen as alien to rural Costa Ricans' understanding of the environment; it accords with cultural ideas about nature and is part of both national and *campesino* rural identity.

Notably, to attest to its credentials, Coopeldos has gained a second international certificate for environmental management of the plant (ISO 14001), to add to the certification for quality. In 2003 Juan Carlos, the manager, was immersed in a project supported by the Canadian government to install solar panels on the roof of the drying section of the *beneficio*. This power would cut the amount of wood required for the furnaces and reduce emissions. Other improvements had already been made to the wet process, which requires vast quantities of water to be drawn from the river. Contaminated by the fruit pulp, this water turns light brown and toxic (*'aguas mieles'*). Encouraged by legislation, Coopeldos has introduced a system of recycling to lessen the impact on the watercourse. Usage has been reduced from 2,000 litres to 350 litres of water per *fanega*, and whereas the effluent was once pumped back into the river, it now goes to sedimentation pools for treatment. By all accounts these measures have been highly effective; Rafael owns land that adjoins the river and on one excursion he talked of water that was once brown and lifeless; he then showed me the clear water and spoke of restored habitats and returning wildlife. The cooperative now combines water treatment with the establishment of small nature reserves, particularly along watercourses. As well as providing a haven for wildlife, the trees help combat erosion, a problem less associated with coffee than with beef and dairy farming, but one that the cooperative has been keen to address.

In the cooperative nursery, a programme supported by NGOs produces in the region of 100,000 saplings a year. Both native and non-native trees are grown, and are sold at subsidised prices to members of the cooperative. Coffee farmers recognise a number of advantages and benefits from planting trees on their land. They are motivated by expediency, but many farmers also emphasis restorative action on the environment. A retired farmer took me on a tour of his farm and gave a graphic description of his efforts to clear the land; he went on to explain that farmers now realised the error of their ways and were trying to repair the damage through reforestation. From a utilitarian perspective, trees form a windbreak that protects the coffee bushes and helps open up new areas to cultivation; for this purpose fast-growing non-native eucalyptus are particularly valued. Tree planting also reflects changing agricultural techniques and the expanding market for shade-grown coffee. Fruit trees in the coffee grove (*cafetal*) provide an extra source of food for home consumption, other varieties are favoured because of their nitrogen-fixing qualities, and yet others are planted because they are native species that help restore the environment.

Perhaps the most notable and successful of the environmental activities in which Coopeldos is involved is the organic coffee programme, initially facilitated by funding from the Dutch government. This has involved a number of specific measures and policies, not least subsidies for conversion costs, the provision of training and the encouragement of practices to limit the use of agrochemicals. Because organic coffee production brings with it specific challenges and opportunities for farmers and is a useful avenue for discussing ideas on nature and the environment, it will be dealt with more fully in Chapter 5.

With regard to its professed aims, the cooperative has attained institutional strength, made substantial investments in its area of influence and has wrought changes in the economic situation of its members. The manager is confident that Coopeldos has, in a very real sense, 'sown progress' and wellbeing. The conditions today, he says, bear no relation to those he found when he arrived 14 years ago. More children attend school beyond the compulsory age of twelve. Most residents live in cement houses, and old-style wooden constructions with earthen floors are now uncommon. Roads are improving and stretches of tarmac are encroaching into the highlands, remoter communities are finally getting electricity, private phone lines are becoming available and, by many accounts, standards of living are rising.

PRODUCERS AGAINST PROCESSORS:
THE POLITICAL STRUGGLES OF THE 1930s AND 1950s

The success of Coopeldos is, in part, due to the lack of serious competition from private processors, but managers of other cooperatives, and producers around El Dos, more often attribute it to the dynamism and foresight of the manager. What is certain is that the course of events I have documented – the 'sowing of progress' – takes place within the wider historical process of nation-building, and struggles between different groups involved in what was the principal economic activity in Costa Rica.[47] The cooperative movement that emerged out of those conflicts was largely geared towards providing technical and rational solutions to problems identified in the industry by politicians and experts. In this respect it did not specifically respond to the concerns and demands of small and medium-sized producers themselves. The gap between the rationale of the cooperative system and the political ideology and moral commitments of small farmers is the key to understanding a degree of dissent amongst residents, and some *asociados*, towards Coopeldos.

Analysis of letters, reports, speeches and newspaper interviews with small farmers during conflicts between producers and with processors in the 1920s and 1930s, and again in the 1950s, has allowed scholars to document the official discourse of producers and sources of conflict at times of crisis in the industry (Acuña Ortega 1985, 1987; González Ortega 1987; Paige 1997; Winson 1989). Coffee growers protested against the exploitation they suffered at the hands of the processors, and with the government acting as arbitrators, the commercial relationship between agricultural and industrial interests in the coffee industry was renegotiated. Here I will concentrate primarily on the history of the struggles, the nature of the complaints made by farmers, and the uneasy settlement of the conflict. The moral values and ideology inspiring producers requires deeper analysis and will be dealt with fully in later chapters.

The conflicts and negotiations of the twentieth century involved an agitated but reform-minded group of small and medium-sized coffee producers, coffee processors who had long controlled the industry but whose power was on the wane, and executive and legal branches of the state acting as intermediaries between the two groups. Waged labourers have long played an indispensable role in the coffee industry, but had no voice in these struggles. We are looking at a social movement instigated and inspired by small and medium-sized property owners against the dominant interests of the ruling elite; a class-based social movement in which passions were aroused and different interests played out (Pratt 2003). While there are antecedents to social unrest, detailed documentation of agitation begins only in the 1920s. The early protests and putative organisations are important; they emerged during a period of relative prosperity in the coffee industry and show that the conflict was not merely a reflex reaction to prices (Acuña 1985:186). Nevertheless, the most intense campaigning coincides with significant slumps in the coffee market such as those that occurred in the 1930s and 1950s. Both these periods became occasions for significant mobilisations, intense negotiation over social and economic relationships, and changes in legal statutes.

Between 1928 and 1932 coffee more than halved in value.[48] Anticipating problems, processors cancelled advance payments for coffee and called in debts, and exporters formed an association, the *Camara de Cafetaleros*, to protect their interests. More importantly, evidence suggests they succeeded in passing on the worst effects of the crisis to growers; the decline in prices paid to producers has been estimated to be a third greater than the falls on the international market (Acuña 1985:190). Farmers reacted by demanding government intervention and rallied behind the National Association of Coffee Producers under the leadership of a leading coffee grower, Manuel Marín.

To make their case, the farmers put forward a number of specific arguments. Firstly, they represented themselves as an exploited group, the agents of their exploitation being what they termed the 'trust' of processors:

What is this 'trust' of the Costa Rican coffee processor? It is simply this: the processors meet, do their calculations, all absolutely all in their favour, and without the slightest intervention from the victim, they say: 'this is the price of coffee', and anyone who does not accept it can just swallow his coffee and be ruined or sue us; and since they pay what they call 'current prices' although they fix those prices themselves, the poor farmer finds himself up a dead-end street: he cannot swallow his coffee and he cannot sue. Isn't this a despicable 'trust'? (*La Tribuna* 1921, cited in Acuña 1987:141, my translation)

Government and public employees and the urban middle classes were also blamed. They were derided for their lifestyle, decried for demanding excessive and iniquitous taxation, lambasted for introducing a profligate and unnecessary bureaucratic machine, and condemned for living from the sweat of *campesinos'* toil. But at the same time politicians were potential allies who could protect the social and economic wellbeing of producers from greedy processors.

Secondly, the farmers claimed that unfair prices and taxation would drag them into poverty and destitution. From there, despite naturally moderate and reformist views, the looming threat of communist extremism was used to gain political leverage. Thirdly, and in opposition to this, producers expressed a kind of 'mercantile utopianism' in which just exchange could and should be realised without 'the domineering and wicked distortions of capitalism' (Acuña Ortega 1987:148; González Ortega 1987:172). This economic vision draws on the legend of the yeoman farmer, a persuasive tool in the politics of the growers.

A number of proposals were made to address these complaints; the founding of a regulatory body to mediate between producers and processors and to control prices; access to be made to information on the price of Costa Rican coffee in international markets; credit to be available to small producers through the national bank; and a call in favour of a cooperative system to allow small and medium-sized producers to process their own coffee (Acuña Ortega 1985:186–187). Some of these demands were quickly met, although the growers would have to wait some 30 years, until 1958, for a law to be passed allowing them to form cooperatives.

Acting as spokesperson, Manuel Marín presented two draft laws to Congress that aimed to fix prices and oversee relations between processors and producers. These proposals were rejected, but two laws were passed in 1933. The first established a government department to protect the interests of the coffee industry; this *Instituto de Defensa del Café*, or Idecafé, became the coffee office in 1948, and continues to operate today as the Coffee Institute (Icafé). A second law regulated the relationship between processors and producers and fixed the profit margins allowed to processors. The powerful coffee elite refused to submit to the imposed conditions, and the law was modified to allow processors to deduct 16 per cent of the sale price of the coffee from producers (Winson 1989:83).[49] These events of the 1930s changed the face of the coffee industry. Manoeuvring between the different coffee interests, the state adopted a role as a regulatory body, took up a position that would allow it to raise greater revenues from coffee, and curbed the power of the coffee barons. On the other hand, the margins proposed still favoured processors, a fact that left the door open for future conflict. Although the producer organisations and Marín appeared to lose influence and receded into the background in the latter part of the 1930s, demands for renegotiation and minimum prices did not disappear from the political agenda. As the crisis stretched into the 1940s, President Calderón implemented legislation to exonerate producers from most taxes, and planned to guarantee minimum prices.[50]

The next major period of crisis began in the 1950s with the introduction of a tax on coffee exports, designed to raise revenue for the welfare state and for modernisation programmes.[51] This tax would be passed on by processors and levied on growers.[52] Like the earlier wealth tax, the new legislation met stiff opposition from a coalition of farmers and processors, many of whom were also growers. The Association of Producers experienced a renaissance, and successfully called thousands of protesting growers onto the streets of San José.[53] Under intense pressure the government proposed a compromise. In 1952 the old law that allowed processors a 16 per cent profit was renegotiated and reduced to 9 per cent, with the major part of the difference going to the state, in the form of a 5 per cent tax to be paid as long as the price was higher than $40 a sack. Unfortunately, how this would be calculated remained open to question since coffees from various zones exhibit a range of qualities and fetch different prices. At the same time the state extracted a new levy on exports. Coffee processors claimed that changes in the law represented a 25 per cent increase in costs; certainly some of the financial burden shifted away from producers and on to processors. Declining profit margins favoured larger and more efficient plants and led to a reduction in the number of *beneficios* in the country.[54]

While these measures were introduced, and even supported by processors during the boom years of the early 1950s, they became more hotly contested once recession returned at the end of the decade. Between 1957 and 1961 prices fell from $90 to $36 on the American market. Processors were now subject to heavier taxation, but growers were also under pressure. In the early 1960s, production costs were calculated at 200 *colones* for a *fanega*, but farm-gate prices were 175 *colones*. Although, as we shall discover, farmers have strategies to deal with such situations, it is apparent that they were operating at or close to a loss. Their discontent was fuelled by a failure to implement an electoral promise to introduce a minimum price of 200 *colones* per *fanega*, and by further deductions made by processors. These included a 2 per cent commission charge for administering credit delivered by the national bank, a charge of 20 cents per *fanega* to cover marketing costs, 100 per cent profit on processing,[55] and private deals between exporters and processors to raise profitability and presumably avoid taxation.

It was clear that in the light of the crisis, and to deal with tension between the coffee industry and the state, growers and processors, new legislation was required. In 1961 a Congressional representative, Luis Alberto Monge, who would later become President, proposed and introduced Law 2762: 'Rules Governing Relations between Producers, Processors and Exporters of Coffee'. As proposed, this law took the side of small farmers. It sought to resolve dissatisfaction by providing a just return for farm work, to curb the excessive profits of the processors, and to defend the private property of small and medium-sized growers, while at the same time fomenting the kind of economic and technical development in the industry that would later transform Coopeldos.

Yet beneath the rhetoric lay more complex processes, judgments and motives. Farmers were no longer able to represent themselves as the guardians of Costa Rican democratic stability; relations in the coffee industry, and with it Costa Rican exceptionalism, were now enshrined in statute and it was no longer the exclusive preserve of a smallholding peasantry (Paige 1997:233–237). At the same time a sea change occurred in analyses of the problems of the industry, with the actors providing diagnosis and suggested resolutions (González Ortega 1987).[56]

In the earlier period, farmers' representatives were drawn from the ranks of the producers themselves, but by the middle of the century politicians and experts from the professional middle classes dominated the movement. They introduced a more global and studied understanding of the workings of the coffee industry, including a recognition of the dependency of primary producers on export-oriented agriculture, and problems attributed to unequal exchange relations between North and South. To respond, a raft of more 'technical' solutions were suggested (see González Ortega 1987:184). In comparison to the sophisticated analysis and far-reaching remedies of the professional economists and politicians, the producers' demands remained largely unchanged. They continued to campaign on the national stage for a minimum price of 200 *colones* per *fanega*, and for reduced taxation on coffee production and marketing within Costa Rica.

By the 1960s, then, the conflict between the producers and processors had been sidelined, and groups with greater political power dominated and administered the coffee business, seeking to protect state revenue. In place of the moral outcry of producers against exploitation, these new middle-class actors preached modernisation and progress, a model that was imported to the cooperative sector. Meanwhile, the moral tone of the producers was pushed off the agenda, but not silenced. In the concluding section of this chapter I explore the persistence of dissent by demonstrating that cooperatives themselves are not immune from moral adjudication.

PROGRESS AND GROWTH: CONTESTING THE BENEFITS

As in the discussion of national politics and the case of Coocafé, two sets of ideas are affirmed through the activities of Coopeldos. The first relates to progress, and concerns running an efficient institution, what González Ortega (1987:173) calls technical-economic rationality. The other is social and moral, and is directed towards the question of distributive justice. In commenting on and discussing the cooperative, producers as well as staff draw on and emphasise these two aspects to varying degrees. For example, the manager, Juan Carlos, stresses the need for growth and efficiency, but at other moments accentuates the cooperative's contributions to social welfare. For him, and for many producers, there is little or no contradiction between the two aims.

The most vocal supporters of Coopeldos are usually younger and perhaps more technically minded coffee farmers. They often involve themselves in cooperative activities and may sit on one of the many boards, such as the Administrative Council (*Consejo de Administración*), the Education Committee (*Comité de Educación*), the Appointments Committee (*Comité de Nominaciones*), or the Audit Committee (*Comité de Vigilancia*). Others are employed by the cooperative in some capacity and work their own land in their free time. Even if they play no part in the running of Coopeldos in direct ways, these producers generally attend village-level meetings organised at least once a year by the cooperative to disseminate information. They try to follow guidelines for best practice, attending courses in cultivation techniques, or showing a readiness to experiment with new systems such as organic agriculture. I consider these producers an 'inner circle' who have used Coopeldos in beneficial ways. They are quick to point to the achievements of Coopeldos and are supportive of its policies. As active and vocal *cooperativistas*,[57] these farmers make good, reliable informants on the work of the cooperative for outside visitors from NGOs and other organisations.

Several such growers approached me and invited me to visit their farms to discuss topics related to agriculture; they were articulate, keen to give their opinions on farming and the coffee industry, and often expressed support for Coopeldos. They were also inquisitive about Britain and the consumers of their product. At least part of their reason for pressing their views may be because others are more ready to criticise, overtly, by faint praise or with thinly disguised asides.[58] The farmers who speak against the cooperative are generally from an older generation. The grounds for complaint are similar to those made by producers against exploitative processors and idle bureaucrats, as revealed in the studies detailed above of the political conflicts of the mid-twentieth century; older farmers around El Dos may retain memories of those struggles.

The persistence of voices of dissent is surprising. The literature follows the period up to reforms in the coffee laws in 1961, and although evidence of further unrest is admitted, this date is represented as a watershed, and closure and resolution implied. According to interviews carried out by Paige with the dominant processing families, Law 2762 is eulogised by the coffee elite as a 'hymn of peace', synonymous with the democracy, harmony and the equality of Costa Rican coffee culture – *la cultura cafetelera* – highlighted by farmers in the political mobilisations of the 1930s. Further, as Paige attests (1997:237–239), processors identify with farmers and emphasise the mutual relationship they have with growers. Evidence suggests this sentiment is not always reciprocated. More importantly, the cooperative sector is generally if not universally perceived as a panacea, promoted by farmers themselves as the solution to their problems (Winson 1989:107–108). While this may hold true for the more ebullient of cooperative supporters, and is in keeping with the professed moral purposes of the cooperatives to represent the interests of small farmers, the persistence of dissidence shows that even the cooperative sector is not beyond criticism.

As we have seen, the law regulating the coffee business represents a settlement between particular political and economic interests and remains a reflection of power relations. As is the case with all other *beneficios*, the deductions that Coopeldos is permitted to make for processing the members' coffee are fixed by law at 9 per cent of the sale price. This gives all processors a guaranteed margin for profit. On the other hand, the law demands that the international price must be passed on to the producer. While this can benefit growers in boom years, it also means that when prices fall the losses are passed down from the industrial and export side of the business to farmers. The obvious way to avoid this is to guarantee a minimum price to farmers, something that has been part of political negotiations since the 1930s. Fair trade offers such a mechanism for some of the crop from growers affiliated to Coocafé; what it has not as yet done is meet the aspirations of farmers with respect to livelihoods, or silence their objections to commercial trade as being exploitative.

Without guaranteed farm incomes, growers have to work to diminishing margins as prices fall. Processors, by contrast, always operate at the legally endorsed 9 per cent profit margin. This prompted several residents to present me with the following riddle:

'Who is the best coffee farmer around here? Is it Mr X or Mr Y?' [At this point the questioner would put forward suggestions of several experienced local producers, according them the formal title of *Don*]. 'No,' they would continue, 'these are good farmers, but those who work for the cooperative do best. They have paid holidays, a regular and guaranteed income, sick pay and many other benefits that no farmer receives' (my translation).

Some of the critiques offer a more radical agenda than the reform-minded attitude attributed to coffee farmers in the literature, suggesting the influence of 'communist' ideas. In fact, a number of residents who had worked in the banana enclave at an earlier time in their life claimed to have communist sympathies.

I first became aware of such politically informed criticism of the cooperative in the first few days of my stay in El Dos, during a conversation with a resident who introduced himself as Charles. This man owns considerable land, coffee and cattle, and made the following comment:

I like the cooperative, but in my own way. I think that if you amass a fund, a more or less considerable capital in order to cooperate with those who have nothing and set about driving out poverty and misery, I would be *cooperativista*. But the cooperative is too bureaucratic; there are those who earn a lot of money, and others who live badly, and this I do not like (my translation).

The main thrust of Charles's complaint is that the cooperative does little to alleviate, and even exacerbates, inequalities. Although this runs counter to common conceptions of cooperative organisations, this comment cannot easily be dismissed. First and foremost, Costa Rican cooperatives are made up of landowners. In the case of Coopeldos the majority of these are small and medium-sized farmers, and its primary purpose is to represent their interests. As a result, landless locals and migrant workers can only benefit indirectly from its activities and are excluded from many of the programmes. A case in point is land distribution. Credit to buy plots to plant coffee was available to cooperative members on preferential terms; non-members, on the other hand, required a considerable down-payment to be allowed to participate. Effectively this excluded those who did not already possess assets. When questioned on this policy, Juan Carlos pointed out that he could not offer non-members the same terms and conditions as *asociados*; there had to be perceived benefits of belonging to Coopeldos, and the membership could sack him if he did not protect their interests.

CONCLUSION

These first two chapters have examined institutional relationships within and between cooperatives and allied organisations, at the same time locating them within a specifically Costa Rican political history and emphasising the common concern of various parties to combat sources of exploitation identified with commodity relations. We can best understand the latter by beginning with the commodity form itself. Exploitation, according to one voice in Western culture, cannot originate with the use value imbued in an object by the transformative work that converts raw materials from nature into, say, a cappuccino or latte coffee. Quite the opposite; illicit extraction of surplus occurs in Marx's version of classical political economy because intermediaries seek profit by paying workers less than the value they produce through their creative acts, so reducing them to penury.

Once established, this principle leads different parties to their own solutions, but it is usually expressed as various versions of trade justice, or fair trade. For cooperative managers the cooperative project is a moral pursuit; their expressed aim is to provide the best possible service for members, to promote development in their area of influence and to generate optimum prices for small and medium-sized coffee farmers. In this version, taking part-ownership of the industrial and commercial stages of an efficient business helps producers avoid exploitation, as more of the value created down the coffee chain returns to them. The mission the managers set themselves is informed by and is part of wider political, economic and social programmes in Costa Rica, and fair trade falls within these ambitions. The minimum prices of alternative trade may come from a new source, but are nevertheless inextricably caught up in longer-term political agendas and struggles. More specifically, fair trade for managers becomes a practical tool to pursue a wider ethical imperative; it can be used and is useful for securing better prices at certain times for the benefit of their members in uncertain markets.

But commentaries upon Coopeldos and its operations by some growers show that the neither the coffee settlement – the 'hymn of peace' of Law 2672 – nor the cooperative principle, has abolished conflicts of interest in the industry. Costa Rica may not suffer from the extremes of poverty and coercion experienced in neighbouring countries,[59] but by acknowledging contestation in a country renowned for its commitments to peace, democracy, harmony and equality I open a space for the exploration of small farmers' ideology, in particular moral and political ideas about the creation of value. Eventually, this will allow investigation of what a commitment to fair trade looks like from different perspectives, while acknowledging commonalities across contexts.

Prior to this, it is necessary to understand agricultural production and coffee cultivation more fully. For farmers and labourers economic activity is an uncertain affair. Whereas the profit margin of processing remains fixed, and the pay and conditions of employment are more or less guaranteed, growers must tailor their agricultural activities to market prices, cope with fluctuating labour needs over the year, and face the uncertainties that result from interactions with nature. Market agriculture as a business is fraught with risks; as producers lose sight of their product in global commodity markets, so the value of the return they receive for their work through their product, and their livelihoods, become uncertain.

3 FARMING FOR THE GLOBAL ECONOMY: 'PLAYING' AND 'JUGGLING' IN THE MARKET

In the first two chapters fair trade was located within the Costa Rican cooperative movement. Pursuing their self-professed mission to promote the interests of small farmers, the managers of Coopeldos and Coocafé developed increasingly successful and efficient organisations. Within these, fair trade has been used strategically as a market opportunity, a sales outlet that can be accessed on behalf of producers to help them escape exploitation. What is not yet clear is how farmers conceive of and proceed in their market-oriented activities in this context. The next three chapters consider agricultural production in relation to the market, to labour relations and to nature, in that order.

Documenting commercial agriculture reveals differentiation in the rural economy; in place of the generic small coffee farmer conjured up by fair trade marketing, we see people engaged in a wide range of economic activities. As an extension of this, the chapters expose different interests, and how these play out are justified and experienced on the ground. One way to consider this is in terms of surplus extraction. We saw in the last chapter how professionals, among whom I include cooperative managers, became involved in negotiations between growers and processors in the coffee industry, and introduced a more sophisticated view of the global economy. Farmers, meanwhile, have a different perspective.

In describing farmers' engagement with the market I draw on local idioms. John Berger has neatly captured the prevailing understanding of farming among peasantries as a series of ambushes of risks and dangers (1979: xvii). In Latin America *campesinos* express this through terms that see agriculture as a kind of game, albeit a deadly serious one (Gudeman and Rivera 1990:31). Utilising local ways of speaking has the advantage of presenting the data in a form that should make sense to those being described. But the local terms also feed into a longstanding theme in social science.[60] Being a practical language, it mediates between strategic, purposive action and the constraints people face in social life, either because of the material limits to their lives or because of the unforeseen consequences of their own and others' actions.

On one level this comes across as a language of options and choice. For example, this chapter explores what prompts landowners to cultivate coffee rather than, say, start a dairy, engage in cattle farming, or grow tomatoes. To proceed, farmers must make technical decisions, adjust activities to changing circumstance, employ trial and error, and manoeuvre their way through the farming calendar. In reaching decisions, as one must in a game, farmers rely on prior experience of markets, utilise contacts, refer to knowledge of the land and local conditions, develop confidence in handling particular farming systems, and express personal preferences, all of which stem from the inheritance of family background and indicate culturally informed ideas and persuasions. Choice and decision-making reflect the values of the 'market-oriented, commercialised peasantry' present within the local economy since the arrival of the first settlers 100 years ago (Gudmundson 1983:152).

However, choices are always framed and limited by circumstance. Firstly, landholdings and other resources that farmers have at their disposal determine options – such as the capacity to secure loans and scales of production – which can be at least as important in making a living as prices. Secondly, the prevailing climate on the farm encourages certain forms of agriculture. Thirdly, farmers consider the fluctuations of various markets, which are unpredictable but exhibit specific characteristics. Lastly, they are influenced by systems of payment and delays in cash returns in the different industries. So farmers mobilise and orient themselves within certain bounds. As landowners they have a limited range of options; they can, in principle, determine the destination of their product, which opens up a space for economic manoeuvre, but in practice their choices are restricted and prices are largely beyond their control. What needs to be understood is who is most likely to be 'ambushed', what risks different parties face, and what they can and can't do about it.

How does this relate to the wider problematic of the book, the grounds upon which fair trade products appeal to us? One issue is fairness. Ethics and justice in the Western model aspire to formal equality, due process and predictable outcomes. For consumers fair trade is perceived to fulfil these conditions by offering guaranteed minimum prices to producers. On the other hand, as the literature sometimes laments, growers appear ignorant or unconvinced of the benefits of alternative trade (Lyon 2006; Murray, Raynolds and Taylor 2003:17; Ronchi 2002). The assumption is that there is a breakdown in communication, which can be overcome by supplying more and better information to producers. I wish to make a different case. Coopeldos has such mechanisms in place; the fair-trade system is regularly and clearly explained at meetings and often referred to in written documents supplied to members.[61] As a result, most farmers know about fair trade, but since it is administered through formal commercial channels it becomes entangled in ideas and experiences of the market. The problem is that, although many growers acknowledged and appreciated consumers' willingness to pay a premium, they do not associate commodity markets with ethics. Whereas the consumption of fair-trade products can be construed as a moral activity, production for markets is hedged by uncertainty, which can only be met by a kind of practical expediency.

A related theme is the desire in fair trade to establish a connection with producers. This can be seen as part of a more general concern in one influential strand of Western culture, most commonly associated with Marx, with the primacy of the value created by labour. From that standpoint a moral order can only be established when people control their productive activities and their products. Conversely, processes of alienation and fetishisation ensue when intermediaries come between producers and the things they make. For consumers, fair trade appears to offer a way out of a conundrum by establishing a direct relation with small family farmers working their own land and operating through cooperative organisations. For farmers it is not so simple; one might say that as they lose sight of their products in the global economy, a process that begins when they deliver their coffee cherries to the cooperative, so they cede control of their product to other people, and uncertainties escalate.

FARMING FAMILIES IN EL DOS

Landowners commonly build their houses on the farm (*finca*), choosing a site close to or adjoining a track, which leads to a dispersed or ribbon-like settlement pattern. Extended families occupy and are associated with certain areas; unmarried children often cohabit with their parents, those that marry build houses nearby, and siblings frequently live near one another. The landowning families of El Dos are described below as discrete units for reasons of clarity, but there are multiple and complex kinship ties between many of the resident families.[62]

There are about ten extended landowning families in El Dos. They constitute more than half the 84 domestic households. Of the 49 families that own land in El Dos, 31 make some income from coffee, almost half earn money from milk production, and eight live from cattle (Table 5, p. 190). These houses represent the family-run, market-oriented agriculture practised in the Tilarán Highlands. A characteristic of the household is the management of the land by men, while women concentrate on running the domestic space. This does not preclude women from employment, owning land or from joining the cooperative, but it is very uncommon for them to work in commercial agriculture, except in the coffee harvest.[63] Economic activity involves maintaining multiple incomes and adopting new ones should others fail. As scholars have long recognised, in Latin America rural producers and households engage in a range of activities to create livelihoods (Deere 1990; Gudmundson 1995; Lehmann 1982; Roseberry 1989). The following view of some of the key families in El Dos indicates the range of agricultural activities practised by landowners, and demonstrates the various avenues for making a living.

THE ALVARADO FAMILY

The Alvarado family fit the image we have in the West, projected by the media and played on in fair-trade advertising, of small family farmers and coffee producers. Carlos, the father, Estefanía, the mother, and an unmarried daughter live in a concrete house they built not 50 metres from where Carlos was born. The house is surrounded by the coffee bushes that provide most of their income. The women work hard keeping house and fill spare moments in the harvest season picking coffee. Carlos, now in his seventies, no longer works, but spends his days in conversation with neighbours and visitors, playing cards and overseeing the management of the small family coffee grove. Over the years he has tried a variety of occupations, including working as an agricultural labourer 'wielding a machete' (*volando machete*), raising cattle, running a general store and transporting produce to market, first with a string of horses, and later by ox cart (*carreta*). None of these enterprises was ever particularly successful, a fact that Carlos now associates with an earlier predilection for homemade maize beer and distilled alcohol (*guaro*). He is now an evangelical Christian and teetotal.

There are six children in all, but only three live in El Dos, and one of these intermittently. Carlitos lives next door to his parents and like them makes a living from coffee. He farms a couple of hectares, enough to provide the cash income his family needs when prices are good, but in the recent depressed market he has had to supplement the family income by doing extra labour for cash. He is fortunate in that his father provides the employment he needs. The two brothers resident in El Dos also work at agriculture. Jorge, the elder, grows coffee on about two hectares and at one time experimented with organic systems, although he has now reverted to conventional practices. He has a second income as owner of a garage, employs a mechanic and sells fuel from barrels. The youngest brother, Wilberth, is the least settled of the children; he has owned coffee groves, but sold one to finance a projected though unsuccessful move to the United States. He is also involved in a project raising cattle on the plains to the north. He is an occasional resident of El Dos and has a room at his parents' house. All the Alvarado households sell their coffee through Coopeldos.

THE LEITÓN FAMILY

The Leitóns are large landowners compared to the Alvarado family. Although some of them grow coffee they specialise in cattle and dairy farming. Amadeo Leitón originally claimed land after he came to the highlands in the 1920s. The children inherited equally sized farms when Amadeo retired. The daughter has sold her share to one of her brothers, and now keeps house and cares for her elderly father and mother. They live in a neat wooden house on the main track into El Dos.

The oldest son, Enar, lives next door and with the aid of his unmarried son, Alex, they keep tough, disease-resistant zebu cattle. Alex calls the system they use a 'double proposition' (*doble proposito*) since it provides both milk and meat. It is based upon allowing cows, calves and bullocks to graze together much of the time and is described by him as 'traditional' and 'more natural'. A second son uses the same system on his farm, an activity that is supplemented by his wife's income from work as a hairdresser and cleaner. A third son, Luis, works a more modern dairy, using machinery, refrigeration and higher-yielding Holstein cows with the help of his sons, who are learning the trade. Their mother runs the household. In the past they have combined these activities with coffee production, but in the light of the recent low prices this has been abandoned and the size of the dairy herd increased. When I first met Luis he had a *cafetal* of just over a hectare, and another smaller one near the house. He was also raising seedlings (*almácigo*) and planned to expand production. However, when I returned in 2003 this project had been dropped, he had cut down his largest grove and the smaller area was overgrown and neglected.

THE MONTERO FAMILY

This family also comprises several independent households. The centre of their activities is the mother's house; Candelaria is now widowed and a pensioner. With the aid of her children she still maintains the more traditional style of *finca*, based upon a model of self-sufficiency described later in the book. She supplements her pension by selling milk and cheese to a limited clientele.

The three sons often work as a team. The eldest, Sabino, runs a local shop. He also grows coffee; part of this is farmed conventionally with his brothers, but he dedicates just over a hectare to his main concern, running and developing an organic system of coffee production. Sabino also has interests in cattle on a larger farm some distance away, but the two other brothers are more involved in the livestock business. The three men are all married and their wives run their respective households, although one of them does domestic labour for another family. Candelaria also has a daughter, Tere, who owns a small area of land, most of which she rents out to local farmers, although she uses a part of it to grow crops and has recently planted a few coffee bushes. Tere's main income comes from renting rooms to travelling salesmen and other visitors.

'PLAYING' AND 'JUGGLING' IN THE ECONOMY

The language the farmers in El Dos use expresses their view of the economy in general, and market agriculture in particular, as a process of strategic engagement, an ongoing process of responding to and modifying conditions. As well as giving farmers the means to describe what they do, the linguistic forms express differing capacities to control outcomes. Four terms are used; each is linked to a common set of ideas, related to the idea of a game, and oriented to the negotiation of uncertainty. They are: *jugar* (to play); *jugarse* (to juggle or gamble); *la lotería* or *la rifa* (lottery or raffle); and *tantear* (to try to calculate or size up). These words came up repeatedly in conversations with and between producers. As such, they formed a backing commentary on discussions about the economy; the metaphors defined and shaped the context within which my research into production systems was set, and undermined attempts to quantify farming.[64] Despite the best efforts of Coopeldos to persuade them otherwise, farmers do not keep accounts and consider cost-benefit analysis a futile and rather foolish occupation. In this respect, one might argue, they refuse the transition to capitalist accounting systems, based upon calculation of inputs and profits, highlighted by Pratt (1994).

The verb *tantear* refers to trial and error, and comes closest to rational procedure. Farmers *tantear* different varieties of plants to see how they perform, and to help them decide what to plant; the inference is of ongoing experimentation, with a view to improving results. However, on entering the market, producers also actively engage in a process of 'sizing up prices' (*tanteando precios*), which involves judgments and consequent choices about who to sell their produce to, and in what quantities. To *tantear* means amassing evidence regarding the imputed qualities of genotypes or the conditions of sale offered by different market intermediaries and making decisions on that basis.

Towards the other end of the spectrum we have references to the lottery, used when future results are unpredictable. This does not mean that outcomes will necessarily be negative; *la lotería* evokes uncertainty, and so it is used when there is a tenuous relation between means and ends, input and outcome. The results of a decision may be entirely beneficial or catastrophic, but there is little ability to control outcomes. It is hardly surprising that tomato production, the riskiest of all crops, is frequently described as 'a real lottery'. This is because of the radical and unpredictable variation in prices, as well as the susceptibility of the crop to pests and disease. Farmers can protect against this to a degree by investing time and money in applying chemicals, but it is not fail-safe, just as buying more lottery tickets improves one's chances of winning, but does not guarantee success. The idea of trying one's luck relates to a more general fascination with lotteries and raffles in Costa Rican life (Sick 1999:87–88). The raffle (*la rifa*) is a central part of almost all social and institutional occasions. At the Annual Assembly of the cooperative the serious business of the day is interspersed with the drawing of numbers, with prizes ranging from colour televisions to sacks of fertiliser. At a course on Modern Techniques of Coffee Production that I attended, the culmination of each session was a raffle of trade merchandise brought in by the guest speakers.

The relation between markets and the lottery was made explicit in a meeting between the general manager of the cooperative and a group of coffee growers in which the former explained how coffee was sold on the open market. 'It is like when you set up your stall in the marketplace and people come along and offer a price for your produce, and you have to decide whether to sell or try to wait for a better deal; it's a lottery.' Farmers understood the observation and it was repeated to me on several occasions: 'the coffee market is a lottery, just like other markets', producers would say. In drawing this analogy Juan Carlos was feeding into a long but now almost defunct experience of exchange, in which producers supplied fruit, vegetables, coffee and sugar to nearby urban centres. This exchange was notoriously fraught, and I was given many examples of great efforts being made to transport produce by horse or oxen down virtually impassable tracks, only to discover the load to be worthless. One older resident recalled dumping the plantain he had taken to market down a ravine, as nobody would buy it at any price; another remembered giving his entire crop of *chayote* (a vegetable similar to a squash) to a distant relation in the town in exchange for lunch. These local markets have now largely closed down. Rather than hawking their wares in town people tend to sell their produce through commercial outlets:

coffee to the cooperative, milk to the cheese-processing plant, beef to traders who tour the area on horseback, or at auction, and tomatoes to wholesalers.

Tantear and *la lotería* represent extremities of control; when farmers wish to express active and conscious experimentation they use *tantear*, when indicating submission to chance or resignation they speak of *la lotería*. By contrast, the verb forms *jugar* ('playing') and *jugarse* ('juggling') seem to operate on the middle ground. Farmers use these terms to refer to attempts to control outcomes, at the same time recognising that circumstances are given. They are agents in so far as they exercise skill and judgment in economic life, but they do not entirely set those conditions, nor do they rewrite the rules of the game every time they act.

Of these terms, the one most often heard is the reflexive form *jugarse*, which has a literal meaning close to our word juggle, but like its English equivalent, it has other connotations. On a general level it is similar to the English verb 'to manage', in the sense of having enough. Tere Montero explained that she could 'juggle' (*me lo juega*) with what she had found when collecting plants for a medicinal infusion. Carlos Alvarado was worried about the future of his younger son, when compared to his other offspring, who were settled and economically autonomous. Only Wilberth had problems since 'he was not juggling' (*no se lo juega*), while his siblings had no difficulties in this respect (*se lo juegan bien*). In a stricter sense *jugarse* suggests the requirement to gamble with the resources at one's disposal, so farmers say they have sufficient, or perhaps not enough, coffee or cows to juggle with.

The related verb form *jugar* is used to denote particular economic strategies. *Jugar* translates literally as 'to play', but a closer equivalent would be the English term 'dabble'. When explaining the crops they grow, employment opportunities they have taken up, or investments they have made in time, money or labour, they claim to be 'playing'; for example, they say 'I play with coffee a bit' (*juego un poco con café*). The idea of playing can also be related to the wisdom of maintaining multiple incomes. To eliminate a potential source of cash, by cutting down coffee for example, is considered an error, since 'one has to keep playing in life'. The long form of *jugar* is precisely 'playing with luck' (*jugando con la suerte*). The elderly and landless Nicaraguan *émigré* we met in the introduction, in describing his application for land distribution under the government programme run by the Institute for Agricultural Development (IDA) said he was 'playing with luck'. Under this scheme plots are provided to the landless for cultivation. A small administration fee is levied, but no charge is made for the land itself. If there are too many applicants then distribution is determined by a raffle, and a successful outcome is literally a matter of good fortune.

The way farmers describe economic life helps us to understand how they think about their activities, but it also throws light upon our own ideas on the economy (Gudeman 1986; Gudeman and Rivera 1990). To speak of 'playing', 'juggling', 'trial and error' and 'the lottery' makes sense to us because we often talk in our own lives in similar ways; parents juggle childcare, we play with different options, try out possibilities and consider aspects of life something of a lottery. Farmers use *jugar, jugarse, tantear,* and *la lotería* in daily conversation and with respect to their main sources of income; it is central to their orientation to economic life. In an ideal world the language would be analogous with economic security; many people are privileged to speak of securing a livelihood, making a living, and having a job. The fact that farmers use a more contingent language graphically demonstrates the precariousness of their position.

The terminology *jugar, jugarse, tantear* and *la lotería* help account for coffee farmers' apparent reluctance to accept the concept of fair trade in commerce; it runs counter to cultural values and contradicts the model of the economy producers work from. Farming, in their view, and according to experience, means using one's resources and abilities to 'juggle' a livelihood under uncertainty; there is a denial of predictability or security of income. The model they evoke encapsulates the idea that success in agriculture is based on luck. Will the product come to fruition and in what quantities? Will the market peak or fall in the coming months and years? Agriculture is a game of chance and a lottery; it requires experimentation and playing on luck. In as much as it demands skill in applying knowledge to resources it also requires strategy and practical competence, but cannot easily respond to appeals to justice or equality.

FARM STRATEGIES AND AGRICULTURAL PRACTICE

In the 'play' of economic life, farmers have different capital resources at their disposal and diverse knowledge and experience upon which to draw, as well as personal preferences to express. But, as we shall see, coffee, beef, dairy and minor cash crops such as tomatoes also have different qualities that must be understood and taken in to account if they are to be worked successfully. In this respect things or products can also be considered agents in economic life (Latour 1993). The rolling hills of the Tilarán Highlands are primarily given over to pasture for cattle and dairy farming, but the meadows are interspersed with groves of coffee bushes, or *cafetales,* stands of original rainforest and belts of exotic tree species, planted to provide shelter from strong winds. Interpreting and understanding this landscape requires knowledge of farming systems, land-ownership patterns and the importance of climatic variations. Information on agricultural production systems allows a better understanding of farming and the place of coffee in the livelihoods of farmers.

To the west of Coopeldos the land rises steeply up to Campos de Oro. On this ridge, which stretches southeast to the communities of San Rafael and Cebadilla, the warm Pacific winds, dry summers and altitude provide good coffee-growing conditions. On the other hand, it is too dry for quality pasture. The land in Campos de Oro is relatively evenly distributed; two-thirds of all families grow coffee and are registered members of the cooperative. There are several larger landowners but only seven landless families. Such data helps gives credence to a 'democratising effect' of coffee cultivation. By contrast, to the north and east of the cooperative it is cooler and wetter under the Atlantic influence, and farming is more mixed. In the communities of El Dos, Esperanza, Cabeceras and Las Nubes coffee is grown successfully, but herds of dairy cows also graze. Land ownership in El Dos is more concentrated than in Campos de Oro; almost 40 per cent of families have no land. Although some households limit commercial agriculture to coffee, the majority keep cattle or dairy herds, and all try to generate income from a variety of sources.

Access to land influences but does not determine agricultural activities. Coffee production is more intensive than beef cattle, while dairy farming can be practised more or less intensively, but it is generally agreed that it needs a minimum of three hectares. Not so with coffee, which can be cultivated on a very small scale as part of a kitchen garden. Data from two parts of the highlands, Campos de Oro and El Dos, show that while some larger landowners combine coffee growing with cattle or a dairy, the majority of coffee farmers specialise in the crop (Table 5). The smallest dairy in El Dos is run on three hectares, less than that owned by several coffee specialists. This farm is managed in intensive fashion by the son of one of the foremost dairymen in El Dos. So although landholdings frame the type of agriculture practised, cultural factors and personal preferences also inform choices. Farmers often emphasise a family connection with production systems, reflecting experience and expertise in a particular endeavour. 'My father had coffee, so I grew up with it', and 'my family have always kept cattle, I know what to do', were typical comments.

Perhaps surprisingly, fluctuations in market price appear to be a secondary consideration when weighing up the attractions of different agricultural pursuits. The timing and regularity of payments, that is, the interval between investment and return, often assumes as much importance as the final sum received. At the time of my initial fieldwork many preferred milk production because the cheque from the factory arrived each month, compared to payments made by Coopeldos, which arrive every two months. Although the cooperative has now changed and also makes monthly payments, these are for the previous year's harvest. As I argue below, the hiatus between delivery and payment has profound implications for the coffee industry.

When making decisions, farmers often prioritise level of investment over return or the stability of a particular market. The highest start-up costs are associated with dairy. Most farmers have now switched away from traditional breeds of cow, which are resistant to climate and disease, to expensive, high-yielding milkers and modern intensive systems. Milking is still done by hand by some farmers, but many have installed machinery, and in any case there are some costs that cannot easily be eliminated: refrigeration units, a milking shed, good livestock, daily labour inputs, fodder and medicines, transport and sufficient land for pasture. Farmers scrutinise the performance of these factors and discuss them with neighbours, since the decision to raise investment leads to greater possible losses. Because of expense, most farmers characterise dairy farming as more risky than coffee, even though milk prices are more stable. As several people pointed out, 'if a cow dies it costs a fortune to replace, if a coffee bush fails you just plant another seedling, which you can produce yourself or buy for next to nothing'.

Among the four main commercial operations, prices for milk are most predictable. Dairy farmers are shareholders in the cheese factory at Monteverde, which is a limited company (*Sociedad Anonima*). They are entitled to deliver churns to the factory on a daily basis, but they must pay for this right, and in return are given a guaranteed price of about $0.30 cents (82 *colones*) per litre.[65] The minimum-price principle of fair trade is not only extended to coffee farmers in El Dos. The price paid for milk rises more or less in line with inflation. Farmers may deliver in excess of their quota but usually receive a lower rate for this surplus, as it comes with the lush pastures and overproduction of the rainy season. Another factor affecting prices is the system of fines for poor quality imposed by the factory for impurities. Complaints about this procedure were rife; it was said to be impossible to maintain a top rating for quality. However meticulous the standards of cleanliness, impurities would be 'found' in a sample and the price tariff reduced.

In beef farming a shortage of pasture in the dry summer months encourages the sale of cattle and a seasonal drop in price at auction. This problem is exacerbated by the lack of rainfall in lowland Guanacaste, which is a prime beef-rearing zone. In the highlands the drought is shorter and less severe, and farmers try to keep their nerve and withhold sale in expectation of a price rise when the lowland

supply is exhausted. In this respect cattle have an advantage over
other production systems involving more easily perishable goods;
they may be held as 'stock' to be sold when necessity dictates, the
market is propitious or when extra income is required (Gudeman
and Rivera 1990:66–68). Livestock offer a relatively stable market,
but there are significant fixed costs: land on which to graze cattle
and capital to build up and maintain a herd. Of the two possibilities
milk provides most cattle farmers with their regular income in El
Dos, while beef production is often carried out in peripheral areas as
an adjunct to other activities. Those with less land can also pursue
primary and secondary activities; tomatoes are sometimes grown in
the hope of generating extra cash. Coffee, on the other hand, is the
backbone of the local economy.

Tomato production, like a dairy, requires significant investment.
Tomatoes can only be considered in the dry summer months, and
then multiple problems ensue due to the number of pests and fungal
infections that attack the fruit in the tropical environment. Although
at least one innovative farmer has experimented with organic
tomatoes, most apply frequent doses of agrochemicals. Sometimes
the return is low and of poor quality. The national market is also
highly unstable. Prices published in the press demonstrate that the
cost to the consumer fluctuated by about 500 per cent over the year
I spent in Costa Rica. This huge variation is less than that reported
by my informants of a range between 100 and 5,000 *colones* for a 9kg
crate, which reflects the scarcity of tomatoes during the rains and a
glut at the end of the dry season.

Farmers try to anticipate market trends and grow tomatoes in
expectation of shortfalls. Unfortunately this tactic can often fail. One
grower ruefully explained how he had heard nobody was cultivating
tomatoes and had invested in a plot, only to discover when he came
to harvest that the bottom had fallen out of the market. When prices
reach their lowest levels it becomes economically unviable to harvest
and the fruit is left to rot, or word is passed around that tomatoes
are available free for the picking. One resident described growing
and selling tomatoes (and peppers) as 'impossible' and 'disgusting',
even though he regularly cultivated these crops. In El Dos those
that produce them try to offset the risks by working on a small
scale, often in partnership, and undertaking most of the labour
themselves. Due to the risk of total failure, this option is taken up
in the hope of generating extra income, but not as a principal source
of livelihood.

The fact that a minority try their luck at cultivating tomatoes
every year bears testimony to the optimism with which the activity
is approached. My main informant on tomato farming considered
1,000 *colones* ($3.60) per box a break-even price. At this rate a

producer with a small half-*manzana* plot could expect a return close to $4,000.[66] If the price rose to 5,000 *colones* ($18.20), the return for the same area could theoretically reach an almost unbelievable $25,000, a considerable fortune for a small farmer in the highlands. On the other hand, a price of 100 *colones* ($0.36) would signify an unbearable loss.

Compared to tomatoes, coffee gives a more reliable income to those without the resources to start a dairy. The coffee crop is mostly destined for export, with only the inferior third-grade beans remaining in the national market. Prices follow coffee futures markets in the United States, principally the New York Board of Trade.[67] Farmers follow current coffee prices, which are broadcast daily in the media and communicated via the cooperative. The price can oscillate between $200 and recent historic lows of around $50 for a 100lb sack. We might assume that price hikes, known as times of 'fat cows' (*vacas gordas*), do not constitute an immediate problem, so I concentrate here on periods of low prices, or 'lean cows' (*vacas flacas*), and producers' reactions to market falls.

The most obvious solution to low prices is to cut down coffee bushes, a tactic often employed by those with sufficient land and resources to switch to milk production. Many farmers in El Dos used coffee cultivation to accumulate capital to start a dairy. But the desirability of multiple incomes makes completely excising one source an extreme measure. The consensus is that it is a mistake to destroy a *cafetal*, and many who had done this expressed regret at their decision. One less radical option is to temporarily abandon all inputs, concentrate on other economic activities, and await better times. A more common solution is to invest less in fertiliser, pesticides and labour. Many farmers reported reducing the number of applications of fertiliser from the stipulated three down to two as a response to current prices, and others were achieving a similar effect by reducing dosages.

Responses to market prices in coffee farming are a complex issue, in which the system of payment, the delayed effect of inputs and the time taken for coffee bushes to come into production all play a role. In Costa Rica the processor pays producers, but terms and conditions are subject to the legal statute and are overseen by Icafé. Payments are made retrospectively. On delivering the crop for processing the farmer receives what is confusingly called an 'advance' (*adelanto*). From the perspective of the cooperative the term is accurate; they make a payment for coffee received, though they have not yet processed or sold it. However, delivery marks the end of the growers' involvement with the coffee; the *adelanto* comes at the end of the investment process, so for them it is a misnomer. After the *adelanto* a series of instalments (*reajustes*) are paid, calculated according to current sales. The 'final settlement' (*liquidación final*) does not arrive until almost one year after the harvest. There is one more payment made at Coopeldos: the premium (*sobreprecio*) that comes from sales to fair-trade organisations. This system gives farmers a regular income, but makes it difficult for them to respond to prices by adjusting production.

The delayed and cumulative effect on production of fertiliser and chemical inputs exacerbates the problem, since investment in the coffee grove is carried forward into crop returns in future years. This means that the financial results do not become evident until at least two years after the initial investment was made. In order to make predictions producers must weigh up the cost of inputs, projected returns on those investments and a prognosis of the market two years or more hence. Although the cooperative manager remains optimistic about prices, and encourages farmers to maintain production levels and inputs in anticipation of future price rises, farmers tend to manage their farms and invest according to current prices.

A final important issue is the time required for the bushes to reach full production. The development of hybrids that mature rapidly and changes in cultivation techniques now permit farmers to react more quickly.[68] Coffee plants in El Dos spend a year in the nursery beds (*almácigo*), which can be reduced to six months if they are raised in bags, after which they are planted out. Two years later a good harvest is obtained, and maximum production is reached in the third and fourth years. By the fifth year pruning must begin if the vigour of the plants is to be maintained. Despite the shorter time scale, the problem of responding to the market remains; predicting outcomes is almost impossible.

Nonetheless, the cooperative policy is that farmers should not neglect their groves in response to the market, and the organisation continues an ambitious programme of expansion in the area under production to increase turnover and improve economies of scale. During fieldwork in 1998 coffee prices were hovering at around $100, a low but not disastrous price. Despite talk of further price falls, the cooperative forged ahead with credit provision for expanding production. When I questioned the manager on the advisability of this, he was adamant that world prices should not be allowed to affect policy on expansion or maintaining inputs. He explained that even if prices were low, experience told them they would rise again and that they must be ready and prepared to take advantage of that future moment. The cooperative encourages producers to ignore short-term fluctuations in the market, but policy is not always followed in practice; as producers experience falling incomes many cut costs or divert attention away from coffee to use time and resources in different ways.

NEGOTIATING THE MARKET

For farmers, one problem with the market is its unreliability. As we have seen, the extent of the variations in market price depends on the product, and each demonstrates a particular cycle and a specific propensity to fluctuate or stabilise. In the case of coffee it is the cooperative and by extension the general manager who assumes responsibility for the processing and sale of the harvest. At the point of delivery producers relinquish control; as one explained, 'we just leave our coffee at the *beneficio*, the cooperative does the rest'. It is the manager's job to place the product on the market, to decide whom to sell to and when. On the one hand, this requires skill, decisiveness and connections; on the other, the movement of prices depends upon decisions taken in New York and London, which he cannot influence.

In order to succeed as an enterprise most Costa Rican cooperatives must compete for the custom of producers with much larger private processing plants and with multinational businesses. Only in choosing between processors can farmers effectively strategise in their articulation with the market, since they control the product of the land. In her examination of the coffee industry in the Perez Zeledón region of Costa Rica, Sick (1999) points to family-based allegiance, credit options and the quality demands made by different processors as the principal motives for selling to one *beneficio* rather than another. Credit agreements often tie a farmer to a particular company, but this does not preclude multiple membership or shifting allegiance. For example, producers may wish to postpone repayment of a debt to a particular processor, and by taking their unprocessed coffee (cherries) elsewhere they can avoid deductions for credit they owe from payments for coffee. Consideration of the quality of services on offer must also be taken into account; the availability of loans, technical support and the final gate price paid by different companies over the years all effect preferences. Political allegiance also pays a part, as some farmers are more inclined to the cooperative model than others. The focus on strategies employed by farmers to optimise credit facilities, services and the terms and conditions of sale, injects agency into the discussion; the ability to choose and move between processors opens up a space within which farmers can negotiate livelihoods.

In the zone of influence of Coopeldos there is a second, privately owned, processing plant, situated in the nearby community of Turín. It is known amongst farmers as 'the competition' (*la competencia*). The final price paid by the Turín facility has lagged behind the cooperative for all but one of the twelve years 1987–98 (Table 2, p. 187). Neither has the private *beneficio* matched the prodigious growth in production achieved by Coopeldos (Table 4, p. 189). Despite this, Turín guaranteed to match the Coopeldos price to attract customers. In the 1998–99 harvest about ten producers took this opportunity, and according to the Turín manager delivered approximately 400 out of a total production of 1,500 *fanegas* to them, the remainder being made up of coffee grown on land attached to the processing plant. This needs to be compared with the turnover of Coopeldos, which for the same harvest processed 15,000 *fanegas* from some 500 producers. Furthermore, most of those who have delivered to the private company also use the cooperative; what emerges is that *la competencia* was no competition at all.

Talk of Turín as the competition is more about ideas about the market than any real challenge to Coopeldos. There is a powerful consensus that 'competition is good'. It provides a yardstick against which the Coopeldos administration can measure the quality and quantity of services on offer. For the producer, competition allows them to compare prices and choose between alternatives; it is an avenue through which they can express power over their product. One coffee grower, who also dabbles in tomatoes and experiments with different genotypes, outlined the three different potential buyers he had in mind for his tomato crop: a market in the national capital, San José; a wholesaler on the Peninsula of Nicoya; and a provincial chain of supermarkets. The choice of outlet provides landowners with an avenue to express agency in the market. But in the case of coffee there is little opportunity to exercise it.

With respect to coffee, 'sizing up prices' (*tanteando los precios*) refers to the initial payment (*adelanto*) because future instalments, indexed to market sales, are as yet unknown. In theory, the advance is designed to allow the farmer to cover costs and pay for harvest labour. In practice it becomes the locus of competition, with farmers attracted to those companies offering higher advances. In areas of intense competition companies pay ever-higher *adelantos* to seduce producers. Some processors, it is said, have even utilised the advance to buy crops outright (*en firme*), an illegal practice in Costa Rica. Larger companies and multinationals are campaigning for a change in the law to allow them to outbid the smaller players in the industry. During the 1998–99 season Coopeldos paid about 30 per cent less as an advance than Turín.[69] Nevertheless, Coopeldos has tried to resist an increase in the size of the initial payment, a luxury other cooperatives in areas of more intense competition may not be able to afford. The cooperative administration argues that the undoubted attraction to producers of a high advance and immediate cash income is undermined by the danger of farmers spending large amounts upon receipt and being left with insufficient funds to tide them over to the following harvest. That is, the system of instalments is intended to assuage the dangers to producers and processors alike of selling a product that is harvested annually, has a relatively long shelf-life and so can be stored, but exists in an unpredictable and fluctuating market. In addition it helps cooperatives with little capital to avoid excessive outlay at harvest time.

In the El Dos area producers know that despite the higher initial payment the final price paid by Turín has consistently lagged behind the cooperative's. This suggests a further purpose served by competition; the space it provides as an avenue for resistance.[70] The producers who were diverting their crop away from Coopeldos to the Turín plant expressed their reason for doing so as discontent with certain cooperative practices. The most common expression of dissent was that Coopeldos 'takes too much'. This is a reference to the 4 per cent social capital deducted from each member for investment back into the organisation. But the bone of contention was not so much the deduction, but the fact that no interest was paid on social capital. One farmer selling to the competition assured me he would return to the cooperative fold if they paid him even nominal interest on the not insubstantial sum he had invested as social capital in the cooperative. He has entered into lengthy negotiations over this, but to no avail. Social capital is sometimes described as 'dead', and contrast is made with the fact that the farmers have to pay interest on loans secured from the cooperative. However, criticism of Coopeldos on this matter is by no means unanimous; at one meeting a farmer suggested that expecting interest on social capital was against the cooperative spirit (*poco cooperativista*).

A second opportunity to 'size up prices' occurs through the sister cooperative at Santa Elena, which is also a member of Coocafé, and is based in the tourist centre near the Monteverde Cloudforest Reserve. Rather than a protest, as with Turín, the growers' approach here appears to be an opportunistic strategy. Recently Coope Santa Elena has achieved higher prices than Coopeldos, due to the greater percentage of output that has gone into fair-trade markets, and because it has traded on its location in a nature reserve to command premiums for an ecological product. By maintaining membership of two cooperatives, a handful of farmers, particularly those living and farming in the grey area at the periphery of both, seek to exploit two options. As members of Coopeldos they can access superior credit facilities and agricultural extension services, from Santa Elena they expect to receive higher gate prices.

CONCLUSION

Farming activities in the Tilarán Highlands involve exploring new commercial avenues, adjusting techniques and switching between production systems. In their endeavours farmers operate within the confines of possibility, depending upon the financial capital they possess, and their resources in the form of land, which can vary in terms of qualities such as aspect, inclination, climate and fertility. Experience, family traditions and competence also influence farm choices. As a practical activity, farming is bounded by material constraints, but the work and preferences of farmers also reconfigure and shape possibilities. As we have seen, drawing attention to farming practice does two things. Firstly, by documenting different activities it undermines the idea of a uniform, undifferentiated coffee producer growing coffee for a fair-trade market on a small plot of family land. Secondly, we learn that in commercial agriculture farmers' attention is fixed less upon the fairness of prices and more upon practices and strategies for gaining a livelihood in uncertain markets.

The language of farmers depicts how agriculture requires them to juggle resources and play on their knowledge; it illustrates competence mustered to offset market instability. Many people would applaud the efforts of small farmers and support their struggles to negotiate unfavourable commodity markets. Farmers can do this because they own land; they control their productive activities, the form of the things they create, and they have some say in the destination of their product. To this extent their work is not alienated. The problem they have is not with work itself, but with the market, since this is where they lose sight of their products.

In the next chapter the theme of uncertainty continues in an examination of different parties in the labour process. Again the important aspects are internal differentiation in the economy and the relative power of different actors. In the market, farmers are often in a weak position when compared to processors, merchants, exporters, supermarkets and other intermediaries. When it comes to labour and employment, however, the initiative usually, though not always, lies with the landowner.

4 LANDOWNERS AND LABOURERS: UNCERTAINTIES, STRATEGIES AND TENSIONS IN THE LABOUR PROCESS

The previous chapter revealed differentiation among farmers and showed that, rather than being passive recipients of fair-trade premiums, they can navigate their way in a complex market economy. To make a living, farmers manoeuvre and juggle between different production systems and investments. Part of this process is the management of labour requirements. I will now describe the distinct ways in which workers and landowners respond to the lack of predictability in the labour market. Local distinctions become more extreme when we consider landless and land-poor *campesinos*, though they, too, actively engage in creating livelihoods. In this respect this chapter continues the task of situating the production of fair-trade goods within wider economic and social forms, exposing the workings of a coffee economy, and revealing the range and diversity of farmers' and workers' income strategies.

Because various parties have divergent and often conflicting interests and priorities, a process of negotiation must take place before important agricultural tasks proceed. Landowners attempt to adjust employment to fluctuating needs, a project that is compromised by the actions of others and dependent upon the social networks they can access. So although farmers may plan and make predictions with regard to labour, workers may not always be available at the moment they are required. For both landless and land-poor with longer-term agreements (*peones*) and daily wage labourers (*jornaleros*), uncertainty is principally the result of shifts in work availability over the year.

One way of analysing labour in agriculture is to see it as a process of bargaining between interested parties (Ortiz 1999). Such an approach again stresses the practical aspect of life, rather than people's moral commitments. Workers with labour to sell bargain for longer-term employment by assuring landowners of their availability at crucial times in the agricultural calendar. In return they are often provided with housing. Farmers and workers claim and draw upon a language of shared responsibility which ensures some degree of trust, however much of a euphemism for power inequalities and compulsion this may be (Scott 1985). Such ties are activated by people with little or no land but who have a history of living and working in the area. For migrant labourers who come to El Dos at coffee-harvest time the situation is not morally grounded. They have no long-term involvement or interest, and labour agreements between them and landowners are often fraught.

In the previous chapter we saw how farmers, as owners of land, could be seen as exercising a degree of control over their lives and work. Landless people do not have this advantage, being alienated from the means of production and separated from the product of their labour, which becomes the property of their employer. Where farmers sell the product of labour, the landless person sells labour itself, so the relationship between the parties has the characteristics of a commodity relation. The landowner tends to treat the worker as a producer of picked coffee and measures the work in terms of the exchange value remaining once the labour is paid for. Workers regard farmers as a provider of employment and wages. They cannot realise themselves in their work because their interest lies only in the quantity of the return to labour, measured in money. A social relationship, for example between neighbours or people who work alongside one another, is constantly undermined as it is transformed into a dehumanised and formal economic one.

Rural Costa Ricans understand wage labour as enforced, and graphically describe it as 'going to be shackled' (*ir al brete*). Of course, this is an exaggeration; 'to be shackled' tends to be said in a joking, ironic fashion since the commodity relationship, at least in appearance, is based upon mutual agreements and complementary interests, but it is a fillip to the liberal model of contractually free labour. Describing the commodity relation established through wage labour usefully indicates the strained nature of different interests in the economy. Wage labour is inconvenient and commonly glossed over in the fair-trade relationship because it introduces class relations into the productive process, as well as a further separation between work and product, things unimagined in the small-producer model.

The chapter begins with a presentation of some landless residents. As with the farming families in Chapter 3, the intention is to give flesh to the wide range of activities engaged in by those without a *finca*, as well as recognise the constraints within which they operate and their ingenuity in generating a livelihood. Following this is a description of work in different agricultural pursuits. Coffee cultivation involves intensive labour and is an important source of income for many in the highlands, but it is also characterised by extreme and troublesome variations in labour requirements over the agricultural cycle. This difficulty is not so acute in the other principal market activities; beef requires very little labour input, while work in a dairy is constant, regular and consequently less problematic.

WORK AND LIVELIHOODS FOR THE LANDLESS

A major benefit associated with coffee farming, and one often referred to by growers, is the employment it generates.[71] As a labour-intensive industry with a high rate of return per hectare it is suited to small landowners with large families, and is said to encourage equity in the social distribution of wealth and resources. This is where Costa Rican 'coffee culture' meets the rural democratic model of national mythology. As many people around El Dos pointed out, a farm of 30 hectares supports only one family involved in milk and beef production, but can potentially supply a livelihood for ten coffee farmers and their families. Largely unquestioned in this representation are structures of power. The yeoman model, with low-intensity methods, limited returns per hectare and large family units for satisfying labour needs is complicit in this. The cultural and romantic associations of peasant modes of production diverts attention away from obvious inequalities between parties with different interests and capacities (Stolcke 1995). To be specific, what is obscured in this representation of the coffee industry, small farming families, the cooperative and, by extension, fair trade, are inequalities between landed and landless, women and men, residents and migrants.

Landless families share with landowners the propensity to generate income from more than one activity and to experiment with new opportunities. The main difference is that, unlike people with sufficient land, they cannot juggle with coffee or livestock and have fewer possibilities than commercial farmers. Those with little or no land find similar work to that done by landowners seeking to generate extra and alternative sources of cash. They become public employees or work for businesses such as Coopeldos, do domestic chores for better-off neighbours, drive trucks, become shop assistants, mechanics, or cooperative *peones*, pick coffee, milk cows, help with livestock, prepare fields for planting with tomatoes or coffee, clear undergrowth, spray herbicide, collect pensions, borrow money, grow crops and keep chickens around their house.

Overlapping the distinction between farmers and landless workers are the differences between the activities of women and men. Women rarely work in commercial agriculture except during the coffee harvest, when they play a crucial role. And despite their association with the domestic sphere, they play an important part in many areas of the cash economy; they take on labourers on inherited land, find work as domestic helpers or employ other women in their homes. Some have small businesses, work in offices or follow professions as teachers. Often one woman, in addition to running the home, takes up a combination of self-employment and buying and selling labour. The majority of men, too, engage in a wide variety of tasks; they are self-employed builders, mechanics or odd-job men, they have office jobs in town, or make handicrafts for sale. Activities such as these add to the main income from agriculture. If they have land and grow coffee, men and some women are sometimes both employees and employers at harvest time; they manage their own *cafetal* and pay pickers, but also work as harvesters for other landowners to supplement their cash income.

Despite the array of possibilities, the examples given below demonstrate that life for the landless in the highlands is precarious. Many complained that there was not enough work; the opportunities for them are limited, primarily to domestic work and coffee picking for women, and all kinds of agricultural labour for men. Without connections and a reputation, it is hard for them to find a regular position as a *peón*, and they often have to remain satisfied with casual day labour as a *jornalero*. The problems to be overcome are acute for single women, particularly those with children, and the elderly.

Juan Pedro originally came from a nearby town, but has lived for many years in El Dos. He has built a basic two-roomed house on a piece of land donated by a local landowner. Juan Pedro is old enough to receive a basic state pension. He supplements this by doing odd jobs around the village, borrowing money when needed and picking coffee with his wife. They have a daughter, who also has a child from a relationship with a Nicaraguan migrant. When this younger man was around he helped the family with extra income, and planted beans (*frijoles*) for them to eat on a piece of spare land on the other side of the valley.

Perhaps more typical is the case of Coco who, at the time of my first visit lived with his wife and two boys under ten in the spare house of a landowner, which he himself described as 'really bad'. Made of wood, parts of the structure were rotting away and the roof was barely watertight. The family clearly had little money and their clothes were worn and threadbare. Coco worked as a dairyman for a neighbour, but supplemented this income by clearing undergrowth from pasture, building fences, assisting with coffee and planting some crops around the house; the typical activities of an agricultural labourer. Coco's wife also worked hard in the domestic space and at the coffee harvest, trying to build up a reserve of cash for leaner times. Often the family went picking together. The two sons were frequently kept out of school to work and were expected to collect coffee for long periods. Eventually the family split up, and Coco moved away.

After such a separation the burden undoubtedly falls upon the woman. Considered unsuitable for the rigours of heavy agricultural work, single women must find other means to gain an income. Susie was particularly ingenious at this. When I first met her she demonstrated some business acumen in successfully selling me a television. A few months later she had started a market stall in El Dos, from which she tried to sell fruit and vegetables to passing tourists and residents. After this business folded she began work as a mechanic at the local garage. The income from these enterprises was supplemented by intensive work picking coffee.

Such sketches give an indication of the range of activities through which the landless generate cash. As we shall see in later chapters, there is an obverse side to this; to make savings, practice thrift and withdraw from the market economy is a recognised, acceptable and even idealised way to proceed. But in as much as some cash is necessary, paid work is indispensable. In the next section I explore factors affecting availability of employment, differentials in bargaining power and the way this can be used in agreements between farmers and farm workers.

THE COFFEE HARVEST

In the commercial coffee industry the problem of labour over the harvest months sets up a series of problems specific to the industry, yet many writers seem to miss or ignore this aspect.[72] The technification of production, which in El Dos reaches back 30 years, means more coffee to be picked. But increasing production has, according to evidence and testimony, coincided with a trend towards smaller families. The average number of children in a family today is two or three, while it is common for older residents to have had 10 or 15 siblings, all of whom could have helped in the harvest.

Although the precise timing and type of interventions vary from farmer to farmer and year to year, coffee growing is specifically tied to an annual cycle, with tasks associated with and prescribed for certain months (Table 6, p. 190). The flowering and the fruiting of the bushes and the rains that accelerate weed growth dictate the rhythm of production. The harvest is a crucial time. It is when farmers learn how much coffee they have managed to produce, giving them an indication of potential income and allowing them to measure against previous years and so assess their attempts to negotiate the intricacies of coffee growing. It is also critical for social relations in production. Since almost no farmer can manage the entire harvest alone, even with the help of immediate family, hired workers must be bought in. After the harvest the pruning is carried out, usually by the owner but often with one or two paid assistants. In the dry summer months from March to July when the bushes flower and begin to bud less work is required and farmers generally manage without wage labour.

This is a time for maintenance work, socialising and recuperation in preparation for the intense activity of the harvest.

The timing and tempo of ripening of the fruit is dependent on antecedent blossoming. Coffee comes into bloom repeatedly with escalating and then decreasing intensity, and each florescence produces buds that will eventually turn to fruit that will yield a bean. The frequency and profusion of the flowerings therefore prefigure the timing and intensity of work in the harvest. Bushes producing many flowers at once will later have larger quantities of ripe fruit appearing at one time. Conversely, frequent flowerings spread over a longer period will require repeat visits to the grove and yield poorer pickings each time. By such criteria harvesters characterise coffee as 'bad' or 'good', a judgment that refers to how much ripe fruit appears simultaneously and so how quickly they can fill their baskets.

The pattern varies from year to year, but maturation is partly dependent on environmental and climatic conditions. On one side of the River Cañas, in El Dos, up to eight flowerings occur, which farmers say is due to the cooler, wetter climate, because the occasional and unseasonable rain showers in the dry season encourage blooming. To the south of the river, where it is hotter and drier, the coffee tends to flower more intensively over a shorter period and so reaches maturity slightly later, but in greater abundance at one time. Farmers say the coffee here is 'more level' or 'even' (*se empareja más*). Meanwhile, away to the east, at higher altitude, the fruit ripens even later and the season continues long after producers in El Dos have finished picking.[73] These broad differences in climate and topography mask more subtle variations in light and shade, exposure and shelter; cropping varies between neighbouring *cafetales*, between rows in the same field and even between adjoining bushes. Several farmers also observed that coffee in a well-worked *cafetal* ripens more slowly than one in which the plants are insufficiently nourished or infrequently pruned. Stressed bushes flower and fruit more quickly and old wood is less productive, so labour requirements at harvest depend upon the quality of previous inputs and agricultural practices. These variables in the timing and size of the crop present pickers with a range of work options; when the season has ended in one area it is peaking in another part of the highlands and harvesters can take the opportunity to migrate.

The owner of the *cafetal* takes decisions about when and where to pick, depending on the number of ripe red cherries on the bush. Although this is not of concern from a financial point of view, because pickers are paid piecework, it is vital in attracting harvesters and keeping them. If the picking is good, workers earn more and everyone is happy. A farmer who sets a team to work on a poor patch will soon see the labour force dwindle as they move away to richer fields. In the early part of the harvest little or no help is required but as the season gathers pace the farmer must be able to attract and retain a workforce. Personal judgment is exercised to assess how many labourers will be needed at a particular time. But growers must also develop a reputation for providing good pay and conditions in order to secure workers in the first place.

While the majority of farmers manage with family labour outside of the harvest, thus reducing costs and ensuring more of the value remains within the house, almost all require some help to gather the coffee (Table 7, p. 191). The picking season extends over a lengthy period, roughly from September to February, but peaks in the middle months.[74] In the early part of the harvest the landowner's family and local residents often fulfil labour needs. The ability to attract workers becomes increasingly crucial as the season intensifies. Many landless residents have longstanding work agreements with a particular *patrón*, and so the structure of work is part of wider social relationships. There are two sources of extra labour: local, landless and land-poor residents, and migrant workers. The number of landless varies from place to place (Table 5, p. 190), but it also fluctuates in one place; those who own no land or house have a transitory lifestyle. These residents may best be described as semi-permanent; they move frequently, but often only short distances from house to house within the locality as they attach themselves to a different *patrón*.

Both women and men pick; it is one agricultural task that is considered particularly suitable for women, as manual dexterity rather than strength is required. A report prepared for the Ministry of Education by the school in El Dos records 44 per cent of women residents pick coffee, a significant contribution in an area where the majority of farmers work in dairies. Children are also sometimes kept out of school to help at this crucial time. If the family own the *cafetal* the husband may 'send' his wife, daughter and other female relatives to pick while he oversees the work and undertakes the heavy task of transferring the sacks of picked coffee from grove to cooperative or to the nearest reception point (*recibidor*). Payment to family members for picking is open to negotiation, depending on the relationship and whether they still live in the parental home. Some families pay relatives to come and work, while extended families sometimes avoid employment costs by working as a group, exchanging labour, and moving from one grove to another. This system of labour exchange is said by residents to have once been more prevalent. It is a particularly satisfactory resolution of the labour problem since it avoids cash payments and obviates the need to rely on outsiders.

The harvest is a key time for the landless; many seek to earn as much as possible to tide them over for the remaining five months of the year when less work is available. The ability to find employment during the rest of the year depends on personal ties and reputation, particularly the capacity to work hard. Occasional work may be found in pruning coffee bushes or applying fertiliser, in clearing land or as a *peón* in a dairy. Promising to help in a future harvest is a useful point of leverage for gaining employment during leaner times. If the demand for labour puts workers at a disadvantage in the dry summer months, then during the harvest the tables are turned and pickers have the upper hand as they can move from one grove to another. Picking conditions and requirements vary, and agreements are made on a day-to-day basis, which leaves room for manoeuvre. One picker refused to work a particular grove, even though he was employed on a daily basis in the owner's dairy. As he said: 'no one can tell me who to pick for'.

Pickers work in teams, which in the smaller *cafetales* of El Dos usually vary from between three or four individuals up to about ten. Each harvester is assigned a row of bushes and removes all ripe fruit from one plant before moving on to the next, and so on down the row. Picking is dirty work and can be cold and wet, so old clothes are worn, with waterproofs or black bin-liners, rubber boots and a hat for protection from sun and rain. The fruit is collected in a basket (*canasta*), which is secured to the waist of the picker by means of a strap made from rope, and an agricultural sack. Most harvesters also carry a wire hook (*gancho*) attached to a length of string. The hook is placed over a branch, which is then pulled down towards the picker who holds it in place by standing on the end of the cord, leaving the branch steady and both hands free to work.

The harvester removes all the red fruit as well as that which is 'coloured' yellow or orange (*pintón*), and therefore ripening. In theory all green coffee needs to be left for future rounds. In practice some of this unripe coffee falls into the basket, as do leaves and other detritus. The aim of the picker is to work at speed but to minimise the amount of unwanted material. The coffee in an individual's basket is scrutinised by the producer and assessed as to how clean (*limpio*) or dirty (*sucio*) it is. For the farmer the purity of the work is of primary interest, but the picker is more concerned with volume, and talk amongst harvesters centres upon how much coffee is available on the bush, how 'good' or 'bad' it is, and how quickly (*rapido*) or slowly (*lerdo*) different people work. In this respect coffee picking can be described as semi-skilled; the work itself is repetitive and monotonous, but at the same time it requires dexterity, and speed improves with practice. The trick is to maximise return (by way of quantity picked) but at the same time meet the minimum requirements for purity. The grower's interest in the quality of the coffee is maintained by the cooperative, which measures the percentage of green coffee and dross in a sample and sanctions those delivering unacceptably impure loads. Since green coffee is paid at a lower rate than the ripe product, the system of surveillance practised by the cooperative over farmers' consignments encourages growers to monitor and control the work of the pickers.

From the basket the coffee is transferred to a sack and finally measured in a box (*cajuela*) at the end of the day. In the 1998–99 season the rate paid per box fluctuated around 275 *colones*, although I heard reports of one farmer paying as much as 400 *colones*. A poor day's picking would yield only four or five boxes, but on a good day a fast picker could gather 12 or 15, and legends abound of individuals picking up to 20 boxes in one day. Income during the harvest therefore depends on dexterity and the experience of the picker, not least in judging where to pick next and managing the social relationships that such movement requires.

Information on harvesting opportunities is an important topic for conversation; I was often given advice about where to move next and about the rates being offered by different farmers. Some owners pay a higher price to compensate for poor pickings early and late in the season. Others argue that keeping the same rate throughout the season is fair as it balances out in the long run. Although farmers claimed to come to an agreement about rates of payment for the coming season, workers and landowners negotiate before work commences. The agreed price per *cajuela* is said to be a reflection of the current market, so pickers bear some of the brunt of price falls. In 1999 coffee prices were hovering at around $100, and farmers were predicting a drop in the rate they would pay. The relation between coffee prices and harvest payments may be one way that fair-trade practices 'trickle-down' to the landless, and at least one farmer made the explicit point that higher prices and fair-trade premiums meant he could afford to pay pickers a higher rate.

In this section we have seen how the fluctuation in labour requirements ties landowners, and particularly coffee farmers, into economic and social relationships with the landless, permanent and semi-permanent residents. Reciprocal agreements to offer work and accommodation and provide labour involve a degree of strategising, yet those who exemplify, are identified with, and can activate a sense of social responsibility always appear to gain access to sufficient work to satisfy basic needs. Many of the more industrious claimed there was always work available, while even people not known for hard work seemed to find occasional labour when they required it. One semi-retired individual was particularly renowned for being work-shy, but he was able to get odd jobs outside the harvest season and sometimes took part in community work projects. As one landowner put it: 'he is not a good labourer, but he needs money, so I give him work'.

MIGRANT WORKERS

As the coffee harvest gathers momentum towards the end of the year, the labour problem intensifies to the point that local workers cannot satisfy demand; from September onwards, temporary workers come to the Tilarán Highlands from Nicaragua. Most immigrants have no work permits and many walk long distances to avoid border controls. These arrivals form part of a larger picture of economic migration into Costa Rica.[75] Because of their transient and illegal status it is difficult to estimate numbers entering the El Dos area, but two separate farmers gave a figure of 'around 300' for Campos de Oro, where there are about 100 coffee growers registered as members of the cooperative.[76]

The first Nicaraguan migrants were brought into the area in the 1970s by the owners of the private coffee enterprise and processing plant in Turín. To run a large estate requires a considerable workforce, and even today the Turín operation employs about 30 Nicaraguans for the harvest season, as well as a dozen or more on a permanent basis. The influx of migrants has escalated over the years, and was exacerbated by the Sandinista-Contra war of the 1980s. A number of farmers recalled finding workers in refugee hostels in nearby Tilarán, and although these no longer exist, Nicaraguans continue to arrive in search of work. Often they come in family groups, or friends join forces and make the trip together. Many visit year after year, some stay to work, and some of these may eventually gain citizenship by taking advantage of government amnesties.

What remains beyond doubt is the reliance of the small coffee farmers on these temporary visitors. The cooperative continues its ambitious expansion programme, and in discussions many residents would rhetorically question who would pick all the new coffee coming into production. The answer, of course, is women and Nicaraguan, or *nica*, migrant labourers.[77] The *nicas* are valued for their strength of constitution and capacity for hard work. They are considered 'good workers' and 'valiant' (*valiente*) when it comes to facing the elements, and they continue to pick through the worst storms and winter squalls. The ability to work hard is esteemed; manual agricultural labourers 'work the hardest, but earn the least', and Nicaraguans are not exempt from this judgment. Yet the central role played by these temporary foreign workers in the economic life of the coffee farmers creates a series of tensions and uneasily resolved problems. Nicaraguans come 'in need of work' and have the necessary qualities, but they are also feared and mistrusted, and their position is an ambiguous one. They are *of* the community, but not *in* it (Kearney 1996:167); they are indispensable to the local economy but come and go as they please, and so are almost impossible to trace or hold to agreements. A house in the village near my own contained three migrants at the beginning of one week, then five, followed by eight, then five again, only to be left empty before the week was up. It is not therefore surprising that a number of rather fraught opinions circulate about these dangerously necessary visitors. Not only do judgments vary considerably from one person to the next as to the merits or otherwise of *nicas*, but also distinct and apparently contradictory views are often voiced by the same person.

On the negative side, Nicaraguans stand accused of being unreliable and untrustworthy. When they begin work, agreements are made and they are provided with shelter, usually a wooden shack, which is generally purpose-built to house harvesters. In return they are expected to pick for the provider of the lodgings as and when they are needed. In slack periods between pickings they are at liberty to work elsewhere. However, since they do not intend to remain after the harvest when work is scarce, they have little incentive to keep to these agreements and in practice tend to follow the harvest as it peaks in different places. One farmer was incensed at a group of Nicaraguans. He had collected them from town and given them accommodation, only to see them leave after five days to work on the other side of the valley where the coffee was purported to be 'better'. Compounding the problem of the Nicaraguans is their perceived association with barbarity and danger – traits easily juxtaposed with the qualities of peace, harmony, tolerance and temperance claimed by locals. To a degree their propensity towards violence is attributed to the war, while in part it is claimed that those who come from Nicaragua are a criminal element on the run from the law in their own country. Others say that violence is a result of drunkenness; although some locals do drink, alcohol is generally viewed in a negative light, and the Protestant converts (*evangelicos*) are strong advocates of temperance. During my stay, a number of brawls and machete fights happened outside the village bar and sometimes involved confrontations between guest workers and local youths. Whatever their merits, stories abound of *nica* involvement in violent clashes and deeds, and *nicas* are generally feared and avoided. Many women will not walk out alone if they know Nicaraguans are in the area, and one farmer claimed to always carry a pistol when dealing with them.

However, the wild reputation of the Nicaraguans has its positive side. They are renowned for their hardiness; they are said not to need beds and it is claimed they sleep happily on the floor, 'like dogs'. Some I met had walked for days over the mountains without money or possessions. In their own country they generally constitute the dispossessed rural poor, and when they can find work there it is often only for food, or a dollar a day if they are paid. They can earn this in one hour working the coffee harvest in Costa Rica. Some have land or a house in their own country, which encourages their return; others remain peripheral visitors to the Costa Rican economy, floating between work opportunities in rural and urban contexts. Fernando is typical of such a marginal migrant. He said he had left his own country after his house was burnt down by Sandinistas and had worked cropping pineapples in the south of Costa Rica, as a labourer in construction in San José, and then found his way to El Dos for the coffee-picking season. He remained there after the season and found work as a semi-employed *jornalero*, but always talked of returning to his own country.

Nicaraguans are drawn into the social relations of production and their role is indispensable. Some growers do manage without resorting to employing the visitors, particularly in El Dos, where conditions for coffee are not so favourable and less of the crop ripens all at once. Other work opportunities, such as dairies and the cooperative, generate alternative employment for locals and the nursery also provides both temporary and permanent work. Resident workers can then be mobilised for most of the coffee harvesting. In the community of Campos de Oro, by contrast, more coffee is grown and more comes to fruition during a short period. This increases the pressure on labour at harvest time. Nearly all residents either own a *cafetal* or are tied into an agreement, which gives them effective rights and responsibilities with respect to a particular grove; it also means most permanent inhabitants have coffee to attend to, and there is less of a floating labour force. It is here that many of the migrants end up working; they pass through El Dos and may even stay a few days, but they soon learn of the more lucrative harvests across the valley and disappear as suddenly and mysteriously as they arrived.

The migrant is an elusive figure, and the limited ability of farmers to control them at harvest time increases the uncertainty of coffee production. To be successful growers require more than agricultural expertise – they also need to juggle the labour process. Landowners and more permanent residents may strategise and negotiate, but their interests are longer-term and therefore more predictable. Temporary migrants need have no such allegiance. Their aim is to maximise return over the two or three months they are required, after which they melt back over the border or are absorbed into the informal economy in another part of Costa Rica. Although they are necessary during the coffee harvest, their informal status compromises the ability of farmers to control relations of production and increase the contingency and unpredictability of the productive process.

WORK IN THE DAIRY

Coffee production has profound implications for social and economic relations because of the employment it generates. Working with cattle is a useful benchmark for comparison. Here we are principally concerned with dairy farming since beef affords few opportunities for employment and is consequently of little significance in terms of relationships; farmers engage in the activity in the knowledge that it requires paying no wages but will provide a supplementary income.

To manage a dairy herd entails rising early for the dawn milking. This is an intense period of work. The cows must be collected from the pasture, strict hygiene needs to be maintained and the heavy 60-litre churns must be carried to the collection points along the road. A period of vigorous activity is followed by a more relaxed time when maintenance work on the farm can be carried out or other tasks attended to. The second shift is a repeat of the first and occurs at about 3pm. The process is repeated every day of the year, leaving little room for holidays or periods of leisure, although paid dairy hands are sometimes employed to cover illness or other eventualities.

A common scenario in the organisation of the work is for a father to milk with his son. Children are free to leave school from the age of twelve, and if they show greater inclination towards farming than education they are encouraged to assist on the farm. Even those who continue into secondary school are expected to help, particularly during the school holidays. The father-and-son combination is a favoured solution to the problem of the regular and reliable labour needed in the dairy, and for the younger member of the team it is a chance to learn a trade; in time he can raise capital by taking out a loan, or inherit his part of the family farm, and may come to own a herd of cows of his own.

In some dairies family labour is insufficient, and a permanent worker must be hired. For the landless, or land poor, milking can provide such permanent employment. By covering the daily shifts a worker can earn almost a full day's wage, but since he is required only between about five and seven in the morning and three and five in the afternoon he remains free for much of the day. This allows time for rest, socialising, attention to business in town or other work commitments. As we have seen, the availability of alternative employment varies according to season, the social networks a labourer is able to activate, and his reputation for diligence. At times a *peón* may be required for tasks by the farmer for whom he milks, otherwise work can be sought elsewhere. However, outside the coffee harvest extra employment is hard to find; these are lean times and a dairy worker will consider himself lucky to have a regular income.

The hiring of workers for milking takes place on the employer's terms. Contracts are verbal, informal and offer little or no security. Workers need to be reliable, efficient and scrupulous if they are to be retained and still the dairy farmer can hire and fire at will and without the need to pay for holidays or sickness. Those seeking work, on the other hand, are in a perilous position; they must continually seek new opportunities and openings, but even this can be their undoing. Two brothers of 14 and 16 had found work for a local dairy farmer and had taken up residence in a room that adjoined the milking shed. As youngsters they were being paid at well below the going rate for their services, so when they heard about a better opportunity in another part of the highlands they abandoned the dairy. Their employer, meanwhile, quickly found a replacement. Unfortunately the work the boys had sought did not meet their expectations and so they returned to El Dos, but they had lost their position and their accommodation.

Farmers running dairies do not deny the heavy workload, the lack of holidays or the early rise required. The attraction for them is the monetary return, which is arguably greater than that from coffee and more regular and reliable, and the satisfaction of working with animals. The sense of identification with livestock is revealed by codes of dress and leisure activities. Those who like to work with cows and cattle tend to possess and ride horses, for both work and pleasure. They wear cowboy boots and jeans, although rubber boots are used for milking, for hygiene reasons. The basic cowboy regalia is even more notable during fiestas, when fringed shirts, wide belts with a large buckle, Stetsons, a bootlace tie, and even spurs are worn. Most fiestas include a *tope*, in which riders compete in tests of horsemanship and are judged on their appearance.

In this respect, the identity of the dairy or beef farmer is notably different from identities attached to coffee producers. The former is associated with larger landowners, many of whom drive large and powerful trucks, and dress more impressively in apparent imitation of North American cowboys. Coffee farmers tend to wear more downbeat clothes, emphasise the peace and tranquillity of cultivating the land, and refer to the small scale on which they work, and often their poverty and marginality. These stereotypes are not clear-cut in practice; there are livestock farmers who wear little more than tattered rags, finely dressed coffee farmers, and in any case several landowners work both systems. But they are clear reference points for resident landowners, a distinction that does not hold for labourers who have no land with which to identify.

SHARECROPPING: FARMING *A MEDIAS*

As a primary resource, for both cash cropping and subsistence-style agriculture, land is crucial. For the landless the issue is how to gain access to it; for landowners engaged in commercial agriculture the seasonal shortage of labour has to be overcome. One way these needs might be seen as complementing one another is in sharecropping arrangements. The most common type of commercial agreement between both kin and non-kin is the 'halves' (*a medias*) system. This takes a standard form, and although it can be inscribed in a ten-year, legally binding document, participants generally rely on the honour of the second party in fulfilling what are the commonly accepted terms.

A medias contracts are most common in coffee cultivation, although they are possible in other undertakings. The system requires the landowner to provide the coffee grove and all material inputs: fertilisers, chemical sprays, lime, seedlings and transport. In return, the landless or land-poor party undertakes the labour required throughout the year. Landless residents enter into this agreement when they have time available to carry out the tasks. They either manage the work alone or have sons of working age who may be enlisted, and in any case the day-to-day work required to maintain even quite a large grove can be managed by a single worker. During the harvest it is up to the landless partner to seek out and contract the necessary pickers, oversee the work, measure and record how much each picker has collected, and ensure that they are paid once the advance has been received from the cooperative. Final remuneration comes equally to both parties, hence the term 'halves'. This is achieved simply by registering half the crop in the name of each partner at the cooperative.

The *a medias* system is particularly common in communities where conditions favour coffee production rather than cattle. In Campos de Oro, which is almost exclusively given over to the former, out of a total of 67 households about a quarter are involved in such agreements, while about ten others have similar arrangements, which are not strictly classified as *a medias*. These are normally cases in which sons or daughters manage land owned by elderly parents. In El Dos, with its emphasis on milk production, there was only one *a medias* contract between non-kin in operation. This was between Luis Leitón (introduced in the previous chapter) and Tobias, a landless resident. The documentation of the history of this agreement reveals some of its features, and some of its pitfalls.

In 1998 Luis explained how he liked to grow coffee as an insurance against failure or losses in his dairy. In his own words: 'if one should fail I still have the other'. But because he managed a sizeable herd, and two of his three sons were in full-time education, he did not have time to tend his grove. Tobias, his *a medias* partner, was a near neighbour. The agreement began successfully enough; Tobias was working for the cooperative and valued the regular income it provided, but the salary was hardly sufficient to support his large family and he wanted to generate extra income. Luis, on the other hand, could concentrate on milk production, secure in the knowledge that his coffee was being well tended by a knowledgeable and trustworthy agricultural worker. The original coffee grove was renovated and the area under cultivation expanded; shade trees and windbreaks were also planted and a sizeable nursery of new seedlings was established, as there were plans to plant a second grove on a suitable field between the two men's houses. The original grove contained a number of fruit trees and both partners had free access to the crops. Tobias had also planted a local species of tuber *(tiquisque)* between the rows, which he used to feed his family.

When I visited Tobias at work in the *cafetal* he was beginning to regret the agreement. He had put in a great deal of work but the return didn't meet his expectations. The only reason he had managed to make it pay was by using family labour in the harvest. As we were leaving, Luis emerged from his house and an intense discussion ensued. Tobias felt that he should be paid something for all the work he had done; Luis was unwilling to comply as he was already operating at a loss. They had hoped to get a yield of 40 *fanegas* that year but had only managed 25; this, coupled with falling prices, made for poor prospects. Luis was also having second thoughts about the new *cafetal*, and was contemplating selling his seedlings. Eventually it was amicably agreed to end the *a medias* agreement. A short time after this encounter Tobias left the village and moved to the city of Alajuela where his elder children had found employment. Luis meanwhile started a new agreement with a farmer from Campos de Oro. When I left in 1998 the planting of the new *cafetal* was underway, but by 2002 Luis had given up on coffee.

In Costa Rica, with its liberal democratic model, it is easy to represent the *a medias* system as a consensual arrangement in which parties complement each other's needs.[78] However, this does not detract from the fact that negotiations take place over the course of the contract, that the parties will gain differently depending on their respective inputs, and that the bargaining position of each incumbent fluctuates over time. This short case history of one agreement suggests that the mutual element of the *a medias* system is at best one-sided. Although it cannot be denied that working in this way allows the landless access to the means of production and permits them to join the cooperative, there are pitfalls, and power remains with the landowner. After all, Tobias left, Luis remained, and the only attempt at *a medias* in El Dos failed.

CONCLUSION

This chapter asserts that to understand farming activities we must take into account the labour process. A crop such as coffee, with its major variations in work inputs over the year, generates problems in the management of social and economic relations. Although this is offset to a degree by longer-term and more stable agreements based around moral claims and affective relations between local residents, the threat to farmers of being left short of labour at a crucial point in the harvest becomes increasingly present as production rises. The appearance of migrants increases the labour supply when needed, but forces growers to rely on those whom they cannot control. For these reasons coffee growing is difficult for employers and employees alike. By contrast, the lack of inputs required by beef production and the regular, industrial conditions in the dairy make labour relations largely unproblematic. Not surprisingly, farmers most often cite labour shortages as the deciding factor in converting from coffee to milk production, when land and capital make such a project feasible.

In considering labour two possibilities present themselves. In the liberal model production is ostensibly based upon contractually free workers who sell their labour power on the open market. This suggests a 'democratic' process, regulated by contracts between formally free individuals. The second model, drawing upon Marx, exposes the chimera of formal freedom and emphasises constraint.[79] Although in liberal ideology workers choose between employment options and hence maximise their interests, in practice landowners can hire and fire as need and occasion demand. Workers are constrained or 'shackled' at the whim of the employer. Informal labourers have few rights, no recourse to law and no organisation represents them. An element of control does rest with the landless during the coffee-picking season, but this is short-lived, and coffee farmers tend to fix wages by common agreement before the start of the harvest.

Much of the literature and everyday representations of fair trade by activists, ignore the political economy of coffee production; the romantic attractions of smallholding peasant farmers working their own land ensures a kind of wilful blindness to social relations in production. The emphasis placed upon small farmers draws its breath from the contrast between an idealised economic form of family-based peasant production and large plantations employing exploited wage labourers. My evidence shows that small farmers (even those with two hectares or less) employ workers at certain points in the year and in the process extract surplus value from labour. What is more, workers and migrants find themselves in need of that employment. The point to be made is not that there is no difference between farmers with relatively small amounts of land who work in agriculture and sometimes need to employ workers and plantations owned by absentee landlords that are run purely for profit using waged labour. Rather, it is important to understand that both forms operate within and are organised around production for the market, and as such are impelled by the requirement of profitability.

The reason we object to this is that from one cultural perspective we see waged labour as a distortion because it alienates the worker from the means of production and leads people to treat one another as material ends in terms of the profit to be made from them. We misread the peasant mode in its relation to commodity markets because we project on to the small-farmer model our desire for a world in which this distortion and these alienated relations do not hold. A similar process, whereby an idealised form is distorted by the capitalist market and the profit motive can be identified in relation to nature. Nevertheless, in considering the question of the human relationship to the environment the next chapter represents a turning point in the argument because nature is characterised as a starting point for the economic model in which we hope to transcend the dictates of the commodity form.

5 WORKING NATURE, WORKING THE MARKET: SUSTAINABILITY AND ORGANIC AGRICULTURE

In the market and in social relations surrounding production, farmers manage to exert different degrees of control. Similarly, in nature they have a range of capacities to influence outcomes. Farming involves interventions in natural processes, so activities and actions inevitably shape the environment. The principal means to this end in commercial coffee growing is modern 'conventional' agriculture, based upon technocratic solutions and agroindustrial inputs. But how nature responds remains unpredictable, and attempts to manage and fashion the environment have uncertain repercussions and outcomes of which farmers, as well as social scientists, are only too aware (Beck 1992; Giddens 1990; Latour 1993). On one hand, the *campesinos* of highland Tilarán acknowledge the limits of their control and the propensity for nature to respond in unpredictable ways through the metaphor of chance, but they also refer to divine providence and the natural order. Resignation to God's will and purposes is repeatedly expressed through the phrase *si Dios quiere* (If God wishes; God willing).

In the first place, this chapter documents how uncertainty in nature is absorbed into the local economy, and how opportunities are seized upon and losses distributed, which in turn reflects power relations. Farmers undergo a range of experiences in their attempts to steer or override natural processes, and have various commitments and resources they can muster. In recent years the cooperative, and some growers, have explored an alternative commercial method to the dominant model of agriculture; organic coffee production is commonly represented as a fusion of traditional and modern practices, and becomes a focus for discussions on nature, sustainability and livelihoods. Conventional and organic systems are not, however, diametrically opposed. Farmers who administer chemicals, and they are in the majority, often limit their use and at times develop and employ alternative products and techniques associated with organic practices. In part this is to cut expenditure, but most farmers also recognise that chemical products carry environmental costs, despite their apparent efficacy. Equally, modern organic agriculture requires high levels of inputs in materials and labour, but treatments tend to be non-commercial, drawn from the local environment, and there is greater reference made to local knowledge than in conventional farming.

The material indicates a political ecology; one that considers the effects of capitalism on the environment, takes account of the way farmers engage with demands for more sustainable practice, admits to a plurality of ideas and perceptions on how to utilise resources, and questions and at times rewrites the history of exploitation (Peet and Watts 1996a). Here I am interested in debunking the notion that farm activities are inevitably destructive of Costa Rican ecosystems, that farmers have little or no environmental consciousness, and that the environmental history of Costa Rica is solely about the preservation of pristine forest reserves by enlightened individuals and naturalists, often of North American origin (Campbell 2002; Carriere 1991, Evans 1999). Instead, I argue that farmers are aware of the effects of their actions, concerned about sustainability and, given incentives and possibilities for gaining a livelihood, are able and willing to alter practices (Edelman 1995). In this respect they participate in environmental narratives usually associated in the literature with professional conservationists (Campbell 2002; Nygren 1998).

As in preceding chapters, revealing the strategies employed by farmers in their interactions with nature attends to socioeconomic aspects of farming, coffee production and trade. In this respect it supports the view that organic production, like fair trade, is subsumed within market negotiations, market-oriented activities and economic rationalities geared towards maximising returns. Just as cooperative managers engage with and extract benefit from the fair-trade niche market as representatives of marginal producers, so too does 'green discourse' carry with it commercial possibilities that some are better placed to exploit. In this way this chapter continues the theme of differentiation among peasant farmers, combined with the dominant idea of commercial farming as a moral-free zone, in which the motivation is 'environmentalism for profit' (Nygren 1998).

Yet attending to representations and understandings of the environment begins the process of reorienting the discussion towards ethical ideas and values.[80] The land and nature is central to shared identity; it carries meaning with respect to a particular environment and history and connects to local experience and forms of sociality. For many, identity and culture, linked to exotic place, take symbolic form in the global economy (Baudrillard 1981; Hernández Castillo and Nigh 1998). The question is whether the capitalist economy appropriates and exhausts the full value of the sign, so that identity and culture themselves become fetishised (Bernstein and Campling 2006). The evidence is that particular symbolic values, such as origin, environmental sustainability and the social relations of production and exchange are readily attached to commodities; capitalism has enormous capacity to incorporate and subsume forms that ostensibly offer alternatives, and turn them to profit (Guthman 2004a, 2004b, Harvey 2001). On the other hand, the political and cultural critique of the dominant economy persists, as does an ongoing desire to preserve and develop a space as a reaction to capitalism.

This chapter marks a turning point in the discussion; the importance attached to the environment by farmers in El Dos, and the dangers of considering nature only from the perspective of profitability, allows reflection upon values that make alternative production and trade arrangements imaginable. It is fitting that nature should provide this starting point because according to *campesinos*, working in and on nature, and not commodity exchange, is the origin of all value. What is more, in their interactions with nature they see the possibility of transcending economic necessity and realising themselves in a divinely ordered universe. In other words, where Marx thought humans realised themselves through the power of labour to transform nature, and proposed a human secular order in which workers controlled all aspects of their productive activities, *campesinos* identify a similar potential in submission to divine will and purposes.

Connecting these two views is common in Western thought about the natural order and human potential, where the latter is achieved through unmediated labour, particularly agricultural work, and the way that potential is distorted in the modern capitalist economy. In this chapter problems arise from attempts to control nature in an effort to increase 'unnatural' profits which, as farmers 'play God' to influence outcomes, have the effect of increasing the risks.

RISKS IN NATURE AND THE DANGERS OF PRODUCTION

In November 1998, Hurricane Mitch swept across the Central American isthmus, killing thousands in its wake. In the highlands of Tilarán the hurricane caused two weeks of incessant and torrential rain, and uncommonly high winds for the time of year. The arrival of Mitch coincided with the early part of the coffee-picking season, when many cherries were approaching the optimum time for harvesting. An abundance of water causes the fruit to swell, affecting quality and, in extreme cases, causing it to fall to the ground. Farmers estimated crop losses as a result of the hurricane at between 10 and 25 per cent, a drop in production that can mean the difference between profit and ruin.

Apparently random, and certainly unpredictable, natural phenomena are most commonly attributed to God. After the hurricane

I visited a number of farms and was taken to survey the damage. A tree blown over into a *cafetal* brings resignation: 'we must accept what God sends us'. While past misfortune is referred back to divine purposes, so future uncertainty is attributed to divine providence, expressed through the phrase *si Dios quiere*. To translate this as 'God willing' does disservice to the force and frequency of use of these words. The phrase is endlessly repeated in response to any expression of confidence in the course of future events or the outcome of plans, from a proposed meeting to a projected journey. When visiting coffee groves I would often comment on the healthy state of the bushes, the profusion of flowers, or coffee coming in to bud, and express optimism at the size of the coming harvest, but farmers refused to commit themselves or predict outcomes. Their reply to my optimistic predictions was that all things work in accordance with God's will. Assigning responsibility to a higher power implies that farmers deny their ability to control natural processes at all. Yet as I show below, they do have strategies with respect to what Redfield and Villa Rojas once termed 'the beneficient and the punitive, the bounty-yielding and the perilous' sides of nature (1964:128).

When large quantities of coffee fall from the bushes it is an agricultural emergency. Farmers race against time to collect their crop. Fortunately, under normal conditions the more ripe fruit there is on the bush, the more attractive is the work for pickers, as it takes less time to fill baskets. Trouble begins when the coffee starts to fall. Though some of the fruit can be rescued from the ground, this backbreaking, dirty and unrewarding work has to be undertaken by family labour.[81] While paid pickers concentrated on the bushes, the owners of *cafetales* were sometimes seen on their hands and knees, attempting to salvage what they could of the fallen cherries. Even if pickers had a longstanding association with a farmer, it is unlikely they could be persuaded to collect coffee from the ground. One grower dated his decision to cut down his *cafetal* to a previous harvest; much of the coffee had fallen, and he and his son were left to try to rescue the crop. Heavy rain thus exacerbates problems in a time of labour shortage; losses are borne by the farmers, but it has less effect on the already precarious lives of the landless. Rain makes the monotonous work of picking extremely unpleasant, and the more that falls the slower the picking, but workers can move and search for richer fields with more cherries on the bush, an option not open to landowners.

Some of the problems generated by phenomena such as Hurricane Mitch are initially passed on to the cooperative. Adverse climatic conditions reduce yields and hamper the collection and transportation of the coffee for both producer and processor. But pickers and farmers are paid by volume of coffee, with measurement taking place when the bean is still in the fruit (*en cereza*); the more the cherries are swollen with water, the lower is the proportion of coffee bean to fruit pulp (called the 'yield', or *rendimiento*). *Rendimientos* are carefully monitored and fixed by Icafé and are typically set at between 90 and 105lb of dried beans per *fanega* of coffee. A high *rendimiento* is indicative of good-quality coffee. It implies a large bean, a low water content, and a minimal proportion of defective fruit, sticks and other dross, which allows for efficient processing. If the figure falls below the minimum established for each processing plant according to local conditions, Icafé imposes a fine. In any case a low *rendimiento* reduces the utility of the plant, which leads to lower final gate prices to producers.

However, the system used to collect and measure the coffee must also be considered. Unless the producer lives close to the cooperative, delivery of the fruit is made to a local collection point (*recibidor*). Here the volume is measured and recorded, and then added to the harvest of other growers. Each afternoon, cooperative employees empty the *recibidor* and take the coffee by truck to the processing plant. During transfer the fruit settles and the volume drops. A reduction of 2–3 per cent is considered normal, but if the fruit is waterlogged or an error has been made this figure rises. Although a second measurement is carried out to monitor losses, in practice the cooperative can do little to trace the problem, let alone connect it to a particular producer, since the harvests from various farmers are mixed together. So the cooperative as a whole must bear the loss.

Excessive rain has severe financial consequences for farmers; it makes nonsense of controlled outcomes, and forces reference to divine dispensation. By contrast, the industrial process used by the cooperative in order to produce a finished 'gold' bean, ready for export, is unaffected by the weather. Reductions in volume occur in the hulling and drying phases, and overall profits depend on the efficiency of the plant but, unlike the producer, the cooperative is still legally guaranteed its 9 per cent margin. Of course, a further and significant drop in weight and volume also occurs in the toasting, which takes place after export, but this can be predicted and costed within the industrial process.

The effects of prolonged rainfall are less severe in beef and dairy farming. Storms and bad weather have a negative impact on milk yields, but administering more feed and supplementing it with sugar cane and minerals counteracts this, and the problem is generally not considered significant. For livestock, dry summers can be a problem, as grass grows slowly or wilts in the fields; heavy rainfall has little effect on cattle farmers. There are other dangers, though, which are met by reference to divine dispensation; valuable animals, especially those kept on peripheral areas, can be lost to rustlers; death by disease or due to accidents can strike at any moment; and farmers watch the skies for wheeling birds of prey, which provide unwelcome evidence that an animal has perished in a ravine or succumbed to a fatal illness.

As perishable goods, coffee and milk share a common problem. The law dictates that coffee must be processed within 24 hours of picking to avoid excessive fermentation. Accordingly, farmers deliver their crop to the cooperative on the day it is harvested. Likewise, milk must be kept refrigerated until transported by truck to the cheese manufacturer at Monteverde some 20 miles away. In both cases rains obstruct delivery as dirt tracks become treacherous, if not impassable, to vehicles. When this occurs farmers can load sacks of coffee or milk churns on to horses, or carry them short distances themselves, as dairy farmers did during Hurricane Mitch. The pressure to pick and deliver coffee before it falls from the bush or ferments is matched by a need for regular and swift transportation of milk before it curdles. The El Dos dairy farmers have now abandoned churns and grouped together to buy a refrigerated truck, but if the road were to become impassable the lorry would not be able to deliver nor return for the next consignment.

Farmers acknowledge that the various production systems in which they engage are susceptible in different ways to the vagaries of nature, and this remains an important topic of conversation. Unpredictability in nature is unavoidable, but as with the market and with labour needs, farmers strategise and juggle with natural processes; they try to exert control, use experience and experiment with solutions as problems arise, and so farming becomes at least partially amenable to technocratic solutions.

MODERN PRODUCTION TECHNIQUES: DOMINATING NATURE AND EXPLOITING THE ENVIRONMENT

Over the past 30 years farmers have learnt to apply an agroindustrial, technical and standardised package to the land. Although there is some dissent, many farmers acknowledge that this gives a greater capacity to control outcomes, and it improves yields. As part of the cooperative message of 'sowing progress', farm livelihoods and expectations of return have become inextricably linked to modern technocratic solutions to agricultural problems.

Coffee farmers have developed practices and knowledge concerning the treatment of a variety of diseases and conditions, principally fungal infections which attack the leaves (*la roya* and *ojo de gallo*), and nematode worms that damage the roots. The other great coffee pest, the weevil-like *broca*, has not yet arrived in Costa Rica, but the industry is wary of invasion from Nicaragua. In addition to pests, farmers recognise problems caused by mineral deficiencies and apply easily manageable concentrates of fertiliser and mineral supplements to counteract this. Recently, Coopeldos has instigated a campaign to encourage chemical analysis of soil to improve the effects of such remedial action. Finally, growers apply herbicides to keep the floor of the *cafetal* clear and ease working conditions, particularly prior to harvest. Dairy and cattle farmers likewise administer a wide variety of antibiotics and treatments for worm, ticks and other pests. They fertilise pastures, and apply chemicals to fight infestations of caterpillars that destroy and 'burn' the grass.[82] Artificial insemination is widely practised and dairy farmers select and buy sperm from catalogues imported from the United States.

Producers are remarkably well versed in the types of treatments available, how and when to use them and under what conditions. The technical terms and industry-specific brand names are confusing to the outsider, but familiar to coffee growers and cattle owners. Farmers happily spend hours discussing the benefits of particular agrochemicals, successes and failures, even the merits of different nozzles for spraying. The arcane vocabulary is very real and relevant to those engaged in modern intensive agriculture. Nothing, it was pointed out, makes a farmer happier than an effective treatment; they love to see pests killed off, with their 'legs in the air' (*patas ariba*). Many of the talks during my training course in Modern Techniques of Coffee Production at Coopeldos were given by salesmen from the chemical and equipment companies, eager to promote their products. Styles of dress emphasise the industrial and transnational aspects of production. The cowboy style in El Dos is a reminder of reliance on the North American beef market. In the case of coffee farmers the relationship between dress and agroindustrial products is equally explicit. Like Kearney's Mexican migrants, coffee producers 'dress themselves with a hodge-podge of...shirts and hats emblazoned with corporate logos and brand names of beers, cigarettes, tractor companies, fertilisers, herbicides and pesticides' (1996:164).

For advice and technical assistance with these matters farmers feed into multiple networks. A proliferation of institutions advises and trains farmers, while cajoling them into adopting some practices and encouraging them to abandon others. This ties agriculturalists into an array of governmental and non-governmental organisations (Edelman 1999:70–73). For example, the Centre for Basic Agriculture provides formal training in modern techniques and was described as a forum for farmers to share knowledge and experiences; it engages with a complex network of producer groups, teaching institutions, development agencies and government ministries, and helps access resources. Other organisations provide funds for training in agricultural techniques, subsidise transport to meetings and for farm visits, and help to source seed and new crop varieties. The aim is to formalise, expand and facilitate the informal networks in which farmers have long participated. Knowledge is characterised as both an experience of sharing between equals, *campesino* to *campesino*, and institutionalised training.

UNDESIRABLE OUTCOMES, OR REFLEXIVE RISKS

If modern production techniques are driven by the search to increase profits, then success brought about by new techniques, procedures and products is offset by misgivings. The application of science requires practices that can be prejudicial to nature, and of dubious benefit. Technical ways of working allow greater control, but things become complex when unforeseen and insidious side effects occur.[83] Not least is the cost of applying chemicals in monetary terms, effects on human health, and concerns about environmental degradation. Amadeo provided a succinct account of such reflexive effects: 'you cannot escape nature,' he said, 'the more you move away from it, the more it comes back at you'. Implicit in this comment is a belief in and experience of a naturally fecund and active natural world, as a counter reference to the stresses put on the environment by modern production.

To reduce costs and risk, and in keeping with the exercise of thrift in the house economy (Gudeman and Rivera 1990), farmers try to avoid applications of expensive products, which in any case can fail. Low crop prices push their ingenuity to the limit, and put the cooperative technician to the test. To maintain credibility the *técnico* must find ways to cut expenses but sustain production levels. At a meeting in El Dos in 2003 he recommended varying applications of fertiliser according to production levels. This tactic could be combined with low-cost solutions, such as mulching with coffee fruit pulp (*broza*), which is a by-product of coffee processing and an abundant source of free natural compost. Farmers are not always persuaded by the experts' suggestions, however, for at least three reasons. Firstly, some say the *técnicos* are in the pocket of the agrochemical industry and receive commission for their recommendations. Secondly, apparently cheap options such as organic mulches using *broza* are labour intensive and increase costs in wages. Lastly, varying inputs and using cheap alternatives is already central to farming practice. An example is provided by Carlos Alvarado, who, at the time of my last visit, was experimenting with a mixture of lime and water as a foliar spray against rust (*la roya*). This would be used in place of an expensive commercial product. Carlos was well pleased with his 'invention'; if successful it would lead to a considerable saving.[84] The original recipe for the concoction had come from a farmer in a neighbouring community, and is illustrative of the ongoing sharing of knowledge between farmers.

Health issues relating to the use of agrochemicals have become increasingly pressing in recent years. Despite its reputation for ecotourism, Costa Rica has surprisingly poor credentials for environmentalism. It has the dubious distinction of being the world leader in *per capita* pesticide use (Raynolds 2003:34). Much of this is absorbed by the banana industry, but coffee production has long been heavily reliant upon agrochemicals to increase yields (Paige 1997:71–76; Winson 1989).[85] In the Tilarán Highlands it is common to see farmers with spray guns administering concoctions of herbicides, insecticides, fungicides, nematocides, mineral supplements and fertilisers. Although they are encouraged to wear protective clothing, and receive training in methods of mixing and applying treatments, protective measures are commonly ignored. Farmers and technicians openly admit this, and in more contemplative moments attribute it to *machismo* culture. Whatever the reason, pesticide poisoning is sadly recognised by residents as a cause of illness and death.

In addition, the central importance of land to the family and the desirability of bequeathing an improved farm, not one destroyed by malpractice, makes environmental degradation a grave issue for farming families. One of the principal problems associated with agrochemicals is that they 'sterilise' (*esteriliza*) the soil; they are said to work against fecundity and are considered inimical to natural processes. This claim was made repeatedly and, although pesticides were considered particularly iniquitous, artificial fertilisers were also sometimes declared prejudicial. Many also observed that the increasing amounts required to maintain an effect led to spiralling costs.

Another cause for concern in the highlands is soil erosion. Whereas the connection between the application of chemicals and sterility can be contested, the problem of erosion is visible and undeniable. Deforestation of the once heavily forested area is recognised as the principal cause of soil loss. Most of the blame for decreasing tree cover is placed on the larger dairy and beef farmers. Land under coffee is less prone to degradation, as the closely planted bushes help hold the soil together. The landscape bears witness to this fact, as denuded and eroded pastures are interspersed with a green patchwork of coffee. Reinforcing the association between coffee farmers and environmentalism are efforts to reverse long-term trends. For example, Coopeldos has set up reserves along watercourses and produces nearly 100,000 saplings annually in its nursery. Not only do trees help combat soil loss, they are also needed for windbreaks in exposed and windy areas. Tree-planting programmes therefore allow the establishment of coffee groves where previously it was ill-advised. A second anti-erosion measure is the practice of planting coffee bushes on terraces that follow the natural profile of the hillside, in order to control run-off. Farmers receive training from *técnicos* on how to plant in this manner.

For the above reasons, coffee growers, and by implication the smaller farmer, can lay claim to ecological rectitude. As one coffee grower said, 'it is the small farmer and the poor who care for the environment'. This contradicts assumptions that link environmental destruction with the exploitative activities of people, particularly the poor, and calls into question the connection made between land invasion by settlers (*precaristas*) and ecological degradation in Costa Rica (Carriere 1991; Evans 1999). Perhaps more than anyone, farmers and rural people are caught up in multi-stranded narratives, in which environmentalism must encompass concerns about nature, profit, people and a search for alternatives (Nygren 1998). By encouraging sustainable practice, Coopeldos meets the environmental concerns and aspirations to repair damage of many *asociados*. At the same time the cooperative complies with the criteria of sustainability attached to participation in fair-trade agreements, and opens doors to other niche markets, notably the lucrative organic-coffee sector.

THE ORGANIC COFFEE PROGRAMME

In 1996 Coopeldos made a successful application to the Dutch government for funds to convert 25 one-hectare plots to organic methods. The proposal, entitled 'Small Organic Coffee Communities' (*Pequeñas Comunidades Organicas de Café*), pointed to the excessive use of chemicals in the coffee industry and the negative consequences of this upon human health and the environment. To counteract the 'irrational escalation in the use of chemicals', Coopeldos proposed a programme which would harness 'the high level of consciousness amongst producers regarding the negative impact of conventional systems of plantation management'.[86] The programme had four specific aims:

1) To create communities of organic-coffee producers, which will demonstrate the benefits of the approach.
2) To increase the incomes and improve the quality of life of coffee-producing families.
3) To develop sustainable forms of production in harmony with the environment.
4) To develop and market an international brand of organic coffee.

This ambitious programme required a steep learning curve. It was already known from earlier times, and from data from countries such as Nicaragua, where many growers cannot afford agrochemicals, that dramatic falls in yields could be expected. Could the premiums to be gained from organic coffee certification compensate for smaller harvests, and what production levels could be expected once the organic system was in full swing? These questions could only be answered in practice; a group of producers was required who were prepared to take risks to find out.

Organic agriculture employs household and farm waste and coffee pulp (*broza*) as free fertiliser, and cheap locally available 'natural' substances in place of shop-bought sprays. Consequently it requires significantly less cash outlay on such inputs. This makes the system attractive to farmers, who constantly strive to make savings, especially during market recession. Conversely, and to mitigate expected drops in production, the labour expended in applying organic compost is significantly higher than in conventional growing. One farmer applied 20 lorry-loads of *broza* to his hectare of organic coffee, a task undertaken by five people over two weeks. This should be compared to the application of chemical fertiliser, which can be completed by a single worker on a hectare in ten hours. Another farmer estimated that he put five times the work into his organic hectare than into his conventionally grown coffee.

For this reason organic systems are most profitably developed by farmers with money to invest in labour. Organic growers need both significant resources and a desire to be drawn to experimentation with farming systems, factors that determine potential differences between coffee growers. Although the subsidies were designed to cover conversion costs, future results remained far from certain, which made the project risky. The growers chosen for the scheme had reputations as 'good' farmers, as well as close associations with the cooperative; they mostly belonged to the 'inner circle' of functionaries, ex-functionaries and dedicated *cooperativistas* described earlier. In addition, they tended to be better off, and both able and willing to carry the risk, as they had alternative sources of income from business ventures, cattle and dairy farming, or sufficient land to convert only a portion of their *cafetales*.

Although the programme attracted applicants, organic production was an unknown. The main point of reference was practice prior to the green revolution; memories remained of an earlier form of less intensive 'traditional' agriculture, and one or two older farmers continued to eschew agrochemicals. The vast majority of producers, however, relied on commercial products. The cooperative manager considered wholesale conversion highly unlikely, and many farmers persisted with the by now tried-and-tested methods that employ agrochemicals; they were happy with the results. One grower even described the fascination with organic coffee as a sickness.[87] In some respects this is unsurprising; the combination of new varieties, novel techniques and the use of agrochemicals associated with the green revolution has meant that returns of 50 *fanegas* per hectare are not uncommon. Prior to this yields were a tenth of this amount (Hall 1991:162). So, while some producers are committed to organic practices and perceive clear advantages to them, the majority adhere to the dominant idea of technologically driven development.

Despite some optimistic forecasts, the evidence is that organic yields will never reach the levels achieved using agroindustrial products. Nevertheless, experience demonstrates that the catastrophic decline in production levels can be reversed (Table 8, p. 191). A new approach to organic farming is being developed to this end, one that shares common ground with traditional and conventional systems, but also departs from both. Like conventional agriculture, modern organic production relies upon technical expertise, but of a different kind. An explicit contrast can be made between the universal fix administered by experts, demanding only compliance on the part of growers, and an organic or sustainable agriculture that requires active participation of farmers, who pool knowledge, share experiences and interact with their environment in a learning process. Agrochemicals are also in many key respects inversely related to organic products. They are imported and synthetic; organic products, on the other hand, include carbon, are 'biological', 'natural', are based upon caring for the soil, and employ elements drawn from the producers' immediate environment. Technical organic agriculture then becomes a matter of regular applications of organic compost and fertiliser, the development and administration of treatments for disease, and judicious management of shade. Following these precepts, a convincing argument can then be made that profits from an organic hectare can exceed those from a chemically worked grove (Table 9, p. 191). This is because higher prices can compensate for lower volumes being produced.[88] For the 2003–04 season the cooperative expected to receive $160 for organic coffee, compared to $85 for the standard product. In this light the organic option becomes attractive for better-off, diligent, well-placed farmers who were successful in entering the programme and who have persisted with the project.

A distinction, then, can be made between conventional systems, grown in full sun, which may require trees as windbreaks around the edges, often of a single, fast-growing variety (eucalyptus being favoured), and organic coffee, which should be cultivated in light woodland made up of a variety of native species. Trees help contribute to the buildup of organic matter in the grove, counteract the need for artificial fertilisers and mitigate stress; coffee bushes produce more fruit in full sun but the life span of the plants is shorter. As the cooperative technician charged with promoting conversion to more environmentally friendly systems particularly emphasised, tree cover also creates biodiversity and provides a haven for a cross-section of wildlife (Greenberg 1997; Perfecto 1997; Toledo and Moguel 1997). A final practice associated with organic coffee, and the most commonly adopted, is the manual removal of weeds using a machete or strimmer in place of the wholesale application of herbicide. Whereas in the past most farmers had used several applications during a season and favoured a denuded floor to their groves, most now apply herbicide once a year prior to the harvest to aid collection of fallen fruit, and some have abandoned the use of these chemicals altogether.

The organic scheme captured the imagination of many growers, and provoked debate in El Dos. There were three applicants for every place on the programme, and the selection process caused consternation and some dispute; several farmers and some cooperative staff went so far as to suggest that the selection process was unfair or had been badly handled. One explanation for the level of interest may have been the finance made available for the conversion process. However, we can generally discount this motivation because many growers whose applications were unsuccessful decided to experiment with organic systems without being granted subsidies. In addition to stimulating arguments about the need for good returns from land and labour, organic practices also touch upon important themes in the lives of *campesinos*. Organic agriculture is emblematic; it is an example of a niche market that allows farmers to combine financial concerns with their interest in and reflections on nature and their understanding of farming as a process of active engagement with the environment. In this respect agriculture is more than the creation of economic value; it is the activity through which *campesinos* come to define themselves in relation to history, to the world, and their location in it. The practice of farming underpins and forms the basis for the meanings and values to which they subscribe. Transforming nature by agricultural work is the means and the measure of the importance of their actions, which is to say that for them it is the origin of value (Graeber 2001).

Organic agriculture has nostalgic undertones; it evokes a time when chemicals were not applied and were not needed. The process of opening up the highlands, as described in the next chapter, revealed a natural paradise and, given the strong religious persuasion of many people in the area, there is an easy association with Eden. The land the settlers occupied was naturally fertile and could be relied upon to produce without assistance for three to five years. Because of a lack of disease, pesticides were also not required. According to many accounts, tomatoes, potatoes and other crops that are now problematic to produce then grew beautifully and in abundance. Many farmers then noted an increase in the number of pests and a growing incidence of disease, and linked this to biblical prophecy.

Both the proof and the result of humanity's evil, pestilence was sometimes cited as evidence of the 'fall from grace'.

Implicit in the farmers' accounts is the idea that they are caught in a spiral of increasing reliance on expensive agrochemicals. Coffee grown without chemicals breaks this cycle; rather than 'sterilising' the soil it restores natural balance and fecundity. Unsurprisingly, the condition of nature as balanced and giving is often attributed to God. Asdrubel's comment captures this view neatly: 'I believe God made a perfect world', he said, 'and man has destroyed that; by going organic I am helping to restore nature.' The move towards shade-grown coffee, the application of organic compost and the use of natural remedies made on the farm is, for exponents of organic agriculture, part of this restorative process. At the same time it allows for retrospection.

Coffee to which no chemicals or artificial assistance has been applied is frequently described as 'natural, as God made it'. Such an image was invoked, for example, with respect to groves that had been abandoned or were not worked, and was used by a man who had a few plants around his house, which he grew and processed for home consumption and fertilised with household compost. Again, an elderly grower persevered with the system prior to the arrival of chemicals and resolutely refused to apply the products of science; his system was also deemed 'natural' and 'God-given'. A third landowner, Faustino, has a few plants that he leaves completely unattended at the edge of a stand of bananas, and he frequently refers to their health and vigour. These approaches are a precursor, though different in crucial respects, to the organic systems now being developed.

This form of agriculture – 'natural, as God intended' – provides a reference point for organic systems. Yet there is a fundamental difference between coffee grown in this way and modern organic production which, as we have seen, requires significant labour investment to apply heavy and unwieldy organic material to meet current expectations of yields. To make a success of organic farming requires technical competence, resourcefulness and commitment, not least in negotiating the rigours and expense of certification. In this respect it is a world away from an agriculture predicated upon abandoning inputs and relying solely on nature, although organic coffee was taken by some to mean just this; easy money, grown in a traditional manner, without inputs, and with a higher price promised for the crop.

Confusion between the different approaches – the traditional, the conventional and the modern organic – is compounded by a tendency for farmers to avoid expenditure and skimp on inputs by adapting, or only partially implementing, the recommendations of the *técnicos*. It is here that the boundaries between the models break down; despite the rigorous demands of the certification process, in practice farmers draw upon a range of discourses to guide and justify their conduct. In one case a grower had allowed his coffee plants to become overgrown; there was excessive shade and many of the bushes clearly desperately required pruning.[89] Crouching under some trees to shelter from a downpour, Miguel talked of his love of nature; he was, he said, the 'father of hundreds of thousands of trees', a reference to his second source of income, working in the cooperative's horticultural nursery. Like many in El Dos, Miguel's appreciation of the natural world is a deeply held conviction – and he had spoken many times in the past of the power and importance of nature – yet it is entirely possible that with higher prices he would have been less concerned with the beauty of the trees if that were a source of severe underproduction.

Organic agriculture draws upon, emphasises and at times reimagines local knowledge of the environment. Some of these ideas and practices would have been brought from the Central Plateau with the original colonisers, and they are often attributed to 'the forefathers' (*los antepasados*). Other practices are associated with the indigenous peoples that once inhabited the highlands, despite scant evidence of miscegenation. Organic farmers are leaders in excavating and activating this knowledge. Echoing the biodynamic agriculture famously promoted by Rudolf Steiner (Conford 2001), one set of beliefs concerns the effect of the moon on natural processes, which, in turn, determines the most auspicious time for particular tasks.[90] Pruning should be done under a waning moon; Wilberth explained that most people prune during this phase since the old folk had learnt that it encourages better development of the new shoots. Cuttings to be transplanted should also be taken at the time of a waning moon otherwise they will not 'strike' (*no pegan*). To 'take strength', trees should be planted in the days following full moon. For example, Lelo explained that a group of avocado trees had never produced much fruit because they were planted at the wrong time. Animals are said to be more active under a waxing moon, and a full moon helps bring on labour in cows. Differing degrees of importance were given to the lunar influence by various informants, and although it is commonly discussed, some growers claimed to pay it little attention. Others were more willing to admit to trying to organise their work schedules to comply with auspicious phases.

A second set of observations centres upon local climatic conditions. Prevailing winds are noted and predictions made about the conditions that will ensue. Particular attention with regard to the weather is paid to the first twelve days of the year, called *las pintas*, since they are said to 'paint' (*pintar*), that is presage, the weather over the coming year, with each day representative of its corresponding month. The complex interplay of winds and consequent precipitation has an effect on the climate of each community, depending on altitude and aspect, and therefore affects the type of agriculture and specialisations open to farmers. However, these local differences can be further distinguished at the micro level; one of the decisive factors in the sale of small plots made available by the cooperative for coffee cultivation revolved around the microclimatic conditions, specifically wind, likely to prevail in the individual groves. This became the defining factor in determining the qualities attributed to each plot (*parcela*), despite the fact that they previously formed one single farm. Eventually different credit terms were agreed for those buying 'bad' plots to give the new proprietors financial leeway to establish the windbreaks necessary to alter conditions.

Thirdly, treatments and recipes used and developed by the organic farmers draw on knowledge of the medicinal and curative properties of plants. To this extent they are adapted to prevailing conditions and employ plants and products found locally. Brews using dung are concocted to fertilise, and plants are gathered to combat pests and disease. Farmers can then produce cost-effective treatments, gathering round large pots of potions and discussing plants and their uses.

It is difficult to know what weight to give local understandings of nature, primarily because the residents themselves often seemed uncertain as to their accuracy. Most farmers declared themselves neither completely sceptical nor absolutely convinced of these wisdoms, simply stating that there was 'something' in them. Perhaps the greatest room for doubt was reserved for the herbal cures and remedies, which, although much used and commonly prepared, would still be jokingly referred to as 'witchcraft'.

The introduction of agrochemicals in the 1980s led to increases in production, which in turn strengthened the cooperative and aided its expansion. After all, as I have argued, Coopeldos is built on a modernist message of progress. Despite this, in recent years alternative possibilities for working which build upon local understandings have been fostered by and through the cooperative. Involvement in national and global networks means that the demand for environmentally friendly practices and organic coffees, has precipitated and encouraged different ways of processing and working. In the light of this the cooperative has reassessed and reorganised many of its aims and practices, and the way it presents itself within the global network in which it participates, a so-called 'greening of the discourse' (Edelman 1999:21; see also Arrivillaga 1997; Cifuentes 1997; Martinez Torres 1997; Montero Zelédon 1997). At the local level it has encouraged a different approach to working the land under the general rubric of greater sustainability, which in turn finds a cautiously positive group of practitioners in El Dos.

Sustainable practices and organic systems exist in accordance with cultural ideas about the environment and nature, which can be utilised as grounds for funding and repackaged to open up commercial avenues. In El Dos I came across a student from the University of Costa Rica who was carrying out research into 'resistance amongst small farmers to organic agriculture'. In my view this is misguided. Few producers in El Dos object to the idea of organic farming; indeed, I suggest it is remarkably in tune with their ideas regarding nature. Any doubts in their mind concern not so much the benefits of such systems, but their financial viability.

CONCLUSIONS

The tendency to consider all agriculture as necessarily destructive relies on a romantic model of pristine nature. It does not take into account the need for or the right to livelihoods, nor does it consider that human activity unavoidably alters the environment, sometimes in surprising ways that conflict with dominant interpretations (Fairhead and Leach 1997). Furthermore, given incentives, farmers happily draw on their deep identification with the land and their *finca*, utilise knowledge about the way their activities shape the environment, and alter practices accordingly. However, this does not necessarily mean that scientism in agriculture has been abandoned. As Alvaro Borbón at Coocafé explained, the search is for new technical-organic approaches; reason, Peet and Watts argue, 'must be re-reasoned, rather than rejected' (1996b:261).

One response to the perceived problems generated by agrochemicals is to retreat from modern farming techniques and the increased and often uncounted costs these entail and look to nature and a reliance on natural processes. For certain coffee farmers in El Dos this becomes more feasible as the organic coffee market gains ground; the concerns of the European organic consumer find an echo in small farmers' interest in the land and their proclaimed desire to protect the environment. The development of this political agenda emerges from ethical ideas based upon understandings and representations of nature which are often linked to the identities of small coffee growers. On one level, to work in harmony with the natural world is entirely in keeping with the concerns of farmers; on the other they are not immune from the modernist message, and are affected by the requirement to make a living. Changing practices in accordance with demands for 'green' products highlights hazards in conventional agriculture. In the process different interpretations and understandings of nature are brought in to play, compared and contested (Macnaghten and Urry 1998). Stated plainly, and at the risk of oversimplification, we have nature as a resource for extracting maximum exchange value measured in money, nature as a storehouse that provides useful and necessary items for human sustenance, and nature for nature's sake, most commonly identified as God's preserve. The interplay between these contested concepts of natures is complex, but organic agriculture helps farmers to reconcile different interpretations and understandings of their environment.

The last three chapters have explored how farmers strategise and respond to uncertainties in the market, labour needs and nature. This approach has allowed me to describe the political economy of coffee production for the market, and the orientations of farmers. Two outcomes were noted; firstly, in creating livelihoods farmers focus on practical necessity rather than on the moral dimension. Because of chronic uncertainty, agricultural outcomes are the result of a mix of strategy and chance. The connection between farming and unpredictability, made explicit through the metaphor of a game, renders the notion of fair trade in commerce problematic. People are accustomed to locating morality in places away from agriculture, notably in local relationships and in religious life.

Secondly, agriculture and coffee economies comprise a range of actors with different resources, ideas and agendas. Often farmers practise more than one kind of agriculture; a 'small' coffee farmer can also have quite large landholdings under cattle, for example. Developing an extensive coffee estate is constrained more by availability of labour than ownership of limited areas of land. In any case, high labour requirements and equally high expectations of yields per hectare make coffee growing an intensive industry; it is ludicrous to put a farmer with less than a hectare of land in the same category as someone with three, five, or even ten hectares. Similarly, all farmers of my acquaintance employ paid labour at harvest time, and several also hire themselves out as pickers, so challenging the popular conception of small 'family' farmers. In this way detailed study of a local economy generates better understanding of local realities in coffee-producing economies.

On the other hand, it reveals little about the commitments and values established and expressed through the production, consumption and exchange of goods and commodities. Anthropologists have long recognised that these values are framed within personal relationships and by cultural ideas, and authors have become increasingly aware that they are also shaped, informed by and attached to specific physical localities (Graeber 2001; Gudeman 2001; Hirsch 2004; Ingold 2000:25; Peet and Watts 1996a:37). The links between the environment and the economy, and the manner in which human beings interact with, imagine and experience the world, provides the base for people's creative acts and commitments. In this chapter we have analysed this with reference to the implementation of organic agriculture, which draws upon specific traditional practices. In the following chapters I document and contextualise the moral imagination of *campesinos* in the Tilarán Highlands, a discussion that encompasses the basis they establish for a moral order in nature, and the political ideas that result from this, including their adjudication on ethics in relation to trade.

6 ENVISIONING AUTARKY: THE FAMILY AND THE FARM

So far I have detailed how farmers and cooperatives in Costa Rica engage with markets, labour, and nature. For cooperative managers the mission is to maximise prices that can be passed on to the growers who own the cooperative business. This requires an efficient processing and marketing operation. Farmers, by contrast, are concerned with production, and their goal in market agriculture is to get a good return from the land, which may be done by producing greater quantities, as well as by growing different qualities of coffee. In both cases I have suggested that fair trade (and organic coffee) is thoroughly entangled in the market and the commodity form.

Left thus, one might conclude that though some material benefits accrue to farmers and their organisations through alternative trade deals, the moral component is largely absent at the production end of the chain, or at best is subsumed under a social identity that can be turned to profit in the global economy (Hernández Castillo and Nigh 1998). Rather than accept this somewhat reduced model of the ethical, I now focus attention on local forms of sociality and shared principles in El Dos. This will reveal a different way of seeing the world, the economy and the environment, one that is distinct from and contradicts market rationalities, orientations and uncertainties. This consideration of the commitments of farmers and farming families opens up the discussion to values that inform ideas both on the economy and on demands for fair trade. Rather than the fair-trade constructs created by Northern NGOs and projected by consumers on to producers, the ethnography reveals the producers' view of things. This is not to say that there are no parallels between the two; indeed, I contend that looking at rural Costa Ricans' perspective reveals connections made between trade and ethics in Western culture.

An important point of reference is Catholic social thought. In Chapter 1 I demonstrated the significant contribution made by Catholic doctrine to the Costa Rican model of the welfare state. I now identify characteristics of this model apparent in local ideas on society and economy, morality and politics. According to Catholic thought, society is based upon rights to individual ownership, quintessentially of land.[91] Papal encyclicals and pastoral letters produced by Latin American Catholic bishops propose that the importance of landed property lies in the earth, which is the origin of value and is provided by God for human subsistence. The first part of the argument is clearly put in an encyclical by Pope Leo XIII, the *Rerum Novarum* of 1891: 'when man turns the activity of his mind and the strength of his body towards procuring the fruits of nature, by such acts he makes his own that portion of nature's field which he cultivates' (*Rerum Novarum* 1960 [1891]:12).

The second step is to attribute the source of value to God. In Latin America this idea is often promoted in the guise of liberation theology. For example, Catholic bishops make repeated reference to 'God as creator and master of the earth, who puts the earth at the disposition of humanity, particularly the poor, for their wellbeing' (May 1993:28). These philosophical and religiously inspired ideas are then attached to a specific and gendered model of social life, based around a patriarchal and autonomous household. In Catholic doctrine the man is considered the head of the family; he has a duty to provide material necessities and for the inheritance of private property for his children, as well as having ultimate authority. The autarky of the household and the family, as well as patriarchal authority, is reinforced by the claim that the domestic unit is a 'true society' that exists prior to the community and the state (*Rerum Novarum* 1960 [1891]:13).[92]

In El Dos, as in Catholic doctrine and, more broadly, in the Costa Rican national imagination, society is constructed around the idea of the family farm. In the model, ownership of land is claimed by the male household head through labour, with the aim of providing subsistence for the family. This economy idealises the autonomous household reproducing directly from nature, in relationship with a natural world provided and steered by God to sustain human beings.[93] Because it is in accordance with 'natural law', and people appropriate and consume directly from nature, intermediaries are avoided. Also, in as much as economic relations are social relations based upon giving and receiving, and because people attribute socially creative value to things, there is no experience of alienation or fetishisation.

In reality, the idealised model of the autarkic and consensual household tends to fail; in El Dos there are landless and land-poor families, single parents and 'free unions' (*uniones libres*) between non-cohabiting couples, and even in those households that conform to the model there are disagreements, separations and conflicts. What is more, although the rationale behind the family farm encompasses a tradition of an autonomous and independent unit existing out of nature, most farmers have had dealings with the market from the beginning, and have sought profit there. So different economic rationalities, the 'house' that seeks to reproduce, and the capitalist 'corps' that pursues profit, to borrow a terminology employed by Gudeman and Rivera (1990), can be said to coexist.[94]

The concept of a measured house economy, based upon subsistence production by property-owning families, from a fecund, reliable and giving earth, informs much of what locals say about where they live. It allows them to imagine and partially replicate a subsistence base outside the uncertain world of commodity and labour markets, in which they feel constrained to juggle for a meagre livelihood. The identity of small, marginal farmers with knowledge of their environment does not just provide a commercial avenue; the cooperative and other local NGOs actively promote subsistence agriculture as a way of avoiding the market mechanism and as a means of reducing both the costs and the risks of notoriously fallible markets.

This chapter draws out certain ideas that are inspirational to the fair-trade movement, ideas that lead people in various ways to identify with peasant society and buy goods associated with smallholding family farmers. The first idea is that of a 'natural order', in which people 'find themselves', or become truly human, through agricultural labour. In the Catholic model proposed in El Dos, working in nature entails a relationship with God, since the environment is a manifestation of divine power. In the secular version pursued by Marx, human transcendence comes from directly engaging with the world through labour; in transforming the nature of things we transform ourselves, become who we are, and achieve our potential. In both cases a promised salvation is not fully realised. For Marx the distortion comes as other people interrupt, or mediate, labour by treating it as a commodity and profiting from the work of others. Christian religion, on the other hand, identifies the loss of Eden with human sin.

Although there are parallels with and contrasts between the ideas of Marx and those of rural people, it may be more accurate to place the Costa Rican model in the Aristotelian tradition of household provisioning. Aristotle proposed that the moral purpose of the economy was to subsist from nature as an autonomous unit, to allow the exchange with other households of those things that could not be produced, and in any case to avoid immoral profit-making from exchange. Likewise, *campesinos* give moral precedence to production for use and to exchanges that satisfy the needs of households. As we see in Chapter 8, at the same time they condemn the actions of intermediaries who seek to profit by positioning themselves between the value created in production and the use-value required by the consumer.

The second important point to be drawn from this chapter concerns the social purposes of the economy. In anthropology the idea that exchanges create and maintain reciprocal relationships between people is commonly traced back to the work of Marcel Mauss on the gift (2002 [1925]).[95] From this tradition comes the much discussed contrast between alienable, impersonal commodities and inalienable personal gifts that always carry something of the giver and become the currency for social relationships. In Western culture this takes an idealised form in the household, the family and in personal relationships, where giving and sharing is an expression of sentiment and love (Carrier 1995), and in the idea of charity, which has been linked to renunciatory religious ideas about achieving grace through good, selfless, works and acts of generosity (Parry 1986). This is important because we see in these acts and ideas the denial of self-interest, which is now commonly imagined to drive the economy.

The data contribute to the overall argument by identifying elements of a moral economy that consumers seek in fair trade. In peasant livelihoods and moral schemes we glimpse a world in which we imagine that people realise themselves through work on nature, where freedom comes from ownership of land, subsistence is a privileged and measured path to independence, and the aim of economy is social reproduction, typically of the household, maintained through personal relationships and generous acts. In all these things we find a reverse image of the capitalist economy with its impersonal exchanges, self-interest and relentless search for profit.

SETTLING THE FRONTIER: A HISTORY

An official account of the invasion of the Guanacaste Highlands by commercially minded agriculturalists from the western edge of Costa Rica's Central Plateau appeared in Chapter 2. To explore the origins of El Dos more deeply, I now recount the adventures of one of the earliest settlers in the region, and their trials and tribulations of gaining a foothold in uncharted territory. At the beginning of the twentieth century, pioneer farmers, encouraged by land reforms and a tradition of squatters' rights on the frontier, moved to the Tilarán Highlands, took possession of land and began to farm. To endorse legal rights, property owners in El Dos often refer to the struggle, valour and suffering they have endured in living and working on their land. But the descriptions of appropriating private property are balanced by ideologies that insist value comes from interacting with and taking strength from forces God has placed in nature, and that sharing and mutual help, which inspire the family, the farm and local solidarities, take precedence over individual rights.

The story of the settlement of the highlands was recorded during a series of extended interviews with some of the early settlers, the so-called pioneers.[96] The most in-depth and absorbing discussions on this theme took place during visits to the family of Amadeo Leitón, who, at the time of fieldwork, was the oldest resident in El Dos. Amadeo, by his own admission, loves to converse, and recall his exploits and the events he has been involved in during his long life. The details he recounted were not always consistent, nor easy to follow, but the adventures were vividly portrayed, and are a testament to one individual's recollection of the past.

In the early 1920s, as a young boy, and before farm tracks had penetrated the jungle, Amadeo walked into the Cordillera de Tilarán. Born around 1910 to an impoverished *jornalero* with a large family in the city of Palmares in Costa Rica's central plateau, he had been compelled to work from an early age, and began full-time employment in a sugar processing plant (*ingenio*) in nearby Grecia at the age of eleven or twelve. After two years of service, disillusioned with the drudgery of the work and the lack of future, he left and went in search of opportunity and adventure. With his father's blessing and a little loose change in his pocket he caught the train that ran down to the seaport of Puntarenas. There he fell in with an ex-workmate from his job in Grecia, who had previously moved to Cebadilla de Abangares in the highland interior of Guanacaste. A twelve-hour walk through tropical jungle took them to their destination, and Amadeo quickly found employment as a *peón*. He was put to work cultivating *ayote* (a root vegetable), which his *patrón* required for the pig-breeding business he was attempting to establish. After a short time the young Amadeo returned home, but this barefoot escapade by a youth in search of adventure was a seminal moment in his life.

Amadeo returned to Highland Guanacaste in 1932, by which time he was in his early twenties. He had persuaded his parents to move their family to the *Cordillera*, and he was put in charge of the expedition as he had prior knowledge of the area. They travelled by train, then boat, and finally ox-cart, taking with them only basic necessities to cook and clothe themselves as they had sold most of their possessions prior to departure to raise funds. Amadeo found employment and saved enough to buy a small farm of about 4 *manzanas*. He had returned with the expressed intention of working cattle, an enterprise he began with the purchase of two calves. He was not alone in this ambition; a neighbour had imported a type of grass known as *gigante*, which was suitable for the climate, and was sown to pasture. These were the modest beginnings of a long career in cattle management. Amadeo expanded his enterprise over the years and came to own about 100 hectares of land and large herds of cattle.

At the time of my fieldwork and our conversations, Amadeo had long since retired and was looking forward to his 90th birthday. He was still active, tending the small, neat garden which surrounds his house, and cultivating the plot of land he has retained and sown with vegetables and coffee, but this he describes as a mere hobby. He has now passed on the bulk of the farm to his five children and although he can sometimes be seen giving advice or lending a hand, he is most often to be found sitting on the veranda of his house watching the world go by.

STRUGGLE AND THE FORCE OF NATURE

This history, which lives on in the minds of residents such as Amadeo, is couched in a language of struggle. It tells of the application of human will and strength applied to the taming of a pristine and perfect natural world. Almost within the space of living memory the *Cordillera* has been transformed from untrammelled tropical rainforest into modern farmland. Through the practical activity of working the land the people of El Dos have shaped and altered the environment over time, but crucially this also shapes the residents themselves. So 'the landscape is constituted as an enduring record of – and testimony to – the lives and works of past generations who have dwelt within it and, in so doing, have left something of themselves' (Ingold 1993:152, cited in Macnaghten and Urry 1998:167). The history then, not only lives in the nostalgic musings of elderly pioneers, but is a living tale that makes the past manifest in the present, and is central to the representation, identity, feeling and imagination of residents. It indicates a shared socially and symbolically constructed identity, attached to and directly perceived in a specific worked environment, and although this vision is at times problematic, it remains a dominant political idea.

In the *Cordillera* people describe the area around El Dos in the early part of the twentieth century as 'pure forest' (*puro bosque*) or sometimes as 'pure wilderness' (*puro monte*). The settlements were thus built in a 'virgin' environment of unspoilt nature.[97] In part this is evident in the biodiversity that today makes the *Cordillera* a premium tourist destination. Residents themselves often emphasised and provided information on the huge range of plants and fauna, and spoke with regret about the loss of wildlife and the forest that had been destroyed to make way for farmland.[98] This does not stop common and frequent reference to the natural fecundity of the environment; as people often pointed out, 'everything grows here'.

By emphasising the fertility of their subtropical environment the *campesinos* reaffirm the value of the earth as a source of sustenance. Despite pretensions to engage with markets, the early pioneers are taken as representative of a tradition of surviving from subsistence agriculture, sometimes supplemented by hunting. This made them dependent upon the immediate environment, where they utilised their energy to extract a livelihood directly from the earth while at the same time reshaping it through work. Subsistence agriculture allowed them to practice thrift, and reserve cash for items they could not produce. To a lesser degree this model is reproduced today, and applying strength and energy to procure a living from the soil is central to their identification with the environment, not least at a symbolic level. This is clear in Tino's definition of a *campesino* as 'someone who puts themselves in nature and works upon it'.

For *campesinos* work means the application of human energy to the earth, and repeated reference is made to the strength, or 'force', that labour involves.[99] By his testimony Amadeo entered the *Cordillera* out of curiosity; 'to see what was available and what could be done', because, he said 'I came with nothing but my strength.' Humans, so the reasoning goes, have 'strength' (*fuerza*), and are entitled to take from nature, which 'gives' (*da*). But what comes from the environment is also described as strength, and because this is an inherent and latent natural capacity, a more correct translation for the Spanish word *fuerza* is force, or power. The idea is that humans are within and of the natural world, and take from and rely on the strength of nature, just as plants and animals do.[100] God put power into nature, presumably in the making of the world, and this power is the resource that all living beings draw upon, store, and potentially expend, although they have different requirements and capacities. So plants can be described in terms of the amount of force they take; quick-growing trees such as eucalyptus are said to 'suck out a lot of force' while a sickly plant is said to have 'never taken power'. Strength comes to the human body through food, the fruit of the earth; particular foods, such as beans (*frijoles*), are considered superior for the 'force' they contain. When we cooked a chicken for the Jara family, Luís supplemented it with *frijoles*, since without them he said he didn't feel he had eaten. The religious element places humanity within a natural order ordained by God. People are like the natural environment from which they gain sustenance. This parallel was made clear in a discussion on agriculture. I put it to a farmer who was recalling the greater soil fertility of the past that agriculture itself is unsustainable. He replied by making the following comment: 'it is the same with people, over time we also lose strength'.

Campesinos have ample empirical evidence to support the view that nature contains a reserve of inherent force. In traditional slash-and-burn agriculture good returns are guaranteed for three years, after which yields decline and the plot has to be abandoned and allowed to rest, then the land recuperates as the force returns. Unworked land, however, retains its strength. Where there is wilderness (*monte*) the earth is rich, so the 'natural condition' of soil is said to be highly fertile, and it is only when it is exploited by people that fertility declines. Through being worked, through humans taking its power, the soil loses force. The vocabulary employed to describe results attests to this; in talking about yields the word for 'take' or 'extract' (*sacar*) is used. For example, a farmer will say, 'I took 40 *fanegas* of coffee' from a particular grove. At the same time the reciprocal relationship is denoted by the fact that the *cafetal* is said to have 'given' that amount.

The image of a fecund natural environment allows residents to draw contrast with an outside, though encroaching and profane, urban world, and to romantically reimagine and place value on the rural environment. Individuals who moved to the city were worried about or derided; crime was blamed on outsiders and the city has seen as a place of violence and immorality. By contrast, residents typically preferred the country, where there was 'trust' (*confianza*), 'tranquillity' and, as was repeatedly pointed out, people 'live in peace'. The reference to peace emphasises the uniqueness of the place, and a special relation with God. As one line of a poem on a poster prominently displayed in a house declared: 'where there is peace, there is God'.

As well as inheriting and building on a 'pure forest' environment, residents claim that the pioneers found 'free lands' (*tierras libres*) that belonged to no one. Despite archaeological remains that provide evidence of inhabitation by indigenous peoples, the early settlers claim to have encountered no *indios*. In any case, the colonists took the Costa Rican land entitlement laws detailed in Chapter 2 to legitimise possession. The establishment of homesteads entailed fencing off areas of land. The inscription of rights took place in both the physical and bureaucratic domain; whereas working the land might justify possession, inscription leads to papers (*papeles*) and officially documented ownership.[101] Residents today often appear confused about the process of land appropriation and the need for legal ownership. The process of surveying and registering tracts continues and has still not been carried out by some farmers. Surprisingly, only one person seemed aware that the area had once belonged to an entrepreneur by the name of Minor Keith and his associates, who exchanged mining rights for the construction of a railroad, and that a financial settlement by the government had secured the settlers' right to farm (Gudmundson 1983). What is accepted is that claims to particular areas were staked by agreement between neighbours, with fences providing a visible boundary. From there began the clearing of forest for farmland and the felling of trees by hand, a process that accelerated with the arrival of chainsaws in the 1950s.

The first farmers began with a blank slate; as *campesinos* they put themselves in nature and worked upon it. To describe their efforts they speak of 'a struggle' (*una lucha*), a process that began with the first pioneers:

Some time has passed since the death of the pioneers, who entered the virgin forest in what constituted the great colonising adventure, the epic deeds of heroic proportions, the struggle against the swamp and the lightning and misfortune, against the tooth and claw, against the majestic turbulent river in whose overflowing course ran the swirling waters of unending time (my translation).[102]

In this description we learn that possession taken through individual action on nature has heroic undertones, akin to a myth of origin. Struggle is required because farmers interact with a capricious and sometimes dangerous natural world. It is those very same uncertainties that we saw combine with market and technological risks to make farming a lottery, and which forces farmers to juggle. To illustrate this, long histories would be recounted of various enterprises undertaken in search of livelihood. Carlos Alvarado had a string of businesses over the years: a sugar-milling enterprise, a haulage concern based on a team of oxen, a grocery store (*pulpería*), a number of different coffee farms, and a series of adventures in cattle ranching. He recalls repeated disasters. The bank repossessed the oxen when he defaulted on the loan, cattle died after he mistakenly reinjected them with a vaccine, markets collapsed at inopportune moments, crops were ruined by drought or excessive rain, and roads to market became impassable. Such tribulations indicate a tenuous existence, which leads residents like Amadeo to characterise everyday life as suffering. Ultimately, for *campesinos* 'struggle' involves individual efforts to avert disaster; it is 'something personal' achieved in the face of suffering and despite adversity.

Through its association with individual action, *la lucha* is related to the world of work. A man from a poor family, to highlight the iniquity of crime, described the poverty of his family origins, but said that by 'struggling and struggling' both himself and his siblings had managed to 'build' something. The moral imperative is to struggle for things, but 'through work, by working hard'.[103] This depiction of life as a struggle validates a particular distribution of resources and prefigures sets of relationships and circumstances.[104] Residents who have larger farms or have otherwise secured economic success can assert moral rights to their advantage through the language of struggle, while those who have less are sometimes said not to have struggled sufficiently or to have frittered away what money they have earned on strong liquor (*guaro*) or prostitutes. So although the community does support those in difficulty, some argue that they are more than just victims of circumstance. Only by redoubling efforts can workers counteract these moral charges, which helps reproduce a compliant workforce.

The notion of struggle points to two somewhat contradictory processes; on one hand *la lucha* describes the creation of a personal space through individual effort. At the same time it involves shared ventures between friends and family and group action and is circumscribed by the values and relationships so formed. The political commitment to struggle therefore extends beyond the purely personal. What began as an ethic for self-improvement inevitably becomes social; *la lucha* is an expression of the singular person struggling in a state of nature, but it becomes a metaphor for collective economic and political action.

The ethic of individualism applied to community service reiterates the cooperative mission to 'sow progress'. Perhaps for this reason the manager often answers his phone with the comment 'here we are, in the struggle' (*aquí estamos, en la lucha*). The concept of struggle is used by farmers with reference to the imposition of agency on nature; it is also appropriated by the cooperative to invoke solidarity and the struggle for development and inspires the political associations related to communal work. In the next sections I consider the main economic arena in which reference is made to struggle within a social context, namely the challenge of establishing a family farm.

THE FAMILY AND THE FARM

In conversations about the struggle to settle the highlands, God and family were irrevocably intertwined, as Amadeo's testimony demonstrates:

Thanks be to God, here am I telling you the story of all that struggle, but it was a hard struggle, very hard, and I suffered a lot. There are some people around here who appear to be working but they are merely wasting what their grandfather or father-in-law began, they are just taking advantage, but I was not one of those; only God helped me, and my family, I have a very good family. I owe everything to God and my family (my translation).

The first of these factors, the relationship with God, reflects the particular understanding of providence explored earlier through the invocation of *si Dios quiere*. It is also caught up in specific ideas on the way nature and natural processes work, which lies at the heart of *campesinos'* assessments of value, their political commitments and, as I argue below, their moral evaluations of trade. In the meantime

I focus on the importance of the family and the household in achieving aims.

The main site of struggle is agriculture, an activity that entails entering into nature and working it to wrestle a living. The object is to establish an independent family farm (*finca*) centred upon the social and redistributive hub of the home in which people 'pool' resources (Sahlins 1974). But the home (*hogar*) is established and reproduced by men struggling with nature. In this way *la lucha* reflects a gendered model of family life, in which women play a domestic and supporting role. Women are said by men to 'help'; they define the domestic space by 'pushing back the wilderness', by taking the role of household 'administrator', establishing and maintaining the home, and by raising children.[105] To varying degrees women's participation in public life remains limited; many, particularly elderly women, spend much of their time in and around their house and were rarely if ever seen in public. Children play an equally important part in reproducing the home; they provide support in old age and carry on the family farm. For this reason talk of children, especially among the elderly, often focuses on inheritance. Under Costa Rican law, property is divided equally between offspring, regardless of sex. Women who inherit may work their land themselves, although this is most unusual.[106] It is more common for women to come to an agreement with their brothers or husbands who then labour on the farm, or they might sell up, an option that is also open to men.

Working a farm correctly means improving it for the next generation and this validates the struggle. Amadeo and others were keen to advertise the fact that they had handed on good farmland, and ideally each generation should inherit better land. This sentiment was made explicit when referring to the negative effects of poisoning the fields with chemicals and was often referred to in discussions on new methods and ways of working, especially organic systems. Attachment to the land and its value to the family is further illustrated by the preference for selling to immediate kin. Wilberth was planning to emigrate to the United States to work, but to raise funds he needed to sell a coffee grove, so his father bought the land and then sold it back to him when he was unsuccessful in his visa application. In another case, Amadeo Leitón's unmarried daughter sold her inherited land to one of her brothers, an outcome deemed appropriate, as the farms were also 'adjacent' (*colindante*). The importance and value of land to the individual and by extension to the family lies in its permanence. A man who needed to raise cash once set me a riddle: should he, I was asked, sell a cow or a small piece of land to raise some money he required? I suggested he should keep the land and sell the cow, a solution that was deemed correct since 'a cow can be replaced, but land cannot and will always hold value'.

In discussing their families, people often remembered and referred to their provenance and lineages. So, for example, an individual would state that his mother or grandmother came from Palmares, while his father or grandfather came from Alajuela. Similar, but less precise reference is made to the European and mixed ancestry with which residents identify. When I commented on the Indian relics I had seen in people's houses and the remains people had told me about, it was pointed out that evidence of indigenous presence extended even to blood (*hasta en el sangre*). The combination and recombination of bloodlines generates diversity.[107] A similar process can be seen to occur with respect to the family farm. Because of partible inheritance all individuals are bequeathed an equal share of their mother's and father's land; what they are given thus does not replicate what their parents had, and through their efforts to build and improve, a new combination of resources is achieved. Patterns of ownership diversify, farm boundaries change and there is a problem created by shrinking plot size over time.

In many houses the primary income, most often generated by the man, is shared and ensures the continued reproduction of the domestic group. Family members, especially those living at home, usually expect or receive income for working the land; sons may help their father, but only in expectation that title to a portion of the farm will pass to them in due course. Surveys I undertook to try to document land ownership were much complicated by shared family entitlement. A man might lay claim to a particular coffee grove but when pressed would admit his father was the legal owner. Similarly, although people know who actually works the plots, the identity of the owner was not always common knowledge, nor was it deemed important; sons were known to have taken over the management of certain areas, as they would be seen working there. Claims to land established through kin ties often seem to take precedence over individual rights to private property. On the other hand, personal items and incomes generated by informal activities by wives or children who had not yet left home were kept separate, to be disposed of as individuals saw fit.

Household and kin ties operate most obviously in work that does not generate a monetary income. This takes many forms; domestic labour in and around the house is not part of the cash economy and agricultural work on the farm may be pooled between close family. Brothers help brothers, nephews find employment with their uncles and nieces help in the harvest, without necessarily expecting payment. Often children set up home close to the parents and the two families visit each other regularly. Grandchildren spend time with their grandparents, particularly when there is work to be done. Neither are these relationships always limited by distance;

Carlos regularly took the bus to Liberia to visit his son, and would be gone several days. Sonia returned to her family home in Campos de Oro, usually on a Sunday. Visits take the place of more formal holidays, which few can afford, and form part of a wider pastime of unannounced visiting of friends and more distant relations for both business and pleasure.

The web of kinship is close knit, and relations by marriage and of blood join the six or seven principal families of El Dos. As people often said: 'we are all family here'. Ties and lineages extend along the *Cordillera*. Partners often meet and court at the dances and festivals that attract an audience from the surrounding countryside, or at intercommunal football competitions. Marriage brings with it family responsibilities, draws the individual into a different set of material relations and alters expectations. Women often take up a domestic role, while men begin full-time work on the land or take up wage labour to provide cash for the family. Marriage can also create new possibilities; for example, a man will often take over management of his wife's *finca*.

The Costa Rican convention is that civil society is made up of a succession of independent family-farming units, each similar and equal to its neighbour.[108] Such formal equality contradicts extreme inequalities in resources, especially land, and the benefits different families and individuals can extract from the market. On the other hand, the centrality of the house as the site for reproduction, the historical importance of subsistence agriculture in establishing and maintaining the farm through difficult times, nature rather than the market as the origin of value in agriculture, and the symbolic importance of these things cannot be denied.

PRODUCTION FOR CONSUMPTION: THE LURE OF SUBSISTENCE

I have argued that in the highlands the family is imagined and represented as a self-reproducing unit, at the level of both biology and economy. Since subsistence-style agriculture has historically been considered the basis of household reproduction, the accent is often placed on that activity rather than market-oriented agriculture. Even though almost everyone now gains their primary livelihood through some kind of engagement in the monetary economy, reference is continually made to practices and possibilities that suggest this need not, nor ought to be, so. The ideas and images conjured up by non-market spaces may mask exploitative relations, but are a key part of the way residents identify with each other and the place in which they live, and are expressive of moral ideas on the economy. The most direct ways to understand the centrality of subsistence agriculture in everyday life is through the concept of the model farm and the symbolic importance given to crops produced for home consumption.

On visits to farms people often emphasised the variety of crops they grew or the animals they kept for direct consumption, rather than the quantity of coffee or number of milk cows they possessed. Soon after we arrived in El Dos, my family was taken on a visit to a 'model farm'. This accolade was not based upon efficiency or commercial success. The owner was an elderly woman who sold a little cheese locally, lived on a pension and relied on help from her children. Much of what was consumed was produced on the land. Its status as a model rested upon reference to a subsistence-based prototype and the range of fruit, vegetables and animals produced for home use. All farms to a greater or lesser degree follow this model; two in particular stand out. In the first a man refused to grow coffee and dedicated his land to maize for home consumption and sale to neighbours. He supplemented this income with wage labour; even though he had enough land to gain a reasonable income from commercial farming he said he did not like coffee farming and considered it unreliable.

Another case is the Jiménez family, whom we met in the Introduction. The father, Felix, claimed to have once owned and farmed large areas of land, but to have been dispossessed. The family now survive on a meagre pension and by growing a wide range of crops in the tiny courtyard of their house, squeezed between the confluence of two tracks. They have several coffee bushes, and dry-process and roast their coffee at home, the only family I came across that persisted with this tradition. Their diet was supplemented by chickens and by a cow that produced milk, some of which they sold as cream cheese (*nata*). Because they did not have land for grazing, Felix cut fodder with his machete and took it home by wheelbarrow from the roadside or from unclaimed or unattended areas of land, an activity that led my children to give him the nickname 'Mr Wheelbarrow'. When he died the daughter of the house took up the subsistence work.

In common with peasant agriculture the world over, farmers around El Dos have a historical legacy of agriculture that combines subsistence with commercial agriculture, although crops grown for home consumption take symbolic precedence and are in many ways the idealised form of economic activity. Evidence regarding the agricultural practices of the first settlers comes primarily from oral testimonies, and points to similar objectives; all were seeking access to land for agricultural purposes and hoped to achieve this without cost or at a reduced price. They came with a variety of activities in mind, depending on the experience and traditions they brought with them, but shared a commitment to market-oriented agriculture to raise cash revenues, combined with subsistence activities to reduce costs and ensure reproduction.

Some residents arrived intending to plant coffee; German Montero, for example, came from San Ramón de Alajuela in 1947 with the necessary seeds in his baggage. Others, like Amadeo, wanted to start cattle ranching; the animals provided milk, meat and cheese, both for home consumption and a cash income. Thus the two main market-oriented activities practised today were already on the agenda from the middle of the last century. According to Carlos Alvarado, sugarcane (*caña*) provided many families with their most important source of money in the pre-1940s economy, although it has now declined in the face of competition from the industrially refined product. The cane was sold as cattle fodder, milled in a *trapiche* and sold in block form (*tapa de dulce*), or illegally distilled into hard liquor (*guaro* or *contrabando*) for local consumption or to be sold to the gold miners in nearby Las Juntas. Tobacco, another cash crop, is no longer grown. The hardwood timber felled in the land clearing process was also lucrative and there was once a sawmill on the site of the present-day coffee-processing plant, although it was destroyed in a flash flood.

For subsistence the residents relied on the staples of maize and *frijoles*, but a great range of other foods were cultivated, which provided a varied diet. Foremost amongst those listed for the pre-1940 period by a long-term resident were the root vegetables *chamol* (also called *ñampí*), *malanga*, potatoes and *ayote*. Other vegetables included *chayote*, which was also marketed in the towns of Tilarán, Las Juntas and Cañas. Peppers and tomatoes were grown, along with a wide range of fruits, including bananas, plantains, oranges, mangoes, avocados and guava. Today many families keep pigs, primarily for home consumption, but also for sale, and almost every farm has chickens in the yard. Others keep cows to produce milk and cheese. Some families have also constructed pools in which they breed fish (*tilapia*).

The tradition of an autonomous household practising production for consumption is maintained to varying degrees; many farmers grow as much of their food requirements (*diario*) as conditions allow, while others are almost completely dependent on retail purchases. In any case, the origins and reproduction of the community are founded upon the idealised goal of self-sufficiency. To highlight the difference between cash crops and subsistence items a classificatory distinction is made between things earmarked for auto-consumption (*por el gasto*) and those destined for sale (*para vender*). It is difficult to convey the poignancy and satisfaction with which the term *por el gasto* is pronounced; it provides the most perfect solution to the 'problem' of the market; that is, dependency on an economic system that often seems to work against them. The gesture that accompanies the expression captures the inherent logic of auto-consumption. It involves bringing one's hand up to the mouth and wiggling the fingers; the arm thus forms a circle and provides closure, just as production destined for direct consumption creates a closed circuit of reproduction of the individual and the family.

In El Dos, as in Central America generally, the crop that best encapsulates and evokes a sense of tradition, of identities pertaining to an earlier time of subsistence agriculture and beyond and to indigenous forms of life, is maize (Annis 1987).[109] Many houses still possess and often display a traditional grinding stone, as well as having the metal hand-operated mincer that replaced it. Neither of these tools are much used as many residents can buy ready-made tortillas in the local store. Today maize is commonly grown, but generally in small quantities to extract the more highly prized 'soft' corn (*maíz tierno*), which is then made into homemade *tortillas*. The maize plot, often intercropped with roots and other vegetables, called a *milpa*, provides an additional source of food for the family, although its symbolic importance is often greater than its nutritional contribution. Explicit reference is often made to local, family and even Indian traditions when talk turns to the *milpa* and homemade *tortillas*.[110]

The *milpa* acts as a site of resistance to the power of the market and its character is therefore as much political as economic. It was, for example, invoked as a sign of indigenous practice, and even though the percentage of Indian blood in local residents is small or nonexistent, informants actively identified with Indian heritage; some even said that they considered themselves more Indian than white. Several farmers, particularly those drawn to organic methods, claimed to be revitalising indigenous agricultural techniques. The association with indigenous peoples and practices by white and mixed-raced farmers suggests political resistance both to commercial and industrial agriculture. The *milpa* represents producing food *por el gasto*; it suggests a time before market domination and a symbolic space outside exchange and monetary value. Whereas the market is often associated with supplements and luxuries, subsistence agriculture is symbolic of the serious business of family reproduction and guaranteed access to the bare necessities of life (Scott 1976). In the year of fieldwork I was told that the number of *milpas* being established had increased significantly, a fact that was specifically linked to a fall in coffee prices.

The appeal of the subsistence economy for residents has deeply romantic undertones; it reflects a particular relationship with nature, now deemed to have been lost in a technologically driven world. People in El Dos spoke with nostalgia about a previous way of life, epitomised by the family farm, communal help, the sharing of tasks and togetherness in adversity. Residents often evoked an image of a poverty-stricken past; houses were wooden shacks made from local materials, clothes were ragged and possessions minimal. But, despite material deprivation, people also associated the past with contentment. As one resident put it; 'we were poor but we were happy; we had *fiestas*, we danced, we sang and food was abundant'. Although crops came in season, those deemed of most value could be preserved; stacks of maize and stocks of *frijoles* and potatoes were often recalled as an image of sufficiency. A common device for expressing abundance was to focus on the size and quantity of crops and the food available. The maize tortillas were huge and potatoes were harvested in great quantities. Older people remembered sitting on stacks of tubers, and individual examples were said to be of huge dimensions. Today very few potatoes are grown and fertilisers are employed to get any kind of return, and even then the specimens are so small the effort is hardly considered worth the result. Like tomatoes, they were once grown 'naturally', that is, without chemicals.

Surprisingly, despite these tales of abundance, informants agreed that the level of material wealth for most residents is higher today than it has ever been. This is by no means to claim that poverty has been eradicated; there are still those who eke out a marginal existence and the quantity of material possessions owned by most would be considered basic to most Northern sensibilities. Nevertheless, concrete-block housing, running water, electricity and a television are now the norm rather than exceptional. It is also generally agreed that prosperity has accelerated since the late 1980s, a success that is claimed by the cooperative and linked by some to preferential trade deals.

What sense can we make of the apparently nonsensical claim that people are now materially better off but that the past was a golden age of abundance and contentment? In the first place there is the possibility that a reduction in absolute poverty goes hand in hand with greater relative poverty.[111] Different capacities to purchase consumer goods and profit from new-found opportunities unsettles a model of formal equality between autonomous households. In part, too, the answer must revolve around the notion of value; a scheme which gives moral precedence to people producing and consuming directly from their environment problematises the value created by exchange, measured in money. Related to this is the idea that subsistence inures families against the risks of the market; it creates a space for the minimal requirement of reproduction and inoculates against danger. A powerful appeal is made to a different set of economic 'goods', a space apart from the modern risk economy geared to individual maximisation. Profit stands in opposition to a measured household that seeks other goals: autonomy, affinity and leisure.[112]

CONCLUSION

This chapter begins the process of linking *campesino* politics in the Tilarán Highlands to cultural background. The *Campesinos'* goal, held since their arrival, has been to farm and improve areas of land by working with the force perceived in nature. People place value on their agricultural and domestic labour because through this they shape the world around them, and the importance of their actions becomes manifest (Graeber 2001). What has been achieved can then be passed on as an inheritable good. In this way, symbolic relationships of blood and name and religiously inspired meanings and values intertwine with material interests. This is most clearly the case in the idealised family farm to which some residents are heir, and that they then maintain and seek to advance. The fact that gender and class inequalities are masked in the model detracts little from its power.

People in El Dos have a complex relationship with markets. They are inextricably entangled in commercial agriculture and rely on exchange to live, but they express values and are committed to subsistence from direct and unmediated interactions with nature. The economic autonomy that this implies is part of the political independence often associated with pioneers and an expanding frontier. The parallels, for example, with de Tocqueville's writings are striking: Americans, he said, conceive of themselves as owing 'nothing to any man, they expect nothing from any man; they acquire the habit of always considering themselves as standing alone, and they are apt to imagine that their whole destiny is in their own hands' (cited in Stirrat 1989:100).[113]

In this chapter we have seen how economic independence involves the family as a unit whose existence has an idealised basis in a divinely ordered natural environment, beyond the rigours and uncertainties of commerce. The suggestion is that such cultural values are recognised and bought into by consumers, played upon, whether consciously or not, by activists concerned at the inequities of the market, and appropriated by commerce for profit. In the next chapter we turn to the political autonomy and oppositional politics of local organisations, operating against the background of a perceived failure of government. These organisations are important, since they are motivated by moral and political ideas that, like the family farm and subsistence agriculture, question the dominant values of the market and set up alternative avenues to access and distribute resources.

7 CIVIL SOCIETY: LOCAL DEVELOPMENT AND THE LIMITS OF GOVERNMENT

The smallholder model and social reproduction from nature carries with it and is sustained by an imagined formal equality. This no doubt adds to its appeal for purveyors of fair trade; the family farmer can be imagined as compromised not by differentiation at the local level but by unfair global commodity relations. In Costa Rica, too, national mythology insists the country is a nation of smallholders, made up of independent, equal, landowning units. This chapter is concerned with relations between people and households, mainly at the village level, and the way relationships are formed, lived and regulated.

There are clear links between the family farms that were the focus of the preceding discussion and local-level associations. Where homesteaders meet they find common interests, which on the surface indicates formal equality. Most obviously, groups gear activities towards providing services that all need to further the goals of their various families. But the language of complementary interests is insufficient as an explanation, not least because, as we have seen, residents are not equal. To compensate for differences both the family farm and village organisations appeal to notions of affinity, moral sentiment and service to others. In the process they endorse the Catholic doctrine that God created the earth for humans, but for the benefit of communities or collectives, not individuals (May 1993:24).

Voluntary associations constitute and express forms of self-reliance that operate outside both formal markets and the state; they correspond to 'civil society' as it is commonly conceived.[114] In the process they fill the space abandoned by corrupt government agencies as they neglect their duty to hardworking, taxpaying, marginal farmers. Informal networks, exchanges between neighbours, personal friendships, as well as more formally organised local associations and committees, are a focus for accessing and regulating resources at the village level. As agriculturalists with a similar background and common experiences, residents share problems, concerns, possibilities and aspirations. Neighbours address these issues during informal visits to each other's houses, or when they meet in public spaces; on the road to work or to town, in the bar, at festivals and football matches, after church, at the village shop (*pulpería*),[115] or in the many meetings organised by the cooperative, village associations and church-based groups.

At the same time, the ideal of formal equality is threatened by differences in opportunity and the ability to exploit resources in market activities. In El Dos the strong Christian ethic offers residents a way to negotiate tension, identified by Hann in civil society 'between the selfish goals of individual actors and the need for some basic collective solidarity in a moral community' (1996:4). The Catholic doctrine laid out in the papal encyclicals and pastoral letters encourages benign and voluntary associations for employers and working people, particularly Catholic groups, while the role of the state is limited to safeguarding property and ensuring self-preservation by guaranteeing and regulating rights gained through labour. Last, but by no means least, the doctrine pursues social justice by promoting moral duties to help the poor, placing limitations on the accumulation of wealth, and extolling the virtue of charity (*Rerum Novarum* 1960 [1891]:16–42). Similarly, conflicts raised by inequalities in El Dos are negotiated through a language of moral conduct. This can be used when people wish to claim rights and remind others of their duties to provide access to resources (Cohen 1985; Li 1996). More importantly, for the purposes of this book, it clearly indicates an ethic that moderates capitalist values of self-interest and personal accumulation.

Where civil society is identified in this chapter largely at the institutional level in forms of public action, non-market, non-state activity also operates when people share, give away, lend, sell and otherwise distribute goods and services. In so doing various kinds of relationships between individuals and households are created in an informal economy. Things often move in personalised exchanges between producers and consumers; for example, maize for secondhand clothes, *frijoles* in lieu of rent, housing or land to work as part of an employment package, and cheese or an old TV for cash. In these cases, it might be argued, there is a formal reckoning of monetary worth, but prices and terms vary according to ability to pay – and this is the case with respect to many goods, from oranges to rent. Finally, things are frequently given away or lent without any apparent or explicit expectation of recompense. Furniture can be borrowed and then returned, and fruit that is produced 'spontaneously' by nature, without human intervention, is often freely taken or given away.

This chapter examines what happens when the formal model of the smallholding family farm meets the reality of social inequality and differing capacities for people to pursue their own interests. Positive and negative responses are noted. The first is to set up associations and groups to offset disadvantages or provide charity in cases of particular need. The ethic is one of service, like that driving cooperative managers or charitable giving of time and resources. The effect is to forge a web of reciprocal relationships between known people. Partly, there is the duty for the better-off to help the poor, but there is a more general principle of giving, receiving and sharing that ties people to one another. I see this as exemplifying Mauss's ideas about gift-giving, generosity and personal sacrifice, a reversal of the capitalist spirit and market ethic. Fair trade follows similar principles; the advantaged use their consumer power to help the disadvantaged and powerless by choosing to give generously. In the process, by paying more than they need, shoppers can see themselves as refusing the market maxim to pursue selfish interests.

The second response is more Marxian; it warns of the dangers of maximising individual satisfaction in the market. What happens when you put personal fortune above social relationships or are consumed by the importance of objects, so that you live your life through them and fail to see they are the result of specific acts of labour and are a source of satisfaction, livelihood and a means to create bonds between people? In El Dos there is a vocabulary that warns of the social and moral consequences of excessive materialism and self-interest. One way to think about it is in terms of alienation and fetishisation. In using these terms Marx was concerned about experiences under capitalism; how people lose sight of their social selves and the way objects are given independent life and the power to create people, rather than the other way round. But the warnings imply the opposite; people should relate to each other as social beings and not as instruments, and they should peer behind the product to see the social relations so easily hidden in production, exchange and consumption.

The relevance of this discussion to fair trade is that it entertains the possibility of economic acts driven not by self-interest, but by self-sacrifice in spending more in order to benefit others in need; it allows a role for things in making social and moral connections to other people; and it recognises the limitations of the market as a distributive mechanism for goods. In El Dos an alternative is offered by a non-state, non-market arena of public action we can call civil society, which is regulated using a vocabulary that critiques capitalist values and places restraint above personal satisfaction and generosity above self-interest.

LOCAL CIVIL SOCIETY AND THE PROBLEM WITH STATE
GOVERNMENT

The greatest obstacle to the opening up of the *Cordillera* to the market
during the last century was the state of the dirt tracks, which at best
were passable to a team of oxen, and at worst no more than footpaths
to be negotiated by packhorse. The latter method was at one time a
common means to haul produce, and some local residents specialised
in running strings of horses bearing their own and neighbours' goods.
The problem of infrastructure was a repeated complaint from residents
and was of prime importance to farmers whose income depended
on getting fresh products to market or to processing facilities in
good time. One man recalled journeying to Tilarán via Cañas, an
absurdly long detour. This difficulty continues today; the infrastructure is such that horses are still widely used, while vehicles are by
necessity either motorbikes, quad bikes or 4WD. The torrential and
extended rains in October, November and December have always
exacerbated the problem of keeping tracks in order. These deluges
quickly transform the dirt surfaces into quagmires and make access
difficult if not impossible. Neighbourhood work teams, armed with
picks and shovels, were once organised to maintain, improve and
build the necessary roads. This is a function that is now most often
accomplished with machinery, and responsibility has ostensibly been
assumed by the state. But villagers still make efforts to fill potholes
and continue to have much to say on the subject.

If the problem of infrastructure was met by road maintenance
schemes and joint action, so too was the establishment of public
spaces. Erecting the buildings required shared effort, fundraising and
teamwork. El Dos has three churches that fulfil the needs of separate
congregations (*cultos*): the official Catholic and two evangelical
denominations. There is a health centre and a semi-abandoned
police station containing two cells. The voluminous communal hall
(*sala communal*), which allows functions and events to be held in
all weathers, has only recently been completed. The village contains
a school, which provides education up until the mandatory age of
twelve. This was one of the earliest permanent buildings. Although
funding came from the Ministry of Education, paperwork and
petitioning was required, materials had to be sourced, transport by
oxen arranged and skilled and unskilled labour were needed. Locals
provided these services on a voluntary basis.

Such efforts are both an expression and a locus for common identity,
ethos, interests and concerns. The legacy of this work now continues
under the auspices of the many committees in each named settlement.
The Integrated Development Association (*Asociación de Desarrollo
Integral*) is a coordinating body that controls the accounts of a number

of committees and communal facilities, and the organisation that formulates and implements village-level development initiatives. At the time of fieldwork the *Asociación de Desarrollo Integral de San Ramon* (which roughly corresponds to El Dos) ran several separate financial accounts: one for the sports hall, one for road maintenance, another for the health clinic, a bridge-building fund, the monies of a sports group, a collection for a new road and the committee accounts for a nearby and smaller village. In addition to financial management, the Development Association seeks funds for specific projects. They have collected money for the construction of a new road, which will allow vehicles into another part of the highlands, and have successfully petitioned for funding for the communal hall. This achievement is seen as the crowning glory of their work. The association not only lobbied the government's welfare institute, or Imas (*Instituto Mixta de Ayuda Social*), who provided the money, they also coordinated the construction effort. The aim of the hall, in the words of one committee member, is to 'provide a communal space for meetings and a centre for entertainment'. It is now the venue for local events: five-a-side football matches, wedding-anniversary celebrations, the annual Mother's and Father's Day parties, and a host of smaller functions. It is also used for business meetings; Coocafé and the shareholders in the Monteverde cheese factory have both used the hall for their annual assemblies.

A final role for the Development Association is the charitable one of 'social support'. The association took it upon itself to locate a spare plot of land, supply wood and corrugated iron and construct a house for a homeless single mother who had been abandoned by her partner. This was not done so much on her behalf, however, as it was felt that 'she had not struggled enough', and was therefore responsible for her own fate; the fact that she had two children was sufficient grounds for providing her with housing.

Although the association is the main avenue for the coordination of local-level action and development strategies, there is a multitude of other groups which organises local activities, raises and manages funds, carries out maintenance work on public buildings, and administers a variety of services. In El Dos there are three education committees. One, the *Junta de Educación* oversees resources, in particular the provision and maintenance of buildings and teaching materials, which in effect involves fundraising. Another provides school meals, pays the cook and organises end-of-year festivities (*Patronata Escolar*). A third (*Comité de Kinder*) raises funds for the infant school. In addition there is a committee that runs the health centre (*Comité de Salud*); the doctor is provided by government but the villagers pay a small sum for each consultation, which then goes towards renovating, cleaning and administering the building.

Another body maintains the graveyard (*Comité de Cementario*), and each religious group has a committee to oversee maintenance of church buildings and lands. Finally, at the village level, there is a volunteer financial officer (*fiscal*) who plays an important role in administering the money earmarked by coffee farmers and the cooperative to maintain the tracks. This sum is proportionate to the coffee production of each village, and the aim is to keep routes open to ensure that the crop can be delivered for processing.

Each of these organisations has a similar administrative structure to the cooperative; there is a president and a vice-president, a finance officer, a secretary, a treasurer and two *vocales*, who may speak but not vote. Election to the committees takes place by ballot, and any local person can stand for office. At the annual meeting of the Development Association in 1998 the entire committee had to be replaced, as the incumbents had reached the end of their three-year tenure. Apparent reluctance to take on this responsibility means that the committees tend to be dominated by people used to administration; namely those who run businesses, are better educated and are confident in their abilities to perform public office. Although women were proposed several times for roles on the committee, particularly the minor positions, they were reticent about putting their names forward for the ballot. Eventually the most important jobs on the Development Association committee went to leading figures in El Dos, who had a proven track record. When voting, villagers must balance personal preference and political expediency. The desire to raise the profile of women in public affairs was an issue for some, particularly with respect to the cooperative which wants and needs to take the issue of equality seriously, at least partly to satisfy NGOs, but deepseated gender divisions are not easily overcome.

Villagers with resources, education and power take responsibility for representing common political interests. Attending the full range of functions often means going to meetings in local towns; it demands time, money and transport and both resources and resourcefulness are required. But because of the large number of councils and committees some position of responsibility is in principle open to all, and men and women who do not take up official posts can help in more informal ways. For example, work groups are often formed to clear and maintain shared public spaces such as the football field and cemetery. The numerous fiestas also mean that many help with the preparation of food, the serving of drinks, the organisation of the music, the selling of tickets and a myriad of other minor tasks.

The role of these committees continually shifts; they adopt new causes as others are completed, and new organisations can be founded as occasion demands. The Development Association is a case in point. It was begun in the late 1990s, in the first instance to meet the need for the community hall (*sala comunal*). Once this had been completed attention shifted to building a new stretch of road. The completion of this project then saw the adoption of a campaign to install telephone lines for private subscribers. As aims are drawn up and strategies embarked upon new contacts are established and novel avenues to resources found. Strategising involves the creative use of networks to seek results. A provisional list of contacts employed by the Development Association in the village of Cabaceras included local, regional and national connections although, as my informant pointed out, the network is incredibly complex and constantly changing.

In common with the image projected and played upon by cooperative managers and fair trade promoters, the political identity and rhetoric of these self-help movements is constructed around poor, marginal *campesinos*, struggling together for improvement. This is thrown into sharp relief by the imputed failure of government to do its long-established duty to provide social support, particularly in the wake of structural adjustment policies in the early 1980s (Rovira Mas 2004).[116] Like many people in Costa Rica, the inhabitants of El Dos have all but lost faith in institutional structures of power, and struggle to defend the social democratic model in the face of neoliberal reform (Edelman 1999; Palmer and Molina 2004:319–321). Cynicism is rife with regard to the political will of the state to effect change, and it is this very failure of successive governments which sets up the need for local initiatives and alternative action. Meanwhile, institutional politics is almost unanimously rejected as a force for change.

Evidence to validate and reinforce lack of confidence in national party politics abounds. Scandals and cases of corruption frequently rock the bureaucratic and administrative levels of government (González and Solís 2001), and are faithfully reproduced in the press. The only village newspaper arrives daily at the shop and forms a focus for discussion. One case of corruption that was often referred to involved the deviation of funds belonging to Fodesaf (*Fondo de Desarrollo Social y Asignaciones Familiares*) destined for the children of disadvantaged families to provide school meals; 100 million *colones* had been siphoned off from the system and was finally traced to a foreign bank account. Similar scandals have rocked the distribution of social funds for housing and the appropriation of money for road-building programmes. Although these instances are the subject of ongoing judicial scrutiny, the evidence of corruption in national public life reinforces distrust of official avenues and justifies overt criticism of institutional power structures.[117]

The cases also underlie and illuminate the numerous comments on politicians; they are frequently referred to as thieves who enter the profession with the express intention of appropriating funds. This corruption is not confined to the higher echelons of the corridors of power but extends to all those in public employment. Repair work to the tracks that serve as roads in and out of El Dos was the focus of much comment for several days; the contractors were ineffectual, it was claimed, since payment was calculated by volume of clay surfacing material shifted rather than the quality of the work. As a result workers were merely dumping loads at random along the tracks and neglecting resurfacing work. Roads form the focus of much dissent, as one informant explained: 'the people of Costa Rica have paid enough taxes to asphalt the whole country, but instead of a road we have a mud bath'. Dissent over taxation reared its head again at a meeting of cooperative members in which mention was made of the high quantities of tax paid by milk and coffee producers in the area (the estimate given was some $400,000 annually). Despite this contribution each cooperative member also directly underwrites road maintenance in the form of a sum subtracted by the cooperative from his payments for coffee. 'Why do we have to pay for road maintenance when we already pay so much tax?' one coffee grower grumbled. 'That is communism, big time.'

Against the background of corruption the local committees and associations take action. Where government and the welfare state fails, shared responsibility steps in. This comes across clearly in the wording of a Development Association mural on the wall of the bus stop in El Dos: 'A United community is a community that prospers' (*un pueblo unido es un pueblo que prospera*).[118] By serving on the various committees individuals contribute to the running and improvement of their immediate area. Securing resources requires strategies to engage with a wide range of external institutions. People access and administer resources for the common good by serving on local-level institutions and by engaging with regional and national non-governmental and state agencies, however corrupt and inefficient the latter are considered to be.

Despite deep cynicism with regard to politicians and the state, the *campesinos* of Highland Tilarán remain reformist rather than radical. Direct action is not unknown in Costa Rica (Edelman 1990, 1999), but in keeping with the country's traditions of stable democratic process, lobbying and political pressure is generally seen as the avenue for change of choice. At meetings in El Dos, calls to start an overt demonstration over roads were tempered by more moderate and conciliatory voices. Better-off, more confident and articulate farmers dominate the organisations; those who in more desperate times and places might lead insurrections (Scott 1976; Wolf 1969). Meanwhile, despite the long history of organised labour and workers' rights in Costa Rica, landless and poorer residents are neither radical, organised nor represented (Miller 1996). They are forced to rely on a social order based upon the ties between patrons and clients to find work, and local-level organisations to gain access to resources.[119] The elderly and single mothers are especially vulnerable in this respect, and are often forced to fall back on charity to supplement pensions and other sources of income. They could not do this successfully if social and moral ideas did not inform economic conduct.

To explore how the above activities are regulated in this moral economy I turn to a series of terms that advise restraint in exercising one's capacity to maximise personal gain. This can be seen as giving voice to that part of the Catholic social doctrine that puts limits upon individual accumulation, warns against making excessive profits at the expense of other people and encourages people to be charitable and generous in social and economic relations.

VALUES AND ANTI-VALUES: HUMILITY, SELFISHNESS AND CONSUMERISM

An important benchmark against which many values and achievements are measured is the quality of being humble (*humilde*). Having been raised in a different tradition it took time for me to appreciate the importance that humility assumes. Eventually I came to see that in *campesino* life the accent on being *humilde* is positive in the same way that success is for many people in the West.

When invited into homes great stress was often put on the humble nature of the family's circumstances. On being shown around people would often point out their 'humble kitchen', and invite my family into the 'humble sitting room', which no doubt reflects perceptions of visitors from Europe and their self-representation as 'poor peasants'. But the emphasis placed on this value is telling. The quality of humility also extends to judgments of others, as individuals were often positively described as humble. It was not applied to those who have achieved success; I was told that one man, the successful son of a small farmer, 'was a very humble man', but has since 'become self-important'.

The value of humility is further accentuated by its inverse relation to material wealth and conspicuous consumption, made explicit by the negative connotations of consumerism (*consumismo*) and luxury (*lujo*).[120] My attention was first drawn to this in a report drawn up by the head teacher of the school for the Ministry of Education. In a section on 'anti-values' (*antivalores*) she wrote:

There is also much consumerism, as most houses contain the most fashionable electrical goods as well as expensive and luxurious ornaments; the people dress very well and in a costly and ostentatious manner, especially the women and children; in this respect the men are more humble (my translation).

Relative prosperity in recent years, particularly among dairy farmers, no doubt accentuates the perception of increasing ostentation. But it is also reflects the anti-materialist and renunciatory ethic of Christian tradition (Parry 1986; Parry and Bloch 1989). As is well known, concern about excessive accumulation is an important part of Christian doctrine, most notably in the famous pronouncement in Timothy that 'the love of money is the root of all evil'.[121] Bible study is an important part of intellectual life in the highlands, and the Book strongly influences ideas and attitudes. Many people spend a good deal of time reading and discussing passages, they readily quote from the Bible, and are highly familiar with Christian doctrine. There are Bible study groups, particularly amongst the Protestant *evangelicos* who make up about half the population. *Evangelicos* distinguish themselves from Catholics by reserving the right to read and interpret the Bible for themselves, and by deriding Catholic received religion and its superstition with regard to miracles, visions and the deification of saints.

Many of the older residents saw fashion as the most pernicious form of *consumismo*. While attractive to some, particularly the young, fashion was often derided by older residents as wasteful frippery and associated with avarice. Carlos told me of his nephew, who lives in the provincial capital and wears $100 shoes, although he has never worked. By comparison, Carlos's own footwear cost only $20 and so, he stressed, he had saved himself a fortune. Likewise, many farmers wear little more than rags for their daily agricultural tasks, and so mirror the way fair trade likes to represent them. The positive value of thrift and humility stands against ostentation and excess, as was graphically illustrated by a man who believed 'all that you accumulate turns rotten'. Objects are recycled, reused and passed on, but seldom if ever destroyed. As Luís pointed out: 'even the oldest and most charred and battered of cooking pots is useful and has value'.

In El Dos, and in keeping with its Christian traditions, a moral order portrays excessive materialism as negative, despite the attractions of consumer goods.[122] The association between poverty and humility is further endorsed by the absence of any stigma attached to penury and by the disarming way that many residents emphasised their lack of possessions. Poverty has its own status, since it implies that one has not, indeed cannot, fall into the sins of *consumismo* and *lujo*. The discomfort I felt when friends and acquaintances openly, and without embarrassment, emphasised their impecunious state or admitted they lived in a terrible house was all mine, coming as I do from a society in which these things are generally shameful and to be hidden.[123]

However, there are other connotations and repercussions underlying the requirement to be humble beyond ambivalent attitudes to poverty and wealth. We can see this in common reference to other negative values, apart from *consumismo* and humility. Principal among these are the sins of pride (*orgullo*), ambition (*ambición*) and selfishness (*egoismo*). Pride is most often referred to in a religious context; it implies one has lifted oneself above God and manifests itself in spending too much time working in the pursuit of material gain. Farmers speak of resting and taking time to contemplate the natural world, and some deride those who work too hard in the pursuit of wealth. In succumbing to pride one fails in the duty to give time to the worship and contemplation of God. Those who are proud are, however, said to be deluding themselves, as the religious ethic decrees us all to have been 'born equal and in the image of the Lord'.

Similar stigma is attached to ambition. Amadeo was told by his father on his death-bed to 'beware of *ambición*'; since the desire to get ahead and do better than your neighbours leads to 'the abyss'. Instead it is preferable, and ethical, 'to live within limits'. As Amadeo pointed out, 'some people are ambitious and build up capital and large *haciendas*, but it serves them nothing'. He was careful to explain that he was not against self-improvement, but this should not be achieved at the expense of others. Ambition is also closely linked to luxury and consumerism, earthly desires and the collection of material possessions. For Amadeo, it is ambition that is destroying Costa Rica; the rich grow richer as a result of their ambition, which is then directly linked to increasing poverty.[124] Similarly Carlos saw ambition as unsettling and a source of unhappiness.

More commonly mentioned than pride and ambition was *egoismo*, a term that comes closest to being an antonym to humility. Another moral malaise attributed to the population and held to account for the loss of values, egoism is characterised primarily as a reluctance to share and contribute. The charge of *egoismo* is used as a form of redress for considering oneself, or one's own family, group or village before others. One woman clearly illustrated the folly of *egoismo*: as she pointed out, 'we are all equal before God'. At a meeting of coffee growers the cooperative president explained how he had quizzed a certain coffee farmer and long-time member of the cooperative on his motives for switching allegiance to the private processing plant. The reasons he was given for the move away from the cooperative revolved around the deductions made from cooperative payments to fund roads and old-people's homes and to build social capital. The response from the other participants in the meeting to this was predictable: how selfish (*que egoista*)! In another case, a discussion about the site of the secondary school was said to reflect the self-interest of communities (*egoismo entre comunidades*), since different groups wanted a convenient location for themselves.

CONCLUSIONS

The above language usefully indicates social and moral aspects of economic thought. Farmers who exploit workers or fail to guarantee rights to less well-off neighbours can be accused of egoism, which is just another word for self-interest, and implies a failure to subsume economic relations under social and moral ones. Similarly, those with a penchant for expensive possessions or who appropriate excessive wealth may be said to be falling prey to *ambición*. This brings to mind Marx's concept of alienation; the failure to recognise that products are first and foremost the outcome of specific social activities and that productive activity is about relationships. *Consumismo*, on the other hand, implies a particular way of relating to objects. It draws on an older and negative reading of consumption in our cultural repertoire in which to be 'consumed' meant to be used up. But *consumismo* is really just to grant the things we create a power over us, to be consumed by and live our lives through them; in other words it is the fetishism of commodities.

In El Dos, values reflect a Christian culture that prioritises humility and personal sacrifice over profit. The tension in civil society between self-interest and moral and social purposes is here mediated by individuals using their talents to contribute to the wider good through service to local associations, and through values that set moral limits to individual accumulation, curb ambition and extol the virtue of humility and poverty. Of course, neither of these devices is entirely successful; people do fall prey to *consumismo*, indulge in egoism and fail to exhibit humility. The point is that the terms give currency to talk about duties, rights, and human failings. So while one may need to guard against allowing peasants to stand 'vicariously for our own resistance to commodification' (Miller 1995d: 146), we ought also to recognise that they themselves are resistant and, having a common cultural background, we share concerns.

It is surely the case, for example, that fair trade also provides a cultural critique of the mainstream and proceeds on that basis. It asks us to consider the social lives behind the product and suggests that we act generously when we shop. In this respect it operates in a space outside and in opposition to the impersonal market with its asocial, alienating tendencies. One irony is that the more impersonal the market becomes, the more profound and widespread is the desire to escape, the greater is the commercial success of products that espouse social and moral ideas. But it is one thing to recognise that fair trade is easily incorporated into the profit-making strategies of capitalist companies as a marketable quality and another to identify the cultural ideas and politics that make it oppositional in the first place.

Locating moral ideas in civil society outside the domain of the market and the state raises issues for the cooperative. One part of its remit is precisely to trade coffee successfully on international commodity markets. In doing this it becomes caught up in the profit-making of trade and is forced to collaborate with state institutions that regulate the coffee industry and demand taxation. In the next chapter I describe expressions of dissatisfaction and dissent with respect to Coopeldos and locate this in the values and commitments outlined above. Principal among these is a negative view of the market and formal government and the 'anti-social' values they promote. As a benchmark for comparison we return to the idealised subsistence economy and probe further ideas that agricultural labour is the origin of value, ideas that inform political commitments and judgments, not only about the cooperative, but also in regard to trade and justice more generally.

8 CREATING AND CONTESTING VALUE: THE EARTH, LABOUR AND EXCHANGE

Many coffee producers in the highlands reject the proposition that exchange can be just; the idea runs counter to their historical experience of agricultural production for the market. Justice, as a normative ethic, requires consistent foundations and predictable outcomes, the kind of conditions that have long been denied to marginal agriculturalists in market relations.[125] In Chapter 2 the complaints and proposals for reform of Costa Rican coffee growers were examined in relation to national struggles between farmers, processors and the state. This chapter picks up that theme in the context of El Dos. It demonstrates that elements of the ideology and official discourse of coffee producers, documented by scholars through the examination of speeches and newspaper articles (Acuña 1985, 1987; Gonzalez 1987), can be identified in the politics, moral adjudications and everyday struggles of producers today.

Although fair trade has introduced some consistency into aspects of economic activity, its assets and advantages remain opaque to producers. There are a number of reasons for this. Partly it is because fair trade is only one sector of the market and the prices received by growers continue to rise and fall dramatically. A second reason is the lack of scope for meaningful price comparisons, except with a 'ball-park' figure published in the press. Finally, the gate price received for a crop is not known for months after the farmer delivers it for processing, and the fair-trade premium is the very last payment made. These factors complicate attempts to create stable livelihoods or predict outcomes. Under such conditions, allegiance and financial ties to a processor influence whom a farmer sells to as much as do unpredictable projections of financial return (Sick 1999). More importantly, these complications are overshadowed by culturally informed ideas about how and where value is created and the way it is appropriated. This comes to the fore as farmers cede responsibility for market negotiations to the cooperative.

I begin this chapter by outlining a critique of Coopeldos made by some members, which seems to contradict both the scale of the cooperative's achievement and the commitment to service of 'small farmers' that motivates it. In identifying the source of dissatisfaction, I initially focus upon the kind of tasks in which cooperative personnel engage and then move on to look at criticisms levelled at cooperative workers, or rather a particular class of employee. An analysis of the basis for this dissatisfaction returns us to the way *campesinos* define work and the creation of value through interaction with the force of nature. The opposition between those who till the earth and administrators and office workers who do not leads to a discussion of the moral and political dimensions of exchange. The argument is based around a labour theory of value; those who do not toil have no right to appropriate from those who do. In this, farmers seem to share something with advocates and consumers of fair trade; the idealisation of the creative value of working in nature and the right to retain the value so created. The problem is that in the North we miss local distinctions; cooperatives become synonymous with small farmers, and landowners and wage labourers are included in the category of producers.

In the minds of many *campesinos* the conundrum of reliance in the market on intermediaries who do not labour is resolved by emphasising links between production and consumption. This resolution is recognised by coffee farmers and cooperative personnel, and it is inspirational to the fair-trade movement; it can be considered a shared conversation on the politics of value. Here we can discern a scale of circuits or spheres of exchange. The first cultural reference point is a world that spontaneously provides all that we need to survive; and what nature freely gives should be generously distributed. When work (or energy) is expended there is satisfaction when the producer is also the consumer, and needs are realised directly from an interchange with nature (exemplified in subsistence activities *por el gasto*). When exchanges take place between producer and consumer, it is better done through known, local and reciprocal relationships that satisfy complementary needs. The concern is to distribute what is created from nature, rather than profit from the distance between parties that occurs in the impersonal market. The grower creates a use-value from nature and the consumer satisfies their sensual desire for that use value. The surplus value created in exchange appears to be excised from the chain, and life is not experienced as alienation, nor products as fetishised objects, as there is no notion of separation from value-producing activities, the instruments thereof and the things so made. The model is a distributive one that relies on the naturalism discussed in Chapter 6.

In the Christian version we begin with divine dispensation, distributed through nature. The Marxian model starts with human self-realisation through transformative work on natural materials. Both accounts engage with the Aristotelian problem of distributive justice and seek to resolve the conundrum that although nature should provide all that we need, we cannot produce all that we consume nor satisfy all our wants within it. Intermediaries are condemned for their willingness to exploit this failure and to satisfy 'unnatural', unlimited desires. To this extent it is a cultural discussion about the inability to realise an idealised autonomy, to limit wants and so realise them in a direct relation with nature and to live exchanges through personal relationships, all in an increasingly attenuated, less local economy. In the conclusion we will identify this as part of our own cultural repertoire through looking at the history of economic and political ideas about value creation, by considering the condemnation of exploitative merchants and by examining early markets in England. Prior to the eighteenth century these were precisely run on moral grounds and regulated by legislation to ensure the surplus went to the producer; exchanges were between persons known to each other, and professional intermediaries were excluded or regulated (Carrier 1995).

INDUSTRY AND INDOLENCE: WORKING FOR COOPELDOS

The undeniable success of the Coocafé group, and Coopeldos in particular, often conflicts with views of the cooperative expressed among the membership base. In the early days of fieldwork I was struck and slightly puzzled by trenchant criticisms of an administration that pursued a remit to help small farmers escape exploitation and was clearly contributing to development in the area. It is not that the claims of 'sowing progress' were denied; people were generally quick to recognise that the cooperative was a powerful motor for development. Rather, the view of Coopeldos frequently voiced was an ambivalent one.

This was clearly expressed to me one day by Carlos. 'The cooperative is like our mother', he said. 'We want *mama cooperativa* to look after us, to nourish and feed us, we want her to be a good mother, but she is not. She keeps us lean and hungry while she grows fat, and we only just manage to keep our heads above water.' The 'bad mother' image neatly captured a common, though certainly not universal, view of the cooperative. The institution does have a familial air; it belongs to and has an intense and closely wrought relationship with the members and profound roots in the economic and social life of surrounding settlements. At the same time many producers looked askance at the increasing wealth and power of the company they own and sometimes expressed reservations and criticisms about the level of their share of that success.

The ambivalence with which the cooperative is viewed is part of a deeper problem: the position of the cooperative with respect to farmers. The primary activity in which Coopeldos engages, the buying, processing and marketing of coffee, means that it plays the role of intermediary on behalf of its members, which places it in a problematic position as far as ethics and the notion of fair trade is concerned. The role of fair trade at the local and producer level, as administered through Coopeldos, goes beyond the securing of an acceptable price for coffee; it is also entangled in the value attributed to different forms and categories of work. At the same time, the depth of the cooperative's involvement in local projects, the services provided and the fact that many prominent cooperative functionaries are also locally active and respected draws the organisation into the moral sphere, a move which is encouraged by the discourse of loyalty and service to members. The cooperative, it seems, is caught between the requirements of business success and social and moral responsibility.

Coopeldos has about 30 permanent staff and is easily the largest employer in that part of the highlands. It offers a variety of employment in accordance with its range of activities and services. The office staff is made up of functionaries who run the bureaucratic side of the venture, including management, the credit department, accounts and sales. Then there are the retail employees who serve customers in the shops and make up and dispatch orders. The technical aspect of production and processing, such as the running and maintenance of machinery in the plant and agricultural extension services, depends on technically competent staff. A final group is composed of agricultural *peones* who may be permanent or employed temporarily and who work in the horticultural nurseries and coffee plantations belonging to the cooperative.

Although one might assume that the opportunity for employment in the cooperative would be eagerly sought, since it entails a guaranteed cash income, this is not necessarily so. Wages for agricultural work are low; a *peón* working for Coopeldos earns just over 60,000 *colones* (approximately $200 during fieldwork in 1998) a month which, although reasonable by local standards, was below the national average and barely covered the basic living costs (*canasta basica*) as calculated by the government. The cooperative also imposes a rhythm of work that is not to everyone's taste; a six-hour working day leaves little time to see to other business, and if you miss a day, I was told, you could lose your employment. As we shall see, work in the offices of Coopeldos can also carry a certain stigma, which only partially compensates for the secure income it offers.

People in El Dos, as in many other parts of the world, often appraise people by their capacity for work, using the terms *muy trabajadora* (hard-working) and *valiente* (strong, or tough) for a positive assessment, and *vago* (lazy) for negative judgments. Sometimes the word *vago* was used as a light-hearted form of self-admonishment, and it can also be used to describe particular individuals. However, the accusation of indolence also relates to categories or types of work rather than to the qualities of individuals. From the beginning I was struck by the frequency with which the cooperative employees were accused of laziness. For example, one commentator was dismayed by his visits to the cooperative offices; 'whenever I go down there the staff are sitting around, chatting, shuffling pieces of paper around on their desks; that is not work'. If, as this farmer insists, office and administrative duties do not constitute work, then what kind of activity fits this category? An answer was implicit in the way residents talked about people and their jobs. A reputation as a good, or *valiente*, worker is based upon involvement in agricultural labour. For example, as we saw earlier, though otherwise feared and considered untrustworthy, Nicaraguan migrant harvesters were frequently lauded for their resilience and their capacity for carrying out agricultural tasks. By contrast, office workers and administrators at the cooperative were frequently credited with good intentions, and sometimes described as *buena gente* (good people), but they were never called hard-working; indeed, accusations of laziness were most often aimed at those in the offices filling administrative and clerical positions. This was corroborated by the cooperative manager in a discussion on criticisms of the cooperative, of which he is of course aware. As he pointed out: 'they [the producers] do not consider what I do as work; if I go to San José or Europe on business they believe I am having a holiday, they do not realise I am working ten or twelve hours a day'. Similarly, many of my informants considered Costa Ricans to be lazy, specifically because they sought employment that did not require manual labour. For this reason, although the importance of education was not generally in doubt, the motives of those who continued into secondary school was sometimes questioned; 'they just want to avoid work', several people suggested.

At the centre of such categorisations lies a set of values that insists that buying and selling, and related bureaucratic occupations, are not really work. Beyond this, the contention is that those who appropriate most from the productive process are precisely those who do not toil in the true sense of the word.[126] This was made clear in a conversation with Faustino, who is unmarried and comes from a family with a large farm. He lives in his parental home with his widowed mother and his brothers and sisters. Faustino grows some corn, occasionally sows other vegetables and cultivates bananas, all for home consumption. He even has a few coffee bushes that he leaves to produce 'as God intended'. At one time he left the coffee unharvested but he has now taken to adding it to his brother's organic crop. Faustino keeps his costs to a minimum and makes an occasional living from producing artefacts for the tourist trade. He also raises cattle on a remote farm several miles away, which can be sold to cover exceptional expenditure but do not provide a regular income. He has a number of avenues and strategies for juggling a livelihood, but refuses to engage in agriculture on a full-time basis. 'Of course, I could grow crops and sell them', he says:

> But I don't like [commercial] agriculture. If I work and produce peppers, I take them to market and sell them to an intermediary for a pittance, say 1,000 *colones*. Once I have sold them the buyer will tell me to put them in a corner, and he will leave them there until someone else comes along wishing to buy peppers. The merchant will then indicate my produce, still standing in the corner, and will demand 2,000 *colones* for them (my translation).

At this point in his explanation I suggested that the intermediary had done nothing. 'No,' was his response, 'he has not even touched the produce.' In presenting his objections, Faustino is indicating a distortion in the 'natural price' that derives from the labour that has been expended in production, a distortion attributed to the merchant positioning himself between the buyer and the seller. The flip side of a system that relies on intermediaries taking a profit is that idealised situation in which the full value of the crop returns to the producer. Such an idea indicates a kind of 'mercantile utopianism', in which 'equity, distributive justice and harmony are realisable ideals in social and economic relations' (Acuña Ortega 1987:141, my translation).

The *campesinos* of El Dos share with the coffee farmers' movements that became active after the 1930s a hatred of bureaucrats, bureaucracy and taxation, a distrust of processors and the market and a love of rural over urban life. They do not openly articulate a rejection of 'the brute systems of domineering and cruel capitalism', unlike their earlier counterparts and official representatives of farmers in these struggles (Acuña Ortega 1987:149, my translation), but they do present themselves as an undervalued, exploited and marginal group. In the process many question the self-serving ambition and individualistic ethic of capitalism which, as we saw, they identify in institutional politics and associate with the market. This dissent, I want to argue, is anchored in the belief that true value comes from working the earth and interacting with the force God placed in nature. In the next section I highlight how this idea permeates the local economy.

LINKING CONSUMPTION AND PRODUCTION

Suspicion of administrative work and condemnation of intermediaries has serious repercussions for the cooperative and for the notion of fair trade. The fact that selling coffee on the market is a core activity of Coopeldos raises a problem, since those employed by the business do not, following the dominant definition of the concept among *campesinos*, properly work. Wages paid to employees are therefore open to moral challenge, all the more so when the conditions of their employment seem to provide a security that contrasts starkly with the uncertainty of economic return that is integral to agricultural production.

The cooperative, it seems, fails to escape what Evers has called the 'traders' dilemma' (1994). Evers asserts that trade and its possibilities pose a challenge and a conundrum to peasant communities, founded on mutual help and solidarity. Profit sits uneasily with the moral values of the community, in which prices are determined by the use value of subsistence crops rather than the exchange value in the open market. A trader who buys at the subsistence rate through the activation of reciprocal ties and then makes a profit is judged as having betrayed the community by moving from values determined by use to those based upon exchange. Therefore 'any trader who wishes to trade with a view to accumulation – the key to the rise of the modern capitalistic world – faces an acute dilemma in regard to the misfit of his ethic of action (personal accumulation) and the ethic of his peasant society (community-distributive solidarity)' (Preston 1994:48). As we have seen, in El Dos the gap between these different ethics is highlighted and negotiated by promoting humility and vilifying egoism, and by the public works and ethic of service that people, particularly the better off and more influential, engage in.

Rather than take the traders' perspective on the problem I now explore a different rationale behind criticisms of the cooperative. To do this I return to the cosmology discussed in Chapter 6, which states that nature contains a force created by God for human use and benefit. There are three logical outcomes of this view. Firstly, all value ultimately comes from working the soil in accordance with divine dispensation. Secondly, and following on from this, work in nature provides the basis for subsistence. These ideas are implicit in the adjudications of people in El Dos, and are quite explicitly stated in Catholic doctrine: 'it may truly be said that all human subsistence is derived either from labour on one's own land, or from some toil, some calling which is paid for either in the produce of the land itself, or in that which is exchanged for what the land brings forth' (*Rerum Novarum* 1891 [1960]:11). In Costa Rica, where Catholic doctrine has played such a central part in social and political life, and where religious values and ideas permeate the countryside, it is hardly surprising to find shared discourses on the importance of labouring in nature (Barahona Jiménez 1975, Miller 1996; Williams, P. 1989). Lastly, and as an outcome of the two previous points, household autonomy and natural order become synonymous with agricultural production and produce from the land.

If we take the first point as a kind of first principle for farmers, we can make sense of the objections to intermediaries and the condemnation of profit extracted by those who do not work the earth. The definition of value created by agricultural labour is central to Faustino's refusal to produce crops for the benefit of a merchant who does not work – highlighted by the fact that the intermediary does not so much as touch the product. It also clearly informs the documents and letters published during earlier struggles, which state, for example, that 'the public knows full well that up until now it has been the farmers, *or rather their work*, that has provided the ladder for the exporters to reach the pinnacle of wealth' (Acuña Ortega 1987:142, my translation, my emphasis). On this basis farmers can claim 'equitable compensation for all *human effort*' (Acuña Ortega 1987:142, my translation, my emphasis). Of course, contention can then arise over what constitutes 'human effort', but it is precisely on these grounds that farmers make their objections known.

Locating value in working the earth puts agriculture at the centre of society, and with this in mind we can return to the social relations that emerge in and through agricultural production and systems of distribution. As we have seen, farmers grow and have access to a variety of crops and animal products. Some foods, mainly fruits such as mangoes, oranges, bananas and avocadoes, seem to produce themselves, and grow in such abundance that they are considered open to access for all or are freely distributed and even squandered. Other foodstuffs, particularly root vegetables, are grown or produced around the house or on the farm and consumed in the home. Another group of products, including the staple bean (*frijol*), can also be exchanged or sold to neighbours, friends or acquaintances. Finally, things that cannot easily be bought or exchanged locally are sold exclusively for cash on the open market. Coffee is the prime example. In each of these scenarios goods move in different circuits and for different purposes; they can be destined for household or personal use, given away as gifts, exchanged either for goods or services, or sold for cash.[127] Such distinctions have frequently been thought about in terms of the distinction between use value and exchange value, or by reference to money and commodified and non-commodified parts of the economy.

But for farmers the question refers back to whom or what creates value and how the benefits of productive activities are distributed. Problems do not arise when people take and eat directly from nature, since this allows individuals and families to reproduce, and so the idea of autonomy is not compromised. In El Dos the possibility of directly consuming what nature provides gives a strong sense to the environment as a common resource provided by God. Since no one has worked or made any other kind of investment to produce these items, everyone has, at least according to this principle, rights of access. Even when fruit trees are on private land, the owners display generosity by encouraging others to eat the fruit.[128] One man was incredulous that oranges could be bought and sold for money.

When crops and produce are created by human investment and effort, a more complex picture emerges. There is a long history of market activity; today some farmers continue to grow and sell vegetables within the local community or take foodstuffs such as cheeses to town for sale. There was never any suggestion that such activities by farmers were improper; since producers extract the value from nature, and therefore do genuine work, they have the right to dispose of the result of their labour. Neither is the destination of the produce deemed to be of moral importance. Producers may sell directly to the consumer or to an intermediary; they may dispose of the product in the way they consider expedient, since they have extracted it at the human interface with the force of nature. It is the state of being an intermediary – a 'hyena', 'coyote' or 'wolf', as they are sometimes described – who takes value without working that draws condemnation.

In each of these circuits – direct interchange with nature, exchanges in the local economy, and trading on the open market – the *campesino* as producer is linked to the consumer, and production to consumption, but in increasingly attenuated and obscure ways. This implies a scale that runs from foraging directly from nature, an often idealised state in which humans take what God gives generously through nature, to social interchanges in and between local households realised through the production, exchange and consumption of things, to transnational trade in which the consumer and producer never meet, though at times they might struggle or be encouraged to imagine the existence and world of the other.

For small farmers the idea of producing for direct consumption is a moral space in the economy, and labouring in nature to create value is a benchmark for ethical judgments. In practice, in a modern economy, this extreme position is always compromised. Many crops and animals do not reproduce on their own or only with human labour; cash inputs are frequently required. This challenges the view of agriculture predicated upon human interaction with the force of nature, complicates ways of measuring value and suggests something is wrong with the world. Perhaps for this reason organic and natural methods that employ inputs prepared from products taken freely from the local environment are seen as promoting God's perfect world, and pestilence and disease taken as one sign of humanity's fall from grace.

A second compromise lies in the practical limits of the idealised autonomous household. To succeed farmers engage in and must maintain social relations. This is particularly true for economic activities for the market. There are logistical difficulties to overcome, such as transport and processing, and commercial avenues, both for inputs and outputs, need to be negotiated. Doing this effectively requires various forms of expert knowledge. Landowners recognise that they can meet demands and obstacles better through sharing information, resources and expenses, than they can as isolated homesteaders. Relations between farmers are at least formally equal, and based upon complementary requirements and goals, so there is little need to distinguish between the rationality of making a profit from what they produce and the moral goal of reproducing the independent household. The two concepts are encompassed by the family farm.

More problematic are the unequal relations between the landless and those who own farms. The implication of this difference is entangled in personal and family projects of maximisation, and in Chapter 4 I considered work contracts largely in terms of goals and strategies; the negotiation for personal advantage of the short-term and often pressing need for labour, and the sometimes longer-term requirements of employees and employers. But there are limitations to explanations that represent these relationships as agreements between parties that allow them both to maximise their self-interest. Agreements are riven by inequalities and policed through power relations, which problematises the notion that they are the outcome of choices. There may be no compelling reason for farmers to offer anything more than minimum wages to workers; they could presumably use only the iron fist to make the landless poor work for a monetary wage and discard the velvet glove of the fringe benefits they offer employees. Even if satisfactory explanations for this can be given in terms of maximising behaviour and competitive advantage or as a way of disguising power relations it cannot explain why agreements take the particular form they do.

To do this we need to understand how inequalities are also embedded in and encompassed by social and moral considerations and ideas. As we saw, to maintain and support social relations around production, work contracts are underpinned by agreements that facilitate the reproduction of households. Often landowners offer temporary housing or eventually a plot on which to build a house, keep chickens and plant vegetables. They allow access to land on which to grow subsistence crops such as maize or *frijoles* that can then be consumed within the house or sold and they give access to the fruit from trees that grow on their land. Of course, such rights and benefits are given first and foremost to potential and actual employees, local and migrant, just as food *por el gasto* first goes to the family, but they are extended to a general right to subsist. The offer of accommodation, work and access to land and food to families in need is presented in moral terms. The fact that social relations and duties are expressed in the idiom of the independent and self-sufficient household economy, in which production should promote reproduction through direct consumption of what is grown, is due to the central place of the right to be a homesteader in the Costa Rican national imaginary and the cosmology that maintains that view. That is, social relationships and agreements are inspired by the idea that, despite practical limits, all Costa Rican households should equally have access to land to work in order to live and to reproduce; cultivating food from a God-given natural world constitutes a subsistence ethic in which goods circulate in accordance with needs and uses rather than for profit and exchange for money.

THE 'TRADERS' DILEMMA'

The cooperative managers also acknowledge the problem of inter-mediaries but take a different view of the problem. Their concern with the producer-consumer nexus was succinctly spelled out in an interview with Guillermo Vargas, manager of the cooperative in Santa Elena: 'the more direct the link, the more the interests of the consumer and the producer can compliment each other. The more intermediaries with purely economic motives become involved, so the dialogue (between producer and consumer) breaks down.' Cooperative administrators do not consider themselves 'purely economic' intermediaries since they work on behalf of their members; they see themselves less as intermediaries and more as facilitators, since their interests are not solely economic. It is in this light that we need to consider the rhetoric of the cooperative in relation to its members; the *asociado*, according to managers, is rightly the final point of reference for the cooperative endeavour, its very 'reason for being' (*razón de ser*). It is telling that the failure of cooperatives was often accounted for by reference to the loss of this vision of service to the temptations of personal self-interest. In the minds of managers it is not the fact of extracting value without working the land that is problematic; it is rather a question of motive. Because the cooperative acts in the interests of and represents, indeed in some respects *is*, the farmer, they exonerate the organisation and staff from being seen as intermediaries.

Of course, there are practical limitations to the idea that the full value of a product should accrue to the producer. This ideal may be aspired to and approximated in the local economy, where foods may be shared in and between families or where farmers can engage personally with buyers and consumers in markets so that exchange becomes embedded in social and moral ideas. However, there are practical difficulties of access and expertise in engaging with national and international markets for commodities such as coffee. The cooperative is a solution to that problem and it gathers members on that basis. So while many producers are supportive of the cooperative mission and remain staunch *cooperativistas*, other members remain suspicious of the motives, profit margins, and pay and conditions they associate with Coopeldos.

This returns us to the ambivalence expressed towards *mama cooperativa*. Sometimes the cooperative is considered a business (*empresa*) and described in terms of profits and expenditures, capital and turnover. At other times farmers and managers alike emphasise its social dimensions, so it is represented as a channel that moves goods and services on behalf of the members. A similar contradiction exists with respect to Coocafé, but in this case the role of providing both a service and being a channel becomes even more problematic. As we have seen, the conglomerate of different cooperatives that constitutes Coocafé has grown in power and influence, and at the same time the consortium has amassed considerable capital. Many farmers questioned the wealth of the group; 'Why does Coocafé need to develop such capital when it is only a channel and nothing more?' they would ask. It appears producers are wary of what has been created on their behalf, an institution of power and seemingly enormous wealth revealed to them in annual reports. Farmers would frequently engage me in conversation, querying the necessity for such a highly capitalised institution, and some even urged investigation into the organisation's financial dealings.

Here a local distinction between confidence and trust comes into play. One kind of relationship in El Dos is encapsulated in the notion of *confianza*. Early on in my fieldwork I fell into a discussion with a taxi driver on the relative merits of town and country life. In the town, it was claimed, there was no *confianza*. On the other hand, in the country, 'if I give you something then you give me something, that is *confianza*'. The personal relationships in local rural life confer security, since they build upon what has gone before and are based upon face-to-face relationships (Giddens 1990:34). But there is a flip side to this. As quoted in Chapter 2, a *trust* refers to a cartel, a means of monopolising interests, which ignores or denigrates the rights and priorities of others. On this reading *trusts* fix prices, impose conditions and ignore others in the advancement of their own interests; they generate uncertainty for those excluded from the *trust*. The word *trust* is commonly used in journalistic reports, but in El Dos reference is more often made to *argullos* or 'rings'.

We need to understand the ambivalence expressed by the small farmers of El Dos towards Coocafé and Coopeldos against this background of a history of dissent with respect to the structures within which coffee is commercialised. An ideology of independence, based upon direct production from nature, makes reliance on wider institutions problematic. In this context the farmers are particularly sceptical about the calculation of the final gate price they receive. Taxes are seen as iniquitous, since farmers believe they receive little or no benefit from them and the money gets swallowed up in bureaucratic structures or appropriated by corrupt officials. Acuña Ortega and his colleagues have identified a series of anti-fiscal movements among small Costa Rican farmers in the years 1922, 1937, 1947, 1951 and 1961 (1985:137). The principal target of these mobilisations was a profligate bureaucracy.

Growers are keenly aware of the differential between market prices advertised in the media and the final gate price they receive from the cooperative. They also know, and like to point out, that although the amount they get for their coffee fluctuates wildly, the price consumers pay remains constant, or only increases. As they often said: 'someone is making a mountain of money at the expense of both the consumer and the producer'. These comments imply two related things: intermediaries exploit the distance between producer and consumer without really working; and the problem can be resolved by forging direct connections between production and consumption, which is precisely what fair trade seeks to do.

In seeking an explanation for this difference between prices paid to producers and by consumers, some people attempted to enlist my support in researching where the 'missing' money ended up. For their part the cooperative was keen to divulge information on deductions for costs, taxes and the like. Potentially sensitive information was always made available under the policy of transparency, and during cooperative meetings with producers the manager went to some length to explain the mysteries of the commercialisation of coffee, including information on how prices were calculated and what deductions had to be made. Nevertheless, the conviction remained that all was not right in the division of the profits.

CONCLUSION

This chapter has explored cultural ideas behind the dissent expressed by farmers towards market intermediaries and shown how coffee processors and Coopeldos are caught up in such adjudications. Their dissatisfaction echoes earlier complaints against unscrupulous processors. However, my account differs from previous discussions in both its explanation and in documenting the persistence of discontent. The authors who interrogate the ideology behind mobilisations of coffee farmers and their representatives in the middle decades of the last century provide evidence for a distinction made by coffee producers between the 'good' processors, who pay respectable prices, and avaricious ones, who are the target of growers' ire (Acuña Ortega 1985, 1987; Gonzalez Ortega 1987). They explain this by reference to the 'mercantile utopianism' discussed above, but take the farmers' apparent satisfaction with some processors as evidence of a 'bourgeois' mindset. The fact that complaints are still levelled against Coopeldos, a cooperative that has consistently paid prices at the top of the range, therefore merits investigation. One way to explain this is to recognise that these scholars seek to follow shifts in official discourse and, because they are concerned with the grounds upon which agreement were made, their arguments are tacitly informed by negotiation and compromise. My data suggest a more radical 'anticapitalist' subtext, in which *campesinos* value their exclusive right to the worth they get from the soil and take exception to those who appropriate from their efforts.

In forging relationships of a transnational kind, the cooperative places itself in a compromised position. Its local connections and contributions to social and economic life are esteemed but, in engaging in trade for profit, by virtue of its bureaucratic structure, and in its deduction of taxes, it is morally suspect. A fundamental dilemma emerges from the fact that the cooperative was created to give more direct access to the market, yet it requires administrative work and operates as an intermediary between the producer and the consumer, two things that many *campesinos* neither value nor trust. This contradiction creates the ambivalence towards *mama cooperativa* with which this chapter began.

The very existence of the concept of fair trade asks questions about the concept of the economy. By one definition the economic is about formal rationality employed to maximise self-interest. Costa Rican coffee farmers and workers understand this pragmatic side to life; like some economic anthropologists they use a language of chance, uncertainty and risk-taking, which renders life a struggle. *Campesinos* and cooperative managers associate this formulation primarily, though not exclusively, with the capitalist market, and they are by no means alone in this. And since it is in this market that they sell fair-trade products, the moral message is lost. Wires cross between producer and consumer, though this does not mean that fair trade cannot have practical benefits.

Following a different definition, the economy can be understood in terms of social and moral relations between people. Here, I believe, Western consumers and *campesinos* speak a similar language. At least the two worlds can be seen to speak to and so reflect each other.

We can use more scholarly arguments to help understand that process and to explore the appeal of fair trade rather than simply understand what it does or does not do.

From Mauss (2002 [1925]) we get one rendition of the more general principle of social reciprocity; the idea that a gift contains something of the giver and therefore creates a relationship between the giver and the recipient. The sentiment expressed by the gift, and the renunciation of self-interest implied, gives it a different cultural meaning to a commodity. It acknowledges a desire to connect to other people through objects; to the extent that fair trade seeks to forge a relationship between producer and consumer it constitutes part of the gift economy.

While Mauss focuses attention on exchange relations, Marx is concerned with production. He, and other classical political economists, begin with a labour theory of value. Although he stressed the importance of unmediated labour, Marx was primarily concerned with the consequences of living in a world in which we are separated from our productive activities. One consequence of this was exploitation of workers and producers, another was the experience of capitalism as alienation from ourselves from other people and from the things we make. I see fair trade as part of these conversations; analytical ideas which will now be explored by way of conclusion.

9 CONCLUSION:
FAIR TRADE AND MORAL ECONOMIES

What makes trade fair? Case studies from different parts of the world suggest that producers, cooperative managers and alternative-trade organisations have a range of commitments and agendas.[129] Consumers, too, have their own ideas and expectations about fair-trade goods. Because shoppers stand at a distance from production and distribution it would be easy to dismiss them as dupes of cleverly marketed commodities, but this would ignore the sentiments people themselves believe they express when buying fair trade. On the other hand, it cannot be right to automatically champion the opposing and romantic view and depict ethically motivated consumers as heroically resisting and subverting the dominant economic order (Miller, D. 1995c; Mills 1997:41).

Despite evidence that different parties have a range of purposes with respect to fair trade, there are grounds for thinking that participants share assumptions and ideas about ethics in the economy. Of particular concern in this chapter are Euro-American ideas, although parallels may be found in other religious, cultural and intellectual traditions.[130] To interrogate the moral notions that people hold with regard to their relations with things or their commitments to human relationships as mediated by objects, I draw upon central themes within economic anthropology and the history of economic thought. Of course, ethnographic data from one Central American country cannot claim to be representative of the way all fair-trade deals across the globe operate. The point is that the idea of fair trade has attracted many people over time within Western culture.

The key referent in that attraction is the dominant order; fair trade defines itself and only has meaning when framed against the capitalist economy. Market capitalism draws on the metaphor of an invisible hand that guides outcomes and determines our economic fortunes. Because the economy is impersonal, it offers a specific notion of moral responsibility; for it to function properly the only economic imperative is self-interest. In looking after ourselves and disregarding the needs of others, it is thought, we promote general economic growth and, paradoxically, benefit everyone. It is an ethic of personal achievement and merit that has come to be synonymous with the profit motive. The principal way that righteous self-interest can be advanced in the capitalist model is through buying products as cheaply as possible and selling them on at a higher price. Often this takes the form of purchasing wage labour and selling the surplus produced by workers for a profit. Because the aim is to make profit through exchange, the specific qualities that we value objects for are reduced to a general equivalence, expressed in money. So exponents of the impartial market propose one answer to the question of what makes trade fair. They argue it provides everyone with equal opportunity. The morality lies in the impersonality; it is fair because everyone is treated the same at a formal level.

An alternative voice challenges the ethics of the market by pointing out that it ignores social processes.[131] According to this second view, formal equality is no way to run economic affairs since it masks the different endowments and capacities people bring to the marketplace. Instead, critics say, we need to look at the real-life effects of the market on people's everyday lives (Barth 1997). For many people fair trade means opposing depersonalised economic relations, objecting to 'middle-men' concerned only with making profits, and decrying a modern economy in which all things take the generic commodity form. In its place, in the Western imagination, stands an economy based upon personal relationships, where the producer and the consumer know one another, or are the same person; a world where value is imparted to objects by transforming them in meaningful and creative activities; where people through their actions make and appreciate things for their specific qualities and usefulness. In this view fair trade presents an image of the economy in which we look beyond value for money to consider the social context within which things are made, and the role these things play in sustaining meaningful human relationships. What is useful and fascinating about rural Costa Rica is that the idea of a moral political economy remains real and immediate; it is based upon living from a divinely ordered nature with the aim of household reproduction from farming so that economic relations assume the form of personal relationships with nature, with the things produced and with other people. Listening to *campesinos* opens up the debate and reinforces the popular conviction that alternative conversations on the economy remain possible.

This chapter locates the attractions of fair-trade products within a broad political spectrum. For those on the left it is a discussion about exploitation, the power of multinationals and political calls for trade justice. The framework for such analyses derives from Marxist political economy, from where it has been incorporated into value-chain analysis (Daviron and Ponte 2005). It builds upon a negative picture in which capitalists control the means of production and distribution, and exploit workers by appropriating surplus value. Costa Rican coffee cooperatives similarly justify their existence by reference to farmers who are marginalised and impoverished in the capitalist system; giving producers a share in ownership of the means of production was designed to cut out the appropriation of profit by intermediaries who control coffee processing and marketing, and to curb dissent. Pragmatic steps of this kind are underpinned by the conviction that value comes from productive activity, so that a just return should go to the producer. For peasant farmers in Costa Rica value is the result of their labour in God-given nature, a standpoint that informs their suspicion of intermediaries of all kinds, and takes them close to the secular position adopted by Marx.

These ideas, and the image of independent, autonomous producers they imply, feed into a less specifically political agenda that has broad cultural appeal. Fair-trade products (as well as many other 'alternative' and mainstream commodities) are characterised by unease about the separation of production and consumption, and the associated processes of alienation and fetishisation that Marx identified in capitalism (Slater 1997). Imagine a world without that separation. In the first place, it implies a particular and romantic relationship with nature, and a specific relation to ourselves. In an idealised world we take things from a giving natural environment, which provides us with all that we need. In the Christian tradition Eden, before the fall, is exemplary. However, since creating livelihoods entails labour, the privileged circuit would be to consume directly the things we produce, and for us to control the means to that end. This tradition would privilege certain forms of production: artisan modes, petty commodity production and peasant farming. Lastly, the necessity of labour compromises our ability to live directly from nature so the aforementioned production regimes involve relations with other people. The idea that economic ethics entail social, cultural and moral relations between persons has been pursued in anthropology since the early days of Malinowski and Mauss. In contrast to alienation and fetishisation, social and moral relationships are, at least in the Western imagination, established and activated through the idea of connecting production to consumption.

Directly appropriating from nature and producing the things we consume, or the exchange of products between people in social relationships achieves two things. Firstly, it cuts out intermediaries and negates the separation of people from one another, a state usually associated with capitalism but now exacerbated by globalisation (Giddens 1990; Harvey 1989; Appadurai 1990). Secondly, it allows people to realise the value of the things they consume as qualities that derive from nature and from the work put into them. Of course, in the act of consuming things we always realise that objects have qualities, and this is tellingly so in the case of food. But that is precisely the point. Fair-trade goods such as coffee are not just associated with small producers and unstable markets; they are also overtly sensuous and exotic products.

This chapter moves from a focus on production and producers to look at exchange and distribution, and then to finally deal with consumption and the concerns of consumers. Throughout it can be seen that, in keeping with their interests, the parties emphasise different aspects, but since fair trade is embedded in complex and evolving Western notions of the economy and morality there are also significant areas of overlap. I begin by emphasising the importance of creative activity in transforming nature as the origin of value in much Euro-American thought. Producers, according to one view, realise themselves through labour when they retain the full value they have created. In the following section on commodity production I show how in Marxist thought this privileged avenue for creating value is understood as compromised, because the capitalist appropriates the surplus created by labour. The next part concentrates on the experience of producers under capitalism of separation, known as alienation or estrangement. Marx identified four kinds of alienation in capitalism; from the product of labour, from the activity of production, from our 'species life' as creative beings, and from each other. I then explore attempts to culturally subvert the experience of estrangement in the Western imagination through idealised forms of economic activity. In particular, I refer to peasant household production, localised forms of exchange in which the purpose is to redistribute rather than make a profit, and the promotion of social and moral relationships through gift exchange. Whereas reciprocal exchanges and mutuality are given local importance by producers in Costa Rica, it is only consumers who, as powerful choosers, extend gift ideology across the globe to try to embrace disadvantaged coffee growers, a morality that I see as inspirational to new forms of politicised consumption. In the final section I note that certain goods, such as coffee and tea, are especially powerful reminders of our sensory attachment to the world. For this reason they are more obvious vehicles for critical consumption than other goods.

Coffee quality can be understood in at least two senses. Firstly it manifests itself in the physical attributes of a product from a particular place cultivated in certain ways. This emphasis on the diverse character of coffees and the cultivation of taste marks a departure from the generic, standardised product promoted until the 1980s, and marks a return to an earlier colonial model of descriptive language used by roasters and exporters to distinguish coffee types and places of origin (Neilson 2004).[132] Secondly, and particularly with regard to fair trade, quality comes to be associated with specific ways of life and idealised relationships: peasant production, the family and the autonomous space known as the household. Here the activities of production and consumption come together in the guise of reproduction and take on the semblance, at least, of unalienated activity. Here also we like to imagine our economic exchanges to entail selfless acts of giving. These observations provide a route to consider moral ideas on the economy and what attracts us to the message on the tin of coffee – 'from the culture of small producers' – with which I opened this book.

NATURE, VALUE AND CREATIVE ACTIVITY

Ethical ideas attached to ways of life in El Dos begin with nature. In part this is because work on nature provides a timescale for the settlement of the Tilarán Highlands. The stories told of the early years evoke 'pure nature', and this provides a reference point for changes in the landscape and the complex modern world in which people now must live. Christian ideas provide the foundation for social, moral and political commitments in the mundane world, for in imagining nature people draw on the religious motif of a divinely created and bounteous environment, exemplified by Eden, and instigated by God for human benefit. The biblical precedent comes from Genesis, a world where acts of production involved picking the fruit of nature and consuming it; the world of toil, inequality and suffering came after the fall. Nature is conceived of as a force that gives humans sustenance, ideally in a direct and unmediated fashion, with people living directly from the land. Crops are grown and turned into food, to consume and to give strength to work in agriculture. In this way *campesinos* consider nature as the origin of value for themselves and their families, and they rightfully access that value through productive activity.

By formulating nature as the origin of value, *campesinos* are participants in a 'conversation', to borrow the term used by Gudeman and Rivera (1990), with an extended history. There is a remarkable similarity between the ideas of Latin American *campesinos*, the strand of political philosophy that can be traced back to John Locke, and the doctrine of the eighteenth-century French political economists known as the physiocrats, most commonly represented by Quesnay (Gudeman and Rivera 1990:30–37). Both the physiocrats and Locke, like the people of El Dos, and in common with Christian and Catholic doctrine, stress the sanctity of private property and the right to freedom from regulation or state interference (Dumont 1977:42; Tully 1993). Perhaps this is not surprising, given they all subscribe to versions of natural-law theory. Central to this is the emphasis upon land, or more precisely the earth, as the source of wealth.

The political implications are obvious. Marx may have objected to the 'physiocratic illusion that rents grow out of the soil and not out of society' (2000:480), but by arguing that agriculture was the only properly productive activity, the physiocrats laid foundations for political economy. In 1772 Paoletti illustrated the primacy of agriculture. Give a cook some peas, he said, and they will be served up in the same quantity; give them to a gardener and they will be returned four-fold (Bradley and Howard 1982:4). For this reason the physiocrats considered agriculture the origin of surplus, while manufacturing and commerce were seen as sterile activities. The idea that rights are established by work in nature was a key theme in the political philosophy of John Locke. He argued that humans have a right to 'Meat and Drink, and such other things, as Nature affords for their subsistence'. What is more, by the act of appropriation through the exertion of labour power the common is divided up into individual possessions (Tully 1993:27). The Ricardian socialist John Francis Bray, in 'Labour's Wrong's and Labour's Remedy' (1839), echoes the right to minimum subsistence demanded by peasantries (Scott 1976). He proposed that since it was a 'natural law' that the 'raw material of all wealth – the earth – is the common property of all its inhabitants', then everyone was due equal rights (Jay and Jay 1986:31). We saw in the previous chapter how *campesinos* privilege their work in nature as the source of value and make political and economic claims on this basis; Smith, Ricardo and, most famously, Marx also worked within the same frame of reference, and used it to develop their various elaborations of labour value.[133]

In discussions of the labour theory of value many commentators move immediately to the problem of surplus, profit-taking and the capitalist form of production. Of course, as discussed below, Marx did use labour value as the basis of his critique of the capitalist economy, but it is nevertheless also true that the human relationship with nature is the underlying philosophical idea that informs his position. Two projects emerge here; the first is concerned with revealing the operations of capitalism, the taking of profit, exploitation and the appropriation of the surplus value created by labour. The second imagines and appeals to alternative social forms. Marx is generally recognised to have made a significant headway in the first task but to have failed in providing a coherent model of the communist society he envisioned as imminent in the historical process.

By placing productive activity at the centre of his political economy, Marx, like the people of El Dos, emphasises the relationship between humans and nature. Both are committed to the idea that the mediation between humans and their environment takes place through productive activity. For Marx, this provides the foundations for the materialist conception of history; through productive activity people alter nature and in the process transform both themselves and their relations with others. Marx continuously emphasises the central role of nature in the creation of value. He considered the earth our 'original larder' and 'tool house' (2000:494; see Ortiz 1979), but he was centrally concerned with instrumentality and the human capacity to appropriate nature and act on an externally given world in order to change it (2000:493).[134] The language that Marx uses echoes that of *campesinos* who consider themselves dependent upon and part of the natural order, but who also understand that agricultural production requires them to negotiate the agency of nature; in this work they can hardly help but notice that they have an impact upon their environment and alter it.

It is helpful at this point to follow Arthur (1986), and consider two kinds of mediation. In the first people engage in productive activity and through this their relationship to nature and with each other is transformed. No necessary connection is made with actually existing societies; rather a philosophical point is made about the way humans create a material world around them and in the process change themselves. A second-level mediation occurs when work on nature takes a particular historical form, manifest in the social arrangements within which creative activities recreate specific circumstances:

In the present economic conditions we find that productive activity itself is mediated through the division of labour, private property, exchange, wages, in sum a system of estrangement in which productive activity loses itself and falls under the sway of an alien power (Arthur 1986:11).

Here, of course, we are talking specifically about capitalism. The principal difference between the two forms of mediation is that in the first it is imagined that productive activity is realised as self-expression, with the producer in 'immediate unity' with their object; in the second 'labour is immediately confronted by its object as something separate from it' (Arthur 1986:11). In the first case the term 'objectification' describes the situation whereby people contemplate and constitute themselves in the world they have created by transforming nature; in the second, it refers to our engagement with the world through things not of our own making, and so our experience of objects and social relations (as consumers) is characterised by a sense of rupture (Miller 1994:66–67; 1995a:1–2). The clear blue sky I discern between these two kinds of mediation is not, however, always easy to see. Each social formation seems to 'naturalise' its own system of economy and of transforming nature, and this holds for practices underpinned by Christian theology, natural law and market distribution.

In El Dos, I have argued, material production and the production of meaning operate within and emerge from a Christian view of nature and divine providence. Rather than being passive, however, people engage in a struggle with nature and transform it through work. In this creative activity they reproduce themselves and society and make a meaningful world of value around them (Graeber 2001; Hirsch 2004; Slater 1997). I suggest that this takes us closer to the Marxian model than Gudeman and Rivera allow. To argue that Marx worked with the folk model of labour power and used a secular version for the purpose of picking apart the economic workings of capitalism is important, but it is not the whole story (Gudeman and Rivera 1990:104).

To develop the argument we must hold on to the idea that Marx envisioned a world in which the producer directly appropriates the product of labour, in effect reproducing a central motif in Western thought that privileges economic forms based upon an unmediated link between producers and consumers, or acts of production and moments of consumption, since this avoids the appropriation of value created by labour by capitalist intermediaries. At the same time, or as part of this project, Marx set about revealing actual relations of production between capitalists and workers, relations which overshadow and distort preferred avenues for creative activity. Before moving on to outline idealised economic activity in Euro-American cultural life, we first need to look at the critique of capitalist production against which these preferred economic relationships, as social relations, take shape, retain meaning and are activated and imagined.

COMMODITY PRODUCTION

As we have learnt, farmers experience their relationship with nature, with the market and with the labour process as uncertain, and they have a specific vocabulary to express this. But they also make more explicitly moral adjudications about the economics of capitalism and their engagement with markets as characterised by exploitation. I have argued that their justification lies in the labour theory of value, their creative activity in nature. Intermediaries, by contrast, appropriate the greater part of the profit and yet do not 'work'; they live from buying and selling and not by creatively extracting value directly from the natural world through manual labour. Marx's critique of capitalism worked upon related though secular lines. To expose the way capitalist production was organised and the social and ontological problems the system raised he also made recourse to the labour theory of value.

Marx saw that capitalist production is geared towards creating commodities, but that to have exchange value things must also be useful, or have a 'use-value'.[135] Whereas use-values are cherished for their qualities and the purposes to which they can be put, commodities are valued as quantities, measured against the amount of other commodities for which they might be exchanged. Typically, the medium for comparison is money. The attractiveness and power of money lies in its ability to act as stored value, as a quantity and as a vehicle for the representation of choices yet to be made. But there are some useful things, like air or goods we produce for personal consumption, which cannot be bought or sold 'for love nor money'. Some of the most useful of things do not have exchange value at all, so the value of commodities cannot be said to have any relation to their intrinsic properties as useful things. What, then, is the criterion upon which we base the 'fair' value of something as an exchangeable object if not its usefulness? To answer this question Marx adapted the physiocratic and *campesino* notion of value residing in nature and extracted by human work, and said that the value we place on different commodities is based upon the relative amounts of aggregate human labour that has gone into creating them (Fine 1975:20–21; Graeber 2001:55).

To reveal the workings of capitalism, Marx then distinguished between labour and labour-power, or the capacity to work and produce. Under capitalism, labour-power becomes a commodity that the worker sells for a wage. For their part, capitalists purchase labour-power as a useful thing in return for money. Because this is an exchange, labour-power is also a commodity; the use-value being bought and sold is the capacity to produce further use-values. So capitalists buy labour-power as a commodity and use it to produce other commodities that can be sold for an amount of money greater than that paid to the worker. In this way capitalists, depending on one's point of view, 'create' or 'appropriate' surplus value. They can do this because they own the means of production – tools, machinery and raw materials – that the worker needs and uses to produce. So, as is well known, Marx sees capitalism as a social relationship in which capitalists monopolise the means of production and use it to exploit wage earners and extract surplus from them.

The connection between this view of the economy and fair trade lies in the exploitation identified in exchange relations. At a macro level, and according to the kinds of analysis offered by world systems theory and Latin American dependency theory, 'core' capitalist countries systematically exploit and underdevelop 'peripheral' ones. Typically, they do this by purchasing raw materials cheaply and adding value in the industrial stages to sell at a profit. The coffee industry presents a particular problem because of the complexity of processing. To produce quality coffee requires expensive machinery that has long allowed dynasties of elite coffee families in Costa Rica and transnational companies to dominate the market, both in producing countries and in the North, where the toasting, freeze-drying and marketing is typically carried out. So although coffee farmers do have land, and so own one part of the necessary means of production as private property, they are excluded from the industrial and marketing sides of the coffee business. It is in these phases that the surplus is extracted, and it is this problem that cooperatives attempt to circumvent. As is often emphasised, producers typically receive a very small percentage of the final value of their crop (Gresser and Tickell 2002:24). Information of this kind does not often refer explicitly to the appropriation of surplus value, but we are indebted to the ghost of Marx in such analyses.

Compare this approach to orthodox economic models. It is customary in neo-classical economics to locate the value of commodities in supply and demand; how much of a given thing is available and the desire it excites in consumers, measured by the amount of money they are willing to spend on it. Marx followed Ricardo in rejecting this as the source of value. As a dynamic model, supply and demand could perhaps explain price fluctuations, but when prices are stable, Marx and Ricardo argued, it explains nothing at all (Bradley and Howard 1982:9). The shortcomings of supply and demand as a price-fixing mechanism are further exposed by 'real world' practices. Although they can easily be represented as an aggregate of choices freely made by individual subjects, powerful interests easily manipulate both. For example, it is quite possible to stimulate demand among consumers by raising prices. What is more, prices often have little relation to actual supplies or existing levels of demand; they are much more a reflection of subsidies, tariffs and price-fixing strategies. In recent years the more politicised application of the fair-trade concept, usually voiced as 'trade justice', has been promoted by activists, both secular and religious, and by the media. Part of the power of 'trade justice' as an idea is that the rejection of subsidies to Western farmers can appeal politically to those on the left concerned at the effects on the livelihoods of the rural poor in the South, and those on the right who object to any distortion of the 'level playing field' of the market.

A second set of foundational ideas in the neoclassical model is that profit is taken and deserved because of risk-taking, the burden of decision-making, the abstinence required to hoard profit for investment, and innovation (Fine 1975:31–32; Kaplinsky 2000:122). Again, for Marxists these things might be a condition for profit, factors that determine the way it is distributed and the means for it to be accumulated by capitalists, but they are not its source. I have demonstrated that coffee farmers also take risks, make decisions, practise thrift and innovate. These practices can determine how much is retained, but they are not, they believe, where value comes from.

As can be seen, the idea that exploitation occurs in exchange because owners of the means of production appropriate the differential between the value created by labour and the amount paid as a wage has had broader application. Much of the rhetoric of fair trade is based upon political economy of this kind. The opening chapters of this book showed that to participate in fair trade, producer groups are required to project an image of themselves as peripheral, poor, disadvantaged and in need of largesse to counteract the iniquities of the world trading system. So macroeconomic arrangements designed to extract surplus establish the conditions that make alternative trading arrangements both necessary and possible.

The above is common currency in analyses of the coffee industry. It is, for example, used to good effect by scholars interested in the distribution of value down the chain, an approach that derives from world systems theory (Daviron and Ponte 2005; Fold and Pritchard 2005; Hughes and Reimer 2004). The focus on the extraction of surplus provides the broader political and economic framework against which fair trade operates, but it does not grapple with more social and cultural aspects. It addresses how it proceeds, and what it is a reaction to, but tells us little about why the concept appeals to us as a cultural model and about the idioms it uses to attract shoppers. To begin to engage with that problem I make recourse to Marx's work on the effects of capitalism on our experience of the world. For Marx, the commodification of labour does not only have material effects. A second outcome is that human creative activity in nature, as a transformational project of self-realisation, is distorted. That distortion, whereby workers are excluded from the means of production and from the product of their labour, leads to a condition known as estrangement or alienation and a specific relationship with things as fetishised objects.

COMMODITY FETISHISM, ESTRANGEMENT AND ALIENATION

Raymond Williams gives two main meanings of alienation. Firstly, it is a process of cutting off, or being cut off, either from God, or from other people, as a result of a breakdown in social relations. Secondly, it has a legalistic meaning relating to the transference of rights in property, especially by force (1988:33). Williams notes that there is often a loss of distinction between the two usages. Marx in particular is singled out as combining the two senses:

In Marx the process is seen as the history of labour, in which man creates himself by creating his world, but in a class-society is *alienated* from this essential nature by specific forms of *alienation* in the division of labour, private property and the capitalist mode of production in which the worker loses both the product of his labour and his sense of his own productive activity, following the expropriation of both by capital. The world man has made confronts him as stranger and enemy, having power over him who transferred his power to it (1988:35, emphasis in original).

The general sense of estrangement is the product of a specific historical process of separation of the worker from the means of production, through the institution of private property. In the *1844 Manuscripts* Marx identifies four aspects to alienation: people are alienated from the product of their labour, from their 'life activity', from their 'species-being', and from other people. Each form of alienation relates to the others, but all are consequent upon the specific form that the separation of workers from their product takes in capitalism.[136]

Firstly, due to private property, 'the worker relates to the product of his labour as to an alien object' (Marx 2000:87). Because of the transference of ownership workers are 'doubly deprived'; they are denied their right to be subjects creatively reproducing themselves in the material world, and they become slaves to the things that they do produce. People exist as workers and as physical subjects only through objects (2000:89). So although the production of things takes place through specific social and labour relations, these relationships only find expression in and through the commodities. To capture this idea that people enact their social relationships through the objects they produce, Marx turned to the religious idiom of the fetish; an icon created by people but then accorded the power to control human affairs. Marx famously explained the process by which commodities become fetishised in the following way:

[a] commodity is therefore a mysterious thing, simply because in it the social character of men's labour appears to them as an objective character stamped upon the product of that labour; because the relation of the producers to the sum total of their own labour is presented to them as a social relation, existing not between themselves, but between the products of their labour (2000:473).

In the first the worker as subject is separated (alienated) from the object, in the second the object gains 'mystical power' over people. Instead of finding satisfaction in and through creative work, we do so through commodities that unknown people have produced, and our relationship to those products and to other people through them comes to replace and substitute real social relations. It is a moot point whether this tendency for people to live and express relationships through objects is a feature of all societies and whether this is a general condition (Graeber 2001; 2005). Certainly Marx particularly associated it with capitalism because of the total separation of the worker and the product under this system. The second area in which alienation is experienced is the activity of production. Marx relates this to alienation from the product: '[h]ow would the worker be able to affront the product of his work as an alien being if he did not alienate himself in the act of production itself?' (2000:88). Because workers do not realise themselves in their work they avoid it 'like the plague'; work becomes a compulsory and external activity, in as much as it is not owned by the worker but by the employer. The third aspect of alienation refers to human 'species-life'. This relates to productive activity as a process whereby through creative action people transform nature and in so doing transform themselves. For Marx this vital and conscious human activity constitutes our 'species-being'. Alienated labour alienates humans from their 'species-life' and reduces it to the means to individual physical existence. The consequence of the previous three aspects of alienation in capitalist society leads to the fourth; social relations are also alienated relations. When people are alienated from the product of their labour, from their activity as producers, and from their 'species-being', they are also alienated from other people. They relate to others from their position as workers and producers of commodities rather than fully realised human beings.

The people of El Dos do not speak of alienation and fetishisation, but they are constantly troubled by the possibility of being cut off from or losing God, by the breakdown of social ties and by the form their relations with objects takes. Many identified the root cause of this threat in the market economy and were troubled by its effects on social life. Firstly, we can see this in their concern that people give undue importance to material possessions, expressed through *consumismo*. Secondly, *campesinos* stress the importance of owning and working land; when to go to work for a wage is described as 'going to be shackled' (*ir al brete*) and there is no suggestion of labour as a liberating activity in which workers realise their 'species-being'. Finally, the depreciation of *egoismo* is based on the idea that individual self-interest and the denial of moral responsibility to others dissolves social relations.

To recapitulate, we have seen that Marx stressed productive activity as the means by which humans transform nature, themselves and society. Under capitalism, private property, wages and the division of labour mediate productive activity. The consequence is a system of estrangement, in which potentially liberating creative practices become distorted, and alienating activities. On the one hand there is the promise of an ideal state, a vision of a world in which people are in immediate unity with nature, with themselves, the things they create and each other. Against this, we have the idea that under current circumstances we are separated from the goods we produce, cut off from our true natures as human beings and divorced from one another as we relate through objects we did not create.

PEASANT PRODUCTION, SUBSISTENCE, USES AND EXCHANGES

To negate the 'mystery', 'magic' and 'necromancy' of commodities Marx conjures up the image of Robinson Crusoe, alone on his island. All the things that the castaway does to satisfy his wants – tool-making, fishing, hunting and such like – are directly produced by him: 'so the relations between Robinson and the objects that form this wealth of his own creation are here so simple and clear as to be intelligible without exertion ... yet those relations contain all that is essential to the determination of value' (2000:477). In the iconic figure of the shipwrecked hero Marx glimpses an escape from the fetishism of commodities and alienation because there is no separation between producer and consumer, since they are one and the same person. Crusoe appropriates the total value of the things he produces in the act of consuming them.

The residents of El Dos are similarly attracted to collecting and freely distributing food, particularly fruit, that grows 'naturally' and in abundance without the application of human labour or material inputs. Other foods are produced and then consumed as items 'for use' (*por el gasto*) by the household. Farm visits nearly always involved a demonstration of the variety and range of crops grown for subsistence and the animals kept for meat, milk or eggs. Often people lamented a move away from production for consumption and reliance on store-bought food, shipped into nearby towns by container trucks. As we saw in Chapter 6, collecting food from nature or producing *por el gasto* has a telling accompanying gesture. The hand brought up to the mouth makes a circle; what the arm produces by working in nature returns to the mouth and brings with it the sustenance for further work. Here we have a symbolic expression of the economy in which individuals provision themselves directly by extracting things for use from the world around them.

However, Marx realised that every economic relation is also a social relation – Crusoe had his Friday – and in the same passage he discusses two noncapitalist forms organised around economic dependency between people. The first is feudal society. Marx contrasts this with capitalism, not because feudalism was non-exploitative, but because 'the social relations of individuals in performance of their labour appear at all events as their own mutual personal relations, and are not disguised under the shape of social relations between the products of labour' (2000:477). That is, goods are not fetishised and economic relations are first and foremost social relations, albeit of an exploitative kind. In the second case Marx uses the peasant family as an example of directly associated labour. Here production as a social relation is a function of the family; individual labour power is part of the overall labour power of the family and so its social character is stamped upon it. But he objected to the peasant household because he saw it as patriarchal, historically regressive and inefficient, and he rejected ownership of personal private property since under capitalism it presupposes and results in the alienation of labour from the product.

In pursuing his political agenda and critiquing the operations and effects of the capitalist system, Marx was not, in spite of his adherence to the materialist conception of history, concerned with how everyday and scholarly ideas were transformed to accommodate the capitalist transition, as, for example, Dumont (1977) and Tawney (1938 [1926]) have subsequently been. Committed as he was to an evolutionary model of human history, he was still less inclined to look to the past, to non-Western societies or to Western ideas that lie between the cracks, or beyond the ambit of personal expediency and the desire for profit. Many other writers, however, have followed this path. Instead of exposing the injustices generated by capitalism, as Marx did, they have been concerned with the ways people in various societies have constructed social relations with and through objects.

One important area of debate is the extent to which peasant production operates by a different kind of rationality from the market and the degree to which accounting methods and relationships change as the peasant household becomes enmeshed in market exchanges (Carrier 1995; Gudeman and Rivera 1990; Pratt 1994). James Carrier argues that the house economy is 'an orientation that sees the household as the focus of economic action and that subordinates the economic pursuits of its members to the survival of the house as a social unit' (1995:154). In maintaining that the house is a distinctive domain, an opposition between subsistence activities and exchange operations and the distinction between use-value and exchange-value, are commonly played upon.

In *The Moral Economy of the Peasant*, James Scott (1976) argues that an assured though culturally defined subsistence level dominates peasant moral and political thinking. Social arrangements for redistribution and reciprocal relationships help maintain that level, and the demands of landlords, moneylenders or the state are deemed legitimate or illegitimate by making reference to the minimum considered necessary to subsist (1976:10). When the minimum is not forthcoming, Scott argues, peasants revolt. In later work Scott moves away from the 'all or nothing' political model of quiescence or outright rebellion. He argues that peasants engage in low-level, everyday resistance to dominant economic and political forms that draw them away from independent subsistence and reciprocal relationships towards the dependency and exploitation of exchange relations (1985).

Despite some evidence to the contrary (Edelman 1999; Acuña Ortega 1985, 1987), Costa Rican peasantries are often represented as pacific. A materialist explanation for this would refer to the benign welfare state, coupled with fecund nature, which makes a minimum culturally defined subsistence an easily realisable goal. In El Dos, for example, reference is constantly made to an earlier time when people were all equally dependent on the natural world to subsist; the refrain 'everything grows here' is regularly repeated. Material concerns are reinforced by the ideology of formal rural equality, a past in which the right to subsistence was given by God through nature, according to the moral precept that 'the product of the land should be distributed in such a way that all were guaranteed a subsistence niche' (Scott 1976:10). The idea of restraint in seeking personal advantage makes sense within a religious frame that decrees all people are equal before God, who created nature for the general benefit and use of humanity. Such a scheme contests the idea that growth can, or should be, unlimited, or that exchange itself can create wealth. Instead, the limited quantity of goods means any gain must automatically take place at someone else's expense (Foster 1965). A moral economy founded on this basis requires distribution according to socially defined ends, such as need, rather than economic criteria, such as the ability to pay, appropriate or exploit.

As we saw in the previous chapter, for Evers (1994) the opposition between the activity of exchange to accumulate wealth and the distribution of use-value to ensure subsistence results in a dilemma for the trader. Here, the association of subsistence with use-value conjures up its opposite: the exchange value of the commodity form and the appropriation of surplus by intermediaries. Earlier I suggested that fair trade relies upon a sophisticated reading of the market economy and the exploitation that is made possible by the appropriation of surplus value by capitalists. Now we can see that fair trade proffers an antidote to this exploitation by making reference to peasant livelihoods, small farmers and their struggle to survive. For example, a quotation from Miguel Barrantes from Costa Rica states that 'without Cafédirect and fair trade many coffee growers here could not have continued; the price paid by the middlemen was not enough to cover the cost of growing and preparing [coffee]'. Messages such as these are doubly effective in appealing to romantic sensibilities, the persistent attractions of rurality and nationalist identities on both the left and the populist right of the political spectrum (Kearney 1996; Pratt 2003; Roseberry 1989).

But what is really interesting is not the relative use-value of different things, their practical utility or their status as commodities, but cultural distinctions made between goods that serve the same or similar purpose (Sahlins 1976). If, as we have already seen, all commodities as exchange items must also have use-values, what sense is there to moral differentiations on this basis? A jar of Nescafé and a jar of Cafédirect are both equally useful, and they are both commodities; we make a comparison between them as two similar things, and the difference is cultural, social and symbolic. In this respect we can usefully move away from formal differences between uses and exchanges to consider ethical ideas attached to social forms of distribution. To this end the discussion now moves away from Marx and the ethics of production towards moral ideas attached to exchange. As any individual or family struggles to produce everything it needs from nature, so it becomes necessary to exchange. But as ancient Greek scholars argued, exchange itself requires the household to surrender autonomy and so involves moral compromise. Accordingly, I now turn to the moral 'problem' of exchange.

PRODUCTION-CONSUMPTION LINKS AND THE SOCIAL DISTRIBUTION OF THINGS

Whereas distinguishing subsistence from exchange implies a radical disjuncture between the household economy producing for use and capitalist exchange, this contradicts ideas that many people themselves adhere to. Householders in El Dos certainly have no moral problem with exchange; they have a long history of producing goods for sale in local markets and exchanging things between households. For them a distinction needs to be made not between use and exchange, but between direct producers who create value from working the earth and can sell or consume the things so produced, and intermediaries who make money from the act of exchange, do not create anything, and yet live off producers and are perceived to maintain a stranglehold on producers' ability to subsist.

In the literature, these moral and political problems can be traced back to ancient Greece (Booth 1993). Although some early Greek thinkers were attracted to the creation of wealth through exchange (*chrematistics*), many, most notably Aristotle, were drawn to the science of household management (Collier 2001:17–18). It is one of the ironies of economic history that the modern term for the science of profit-making, or economics, has its root in the Greek word for household (*oikos*), which conceives it as a self-limiting unit. The Aristotelian tradition insists the purpose of economic activity is to create autarky for the house and leisure for the household head, which should then be used to carry out civic duties and enjoy the good life. The Greek household relied upon and accepted slavery, and feminist perspectives also expose gender hierarchies in the household (Harris 1984; Mackintosh 1984; Moore 1988; Sahlins 1974). Despite this, a scheme based upon the limited end of self-sufficient reproduction rather than limitless expansion proffers an alternative moral architecture to the liberal fascination with the formal freedom to trade and make profit (Booth 1993).

Aristotle distinguishes between natural and unnatural modes of acquiring goods, and in *The Politics* he proposes a three-part hierarchy placed in descending order of propriety (1962:85–87). Most satisfactory, and deemed as synonymous with natural, is direct acquisition from the environment. Here producers create or gather the things they need for use and then directly consume them or distribute them through the household. This mirrors the kind of economy exemplified by Robinson Crusoe, as well as the satisfaction farmers in El Dos derive from growing food *por el gasto*. Following this, and also classified as natural, is the exchange of goods for goods or money, but only to adjust inequalities and scarcities in nature. The form is equivalent to petty commodity production in which exchange takes place but no profit is sought from the transaction itself. The aim is redistribution in order to meet household needs. Again, this mirrors the ethical scheme of *campesinos* who maintain the right to sell goods they produce from the land to obtain necessary items the household cannot produce. Lastly, and regarded as unnatural and therefore morally iniquitous, there is the practice of trade and the pursuit of monetary gain from exchange. This activity, condemned for seeking profit rather than administering to household reproduction, is the source of the disquiet and criticism commonly levied at intermediaries.

James Carrier's analysis of changes in social relations in the retail trade situates moral ideas about distribution in more recent Western historical tradition. He argues that economic practices and legislation in England prior to the eighteenth century were based largely upon moral precepts and relationships rather than expediency. The model was one of localism and self-sufficiency (see Mintz 1985:75). Most things were produced and consumed by and within households and localities; laws were aimed at preserving local and personal trade relationships within the physical space of the market, and at controlling unscrupulous 'middle-men' (Carrier 1995:63–68). To this end, measures were introduced that favoured local traders. For example, tolls taxed outsiders trying to sell their wares in local markets; these people were in any case regarded as suspect and could be seized as vagrants. Monopolising practices, such as buying up bulk stock before it reached the open marketplace and hoarding it for later sale, were also forbidden. Regulations attempted to ensure that market sales were fair and transparent rather than free; officials controlled weights and measures, quality and the price of goods. At the same time, moral and legislative precedence was given to sellers who had directly laboured upon the goods being traded; practical constraints limited possibilities for making profits by acting only as an intermediary rather than by producing goods and then selling them. For example, artisanship was encouraged by forbidding iron to be sold without the seller changing its form, and 'honest wares' were those produced by people through the application of their skill and toil directly upon the thing produced (Carrier 1995:69). Rather than exchange through impersonal and impartial relationships, distribution was channelled through personal contacts – friends, neighbours and families. Shopkeepers had regular, known clients and payments were made 'by agreement'. Commercial deals were inured by law against causing hardship; if suffering was the result of an exchange it was legally invalid.

The point is that for a good part of English history the dominant voice insisted that value is created in production and producers were accorded the primary right to sell their goods. As in the recently revitalised farmers' markets, the accent has long been on localism, self-sufficiency and producers selling their own wares to consumers; the preferred form of transactions was 'direct transfers from local producer to local consumer' (Carrier 1995:66). Fair prices could therefore be best achieved when goods went from the farm gate or the artisan's workshop directly to the consumer (1995:64). At the same time exchange was considered 'a social matter involving reciprocity and redistribution: competition, in the sense of one man's gaining at the expense of another, was a violation of this traditional ethic' (Crowley 1974, cited in Carrier 1995:65).

What Carrier describes is a set of social relations established for the distribution of things. In this model, while producers control their labour power and so can be distinguished from slaves, they also own their means of production, which distinguishes them from salaried workers. The importance of ownership of these things lies firstly in the formal freedom it suggests, and secondly in the fact that it allows production, distribution and consumption to take place through personal relationships. For Baudrillard this is the defining characteristic of the artisan class: 'a mode of social relations in which not only is the process of production controlled by the producer but in which the *collective process remains internal to the group*, and in which producers and consumers are the same people, above all defined through the reciprocity of the group' (1975:97, emphasis in original).

The nub of the matter is the opposition in our mind's eye between exchanges that follow from and emerge out of social relations, in which objects are invested with expressive significance, and formal exchanges in which no relationship exists except in the act of exchange, which ends once the transaction is complete and the self-interest of the parties is satisfied. There are a number of potential problems with this latter view, not least the possibility that one or both parties might never be satisfied, either the producer with the price received, or the consumer who always foregoes other products with different attractions (Sahlins 1974:4). In this view the attempt to realise oneself through consumption choices and personal desires remains a nostalgic but ultimately dissatisfying and doomed project that is dysfunctional not only for the individual but for society as well, (Friedman 1989; Slater 1997:97–98). The more general point for the present argument is that many people in everyday life seem to object to the formal separation of the producer from the consumer and production from consumption. It is precisely this idea that inspires the alternative distribution networks that have come increasingly to the fore in recent years, of which fair trade is but one example.

Encapsulated in the idea of drawing production or producer and consumption or consumer towards one another are a whole range of cultural associations and recurring political and social commitments. In the Christian tradition adhered to in rural Costa Rica, value comes from the earth to sustain humanity; directly consuming nature's product underwrites divine dispensation and reconnects people to God. The more overtly political conviction is that value is embodied in the work of agricultural producers, so they are seen as the sole and rightful owners of the product. By consuming what they create or by selling directly to consumers, producers avoid intermediaries who reap profits but do not create value. Allied to this is the historical memory of self-sufficient, local peasant communities sustaining themselves from nature's abundance and divine grace and distributing goods through known social relationships. Conversely, intermediaries are seen to take value that is not theirs and threaten the livelihood of producers.

David Graeber (2001) has recently argued that alienation and fetishisation are the result of the separation of the two spheres of home and factory, and the two associated forms of human economic activity, production and consumption. If this is the essence of the capitalist transition (Stone et al. 2000:4), it follows that the idea of reconnecting these spheres and activities will proffer the means, at least symbolically, of escaping the whole system of estrangement outlined above. Whereas formal economics locates ethics in a universal rationality and freedom in the inalienable right to promote individual self-interest, an alternative moral voice seeks to draw together that which the market tears apart: the producer to the consumer and the moment of consumption to the act of production.

In the West we have a protracted history of forms of social and economic life in which the producer and the consumer are one and the same person, or where connection is sought and promoted between the activities of production and consumption. The household has appeal not because it is primarily involved in the production and consumption of use-value, as opposed to the exchange value of commodities, but because it is an arena that combines production and consumption, hence symbolising economic autonomy. When autarky fails and the house cannot produce what it needs other moral options are available; welfare, or, more pertinently here, the distribution of goods directly from producer to consumer. Both these idealised cases, household autonomy and unmediated links between producer and consumer, negate the separation of the two spheres identified by Graeber.

So the first explanation for the attraction of fair trade locates it within a longstanding cultural adherence to an economy based upon direct relationships between people. Images of producers, often labelled family farmers, on packaging and websites evoke a common history and portray a shared present. Many products are marketed in this way, but fair-trade goods play more overtly upon consumers' desire to connect with producers and to ensure them a livelihood. Fair trade thus seeks to counteract the exploitative relations of capitalism and the alienation of people from one another that Marx identified in the market economy. It is no accident that many successful fair-trade goods are associated with small-farmer economies. In their idealised form they escape capitalist production regimes, but struggle with distribution and so are well-suited to imagining and creating alternatives. As we know, a source of a further sense of alienation is the more fundamental separation between people and things; to understand how fair trade implies an escape from this estranged relationship I turn to writings on the gift.

FORGING SOCIAL RELATIONS THROUGH THINGS: THE IDEOLOGY AND POLITICS OF THE GIFT

From the beginnings of their discipline anthropologists have encountered and documented alternative ways of organising the economy. As a result they have often taken issue with the capitalist ethic and used fieldwork data to challenge Western stereotypes. For example, the pioneering ethnographer Bronislaw Malinowski tried to describe Trobriand society from the 'natives' point of view', but he did so using terms of reference from his own society to describe differences and challenge conventional economic wisdoms. In his discussion on kula exchange he attacks the assumption that Trobriand society is constructed around the natural desire to accumulate: '[a]lthough like every human being, the kula native loves to possess and therefore desires to acquire and dreads to lose, the social code of rules with regard to give and take by far overrides his natural acquisitive tendency' (1922:96).

Malinowski is an early exponent of the idea that in other societies the economy operates through the give and take of social relationships and not through impersonal formal exchanges, as is made to appear in capitalist society. Contemporaries of Malinowski with a more radical agenda, notably Marcel Mauss, were not even prepared to accept that natural human acquisitiveness, self-interest and the impartial laws of capitalism had become dominant in the West. Quite the reverse:

Mauss was not trying to describe how the logic of the marketplace, with its strict distinctions between persons and things, interest and altruism, freedom and obligation, had become the common sense of modern societies. Above all he was trying to explain the degree to which it had failed to do so; to explain why so many people – and particularly, so many of the less powerful and privileged members of society – found its logic morally repugnant. Why, for example, institutions that insisted on the strict separability of producers and their products offended against common institutions of justice, the moral 'bedrock', as he puts it, of our own – as of any – society (Graeber 2001:162).

Mauss, like Marx, was concerned with alienation, but in the second, legalistic sense identified by Raymond Williams, that is, of the separation of persons from property. This led to his research on *The Gift* (2002 [1925]), since Mauss wanted to understand what it was that led people to believe that a gift should be returned. To this end he explored the different ways people make connections to one another through the medium of things, and analysed exchange in non-Western societies and the history of legal systems and contract law. In his research he thought he had identified a common theme across cultures and through time; objects, he proposed, continue to contain something of the owner, even when they have been passed on. If this were true, things could never be entirely alienated from the person who created them; they would embody the energy and meaning invested in them and producers would feel the impulse to pursue things they produced. What is more, a relationship would be established with the new owner who, having appropriated something from the producer, would feel obliged to make recompense in the shape of a reciprocal gift.

In his reading of *The Gift*, David Graeber (2001, 2004) characterises Mauss's most famous work as a political tract that seeks ethical spaces in the economy in acts of reciprocity. Mauss's involvement in socialist politics and the cooperative movement are illustrative of his political commitments (Graeber 2001:156). While gifts seem to offer a potential obverse image to the self-interest of the market, it is always possible to assign selfish motives to ostensibly selfless acts, and the range of actions and motivations opened up by ethnographic data complicates the issue (Davis 1992). Sometimes gift economies appear almost entirely competitive. Lavish acts of generosity, such as the Roman practice of scattering gold and jewels into a crowd, seem designed to gain status and demean others (Graeber 2001:160). Even achieving 'balance' often involves calculation, as, for example, when we seek an appropriate gift for a wedding or birthday present (Miller 2001). But in many cases of giving there is at least the pretence of an ideal 'total social prestation', in which creating or maintaining a social relationship is represented as an end in itself.

Part of the controversy generated by Mauss's work over the years is no doubt due to apparent contradictions in his observations. One central tenet of Western ideas about exchange is that gifts and the acts of reciprocity they embody cement social relationships. In this respect gifts are personal and ought to be reciprocated in some shape or form. The fact that gifts are understood with respect to the qualities they embody serves to mask any hint of calculation and impersonality, and at the same time means that commensurability is never reached. To donate exactly the same object you receive as a counter-gift would mean equilibrium and the end of the cycle of obligation. But in our imagination gifts should be freely given, absolutely without obligation, and without expectation of receiving anything back. While it must probably be accepted that giving without some return is not possible, this does not detract from an ideology that says that this ought to be so, nor does it deny the possibility of political or social actions that operate on this premise.[137] Sometimes, for example, gifts are even given to mark the end of a relationship or to try to achieve closure. Because gifts can at the same time be symbolic of interest in social relations and represent absence of self-interest makes them polysemic and hence useful in the play of social life.

Many economic anthropologists now recognise that the value that people attach to things changes as items move through social life (Appadurai 1986; Kopytoff 1986). What determines the scale of value? To say that it lies in the object's 'resistance' to our ability to appropriate it, as Appadurai does (1986:1) is to ignore Sahlins's (1976) warning and submit to a purely practical and utilitarian ethic: the false coin of our own dreams (Graeber 2001).[138] Instead we need to focus upon the range of social, moral and political messages that different things transmit (Stone et al. 2000:4–5). We have two concepts in play. One, alienation, is used to describe a condition under capitalism in which people and things lose their individual qualities and take a generic form, as producers are separated from one another and from the things they make. The implication is that people fail to realise themselves in their social relationships or in their relations with objects. The second, the idea of the gift, can usefully be seen as running in parallel to alienation; gifts are a medium for forging social relations but also of negating personal expediency.

Nevertheless, what does inevitably return is an object with particular, savoured qualities.

The idea of the gift can be used, at a number of levels, to interrogate key aspects of the concept of fair trade as a consumer item. We have already seen that alternative trade deals seek to establish social relations with particular kinds of people, namely peasant producers, and so imply a specific kind of political economy based upon household subsistence and reproduction. The idea of the gift throws further light on the specifically social nature of exchanges, since a gift is precisely a vehicle that cements personal exchanges between people. Gifts can do this because they are attached to an ideology and politics that insists they should be given voluntarily and without hint of self-regard. As such, gifts are clearly distinct from what people raised in the tradition of Western markets are encouraged to imagine as impersonal commodities.

In the anthropological literature two accounts are given for the origin of the ideology of the free gift. The first relies on the distinction between gifts and commodities, the second on that between alienability and inalienability. These terms have been highly problematised, challenged and even reversed in recent years (Appadurai 1986; Bourdieu 1977; Gell 1992; Miller 2001; Weiner 1992), but my concern is not so much with the usefulness of conceptual categories than with the culturally specific ideas attached to classes of things.

The social history of capitalism provides the first location for the idea of the free gift. In this explanation there is a move from an economy embedded in society, in which goods were appropriated through the activation and maintenance of personal and social relationships, to one in which the acquisition of goods became progressively more impersonal. Accompanying this are the changes in production and retail trade outlined above. What is proposed is the historical development of two separate domains; one glossed as 'work', in which interest and impersonal relations prevail, the other called 'home', an autonomous space in which goods are disbursed through reciprocal giving. Gifts in personal life then become the means to create and maintain affective ties to other people (Carrier 1995:152–156). Family ties exemplify personal gift relationships and it is notable that fair-trade literature, publicity and websites often stress producers' families.

Along with the dislocation of home from work, and economy from society, Carrier notes a change in the conceptualisation of the self. Whereas humans were previously regarded as 'situated' beings, in the seventeenth and eighteenth centuries the idea emerged of people as 'autonomous', and morally so. Virtuous acts came to be seen as freely chosen, and from here 'it is only a small step to the argument that free and unconstrained acts are good' (1995: 162). The highest expression of social, as opposed to economic, relations lies in 'the cultural image of the perfect giving of the perfect present' (1995: 145), one that expresses pure sentiment and love, and transcends monetary value.

Jonathan Parry (1986) provides a parallel explanation for the ideology of the gift by scrutinising it in different cultural settings. Parry is concerned less with the division between gifts and commodities than the extent to which gifts are expressions of interest and are hence inalienable and require reciprocation, or expressions of disinterest, and are therefore alienated from the giver. In developing his argument Parry works with Mauss's concept of the 'spirit of the gift'. Mauss borrowed the Maori idea that objects always contain the spirit of the owner, termed the *hau*, as symptomatic of a more general condition of the inalienable quality of things. The principle, whether metaphysical or moral, behind the inalienable gift is that of reciprocity; goods, or their equivalent, should find their way back to the donor and in this path lies material productiveness and wellbeing (1986:465). Standing in contrast to the inalienable gift is the idea of alienability, the principle that the gift is divorced from the donor in the act of giving and that no connection is established between giver and recipient. Parry associates the idea of alienability with the renunciatory ethic of world religions. The Indian gift of *dana*, for example, embodies the sins of the donor, which are passed on to the recipient, and should under no circumstances return (1986: 459–463). Gifts in this scenario are given in a spirit of expiation, so acts of charity, the disinterested giving of alienable objects, come to have moral weight.

Both explanations for the ideology of the gift locate ideas about giving in social and cultural domains, either through religiously inspired renunciation as a route to accumulate merit, or through adherence to the ideology of the home and reciprocal relations.[139] The point, and one that can be used to illuminate aspects of fair trade, is that there is a gap between what anthropology tells us about the gift as a vehicle for establishing and maintaining social and power relations, and culturally embedded ideas about what a gift should be. Parry usefully summarises this distinction by pointing to a common misreading of the text: 'while Mauss is generally represented as telling us how *in fact* the gift is *never* free, what I think he is really telling us is how *we* have acquired a *theory* that it should be so' (1986:458 emphasis in original).[140]

Now, if the gift in Western thought is credited with two apparently contradictory qualities, the power to establish and sustain social relationships through inalienability on the one hand, wedded to a principle of generous giving on the other, then fair-trade goods add a further twist. They combine elements of the commodity form, desocialised and 'rational', with the idea of the gift, and so are not dissimilar to other kinds of charitable donations made to NGOs (Stirrat and Henkel 1997). Jars of fair-trade coffee stand alongside other similar commodities on supermarket shelves but remain distinct from them, and this distinction is manifested in the higher price, or premium, paid voluntarily by consumers who could equally well choose a different brand.[141] It is clear that this extra payment is couched in terms of the social relationship between producer and consumer, but this relationship is represented as devoid of obligation; the gift is freely given, to be used directly by the recipient, the small farmer, without conditions or 'interest' on the part of the donor. In short, fair trade succeeds, at least in part, by distinguishing itself from other commodities, and it does this by being couched in the idiom of the gift.

At this point the argument can go two ways. The first would recognise that the ideology of the gift, although naturally appealing, is precisely an ideology: a set of socially located ideas that systematically obscure the relationships between parties and power inequalities at work, and make them appear natural:

What starts off as a pure gift, an act of seemingly disinterested giving, morally and ethically divorced from the mundane world, becomes in the end an object or a service intimately entwined in the mundane and interested world. Furthermore, in the course of this journey, the gift creates a series of problematic relations, frequently ambiguous in terms of their meaning and often paradoxical in terms of their implications (Stirrat and Henkel 1997:69).

The suggestion is that the uncomplicated 'public transcript' of fair-trade policy as a specific order obscures a 'hidden transcript' of power relations (Scott 1992). Ethnographic study can play an invaluable role by revealing the way projects and development initiatives do not proceed as policy prescribes, but are understood, transformed and used locally (Lewis and Mosse 2006a). For example, cooperative managers and members engage with fair trade on their own terms, which can exacerbate local tensions and inequalities, or cause friction between partners (Fraser 2003; Lewis 1998; Luetchford 2006; Tallontire 2000). In Chapter 1 I showed how alternative trade in Costa Rica is subsumed under the wider aim of securing the best possible prices for members; at times fair-trade deals can be a bind that requires managers to compromise this goal in the short term. Equally, relationships with other organisations, including NGOs in the North, can become fraught due to differences in perceptions of poverty, for example. Part of the managers' remit is to negotiate and broker tensions between representation and practice, policy and implementation. On the other hand, to demonstrate that fair-trade initiatives do not work as intended does not mean that they do not work at all, nor does it allow for the good intentions and political motivations of activists and consumers. To deconstruct fair trade leaves little room for an interrogation of the political and cultural ideas and objectives that inspire it, and of the different discursive forms behind the concept (Grillo 1997; Lewis and Mosse 2006b).

One way to approach this is to stay with the notion of the gift. We have seen how Parry and Carrier provide explanations for understanding gift-giving in a market economy as motivated by a spirit of renunciation and selflessness. In both cases, giving generously takes on an air of sacrifice; rather than personal accumulation, the aim is to distribute surplus for moral or social ends. Of course, it is easy to argue that alms-giving and sacrifice, as well as the impulse to buy fair trade, is motivated by self-interest, the accumulation of spiritual merit or personal status by those with sufficient economic security, but this contradicts how people themselves would explain their behaviour, and it ignores cultural ideas that inform actions.

So, instead of mounting a critique of capitalism from the perspective of production and labour, as Marx had done, we can pursue a line developed in French socialist writings from the early twentieth century. A key theme in this work is the destination of economic surplus, which can take the form of ritual destruction, competitive displays or charitable donation.[142] Mauss was fascinated by alms; the political point he wishes to make is that in many religious traditions '[g]enerosity is an obligation, because Nemesis avenges the poor and the gods for the superabundance of happiness and wealth of certain people who should rid themselves of it' (2001 [1925]:23).

I have argued that the concept of fair trade plays upon particular kinds of economic arrangement; namely those encompassing both production and consumption, or those that imply a direct and personal social relationship between the producer and the consumer. In these forms a specific kind of relation is established between people through the medium of objects. We have contractual obligations to give, to receive and to reciprocate which become the basis of social life in many, if not all, societies. The desire for personal aggrandisement can always explain such activities. On the other hand, in Western culture there does seem to be a connection between the ideal of the perfect gift, defined by giving without expectation of receiving anything in return, and the political intention to help others or to forge meaningful social relationships through exchange. In this way we can see that fair trade is entangled in complex Western ideas about selfless giving within and between families and notions of charity and religious duty, combined with the political commitment to sustaining autonomous households that produce in order to consume.

THE POLITICS OF CONSUMPTION

At first sight making a case for an alternative economy based upon notions of giving, religious duty and a cultural commitment to families and households sounds hopelessly idealistic, not least because these are concerns that seem to appeal to middle-class consumers. One of the ironies of fair trade, and other alternative goods that play on anticapitalist sentiments, is that it attracts consumers who gain much from the dominant political-economic order. While working-class shoppers concern themselves with value for money, the better-off consistently buy products with specific qualities attached to them.[143] Such class-based inflections are often used to express doubts and suggest limits to the transformative potential of distribution networks that appeal to moral ideas.

It is notable that explanations along these lines rely on a particular reading of consumer behaviour. One assumption is that shopping choices are determined by the desire to make class distinctions, which is merely to assume what one might wish to explain; class groups buy certain goods to establish themselves as classes, thereby reducing shopping to an expression of self-interest.[144] While there may be something in this with Porsches and Prada, it does not explain why certain goods are chosen as class-distinctive or, for that matter, why certain kinds of things are marketed as fair trade. A second and related supposition is that shopping is a fetishised activity in which people live out their lives entirely through the objects they consume, without thought or consciousness of the social relations that connect them to the producer. It should be obvious that I do not hold to this position. Certainly, fair-trade goods are sold in ways that directly contradict the idea that consumption practices are independent of moral and political intention, which impels consideration of recent writings on the politics and ethics of shopping.

In a polemical work Daniel Miller (1995b) has argued that we should now regard consumption as the 'vanguard of history'. By this he means that rather than rely on the coming to consciousness of the working class to bring about revolution, we should instead look to acts of consumption as a potential motor for historical change. There are two main justifications for this: the first relates to the power accorded to consumption in economic orthodoxy, the other concerns the nature of the relationships we hold with objects and people by and through our existence as consumers. One of the principal tenets of economic theory, and a key element in the justification of policy, is the promotion of consumer choice. Such is the power of the consumer that Miller, in promoting his polemic, suggests that the consumer who makes daily decisions as to which products to purchase becomes the 'global dictator' of the fortunes of producers

(1995b:8–9). This may be an extreme position, but evidence suggests that activities such as product boycotts, environmental activism and demands for changes in trade policy can influence policy makers, while manufacturers are sensitive to consumer pressure exercised through product choice.

Attached to the power accorded to consumers in the economy is the moral element behind consumption. In the classical economic model, decisions are arrived at on the purely rational grounds of maximisation of self-interest: the desire for the best quality at the cheapest price. The demand for cheap goods then drives the competitive mechanisms of capitalism, which forces down prices. This may or may not be an accurate description of the way the economy works; in any case it is reductive of the desires and interests motivating consumers. While the objects and services we consume may not provide the sole locus of our identity, they do say something about who we are and provide a means to express our relationship to specific people and things (Carrier and Miller 1999:36). This suggests an ethical rather than purely rational aspect to consumption, and provides a counterpoint to notions of impersonal and formal commercial relations.

If we increasingly live out our lives and find meaning in relation to the things that we consume and not through our actions as producers (Miller 1995a:1–2) then the principal arena in which this is carried out is the household. The ethical content of this part of the economy lies in our activities as shoppers. Many people balance hedonistic impulses and desires with the supposed virtue of thrift, and it is this that underpins the ongoing material reproduction and moral economy of the household. The purchases we make for ourselves and for others demonstrate willingness to indulge those closest to us with luxuries and gifts, which in turn establishes a moral relationship with them; at the same time this frippery is justified by the exercise of thrift and the value for money we seek in acquiring the basic necessities required for the household to maintain itself. Consumption hence constitutes a quintessentially ethical moment in our orientation to the world.

It is at this juncture that politics and power enter the argument. As Miller (1995b:9) points out, there is a fundamental contradiction between our actions as consumers, which drive down prices, and our interests as producers. As labour markets shift and firms practise 'flexible accumulation' to produce ever-cheaper goods but sustain profit margins, it is worker remuneration, health and safety and job security that are often the first casualties. Anthropologists come closer than many to seeing and sharing the experiences of workers marginalised by such policies. Harvey argues that it is incumbent upon 'a politically responsible person to know about and respond politically to all those people who daily put breakfast upon our table, even though market exchange hides from us the conditions of life of the producers' (1993:56).

It is in this political and ethical vein, rather than in an emphasis on class-based, fetishised behaviour, that I think we can better understand fair trade. It provides a more nuanced account of what consumers like to think they are doing when buying fair-trade goods, namely supporting producers struggling to support families in increasingly competitive markets. This is not to deny that there are contradictions. Shoppers certainly look for value for money in supermarkets and so increasingly contribute to pricing regimes that push producers to the limits of profitability. But neither should we ignore the fact that there is a political backlash, albeit from the middle classes, against that process.

COMING TO THE SENSES, OR THE PROBLEM OF LIVING IN A FETISHISED WORLD

Up until now I have examined two facets of the cultural ideology that inspires fair trade: forging social relations with producers, and the role of things as the medium through which this takes place. In this final section I look at consumption and another arena in which Marx identified alienation under capitalism, our relationship to ourselves. Inevitably the problem of fetishisation arises once again, as does the question of the particular kinds of goods that are successfully marketed and marked as fairly traded.

A striking feature of fair trade, apart from its class inflections, is the type of products available. We have already seen that fair trade works particularly with specific production regimes, glossed as small, family farmers. This is usually considered sufficient explanation for the targeting of products such as coffee (Calo and Wise 2005:3). A parallel explanation would focus on the close association between fair trade and luxury, and sensuous and exotic goods, specifically foods.[145] A description of coffee provided by Daviron and Ponte illustrates this perfectly: 'coffee with floral notes and deep, lush fruit; blackberry, strawberry, raspberry, currant, sometimes grapefruit; with a very corporal quality, a muscular quality, with an undeniable sensuality to be found in its musky scent' (2005:130). Fair-trade goods seem to succeed best when they have very specific qualities. They are often what Mintz identifies as 'powerful stimulants' (1996:19). They are full of taste and aroma, which trigger memories and associations (Sperber 1975). If such foods can be said to have a purpose, their aim is to awaken the senses, give pleasure and evoke exoticism. They are products by and through which we realise ourselves as sensual beings in overt and tangible ways, through powerful smells and tastes that are then incorporated into our very bodies. Of course, one could also argue that such products are ideally suited to connoisseurs and efforts to construct and maintain class distinctions, but their somatic effects indicate that there is probably more to it than this. We have seen that fair trade can be read as an attempt to negate different aspects of alienation under capitalism; we have yet to look at what fair trade tells us about our relationship with ourselves, or what Marx called our 'species-being'.

Marx addresses this issue in the section of the *1844 Manuscripts* on 'Private Property and Communism'. The argument has a number of components, but is grounded in the positive abolition of private property, which he sees as the key to escape all forms of alienation. Under private property, human essence and human life is necessarily distorted and reduced to an unhealthy preoccupation with personal pleasure and the 'sense of having' (2000:100). By contrast, in true teleological fashion, Marx claims 'the whole of history is a preparation for "man" to become the object of sense perception and for needs to be the needs of "man as man"' (2000:102). Beyond the abolition of private property Marx envisions a world in which people develop their true and directly sensuous nature: '[t]he ongoing formation, even cultivation, of the senses was for Marx a recovery of that power of the body lost to the alienating effects of private property' (Stewart 2005:63). The need, then, is for humans to move beyond a relation with objects based upon personal utility and egoistic need towards social utility, human need and enjoyment.

The assertion that the abolition of alienation begins with the senses may help explain why fair-trade goods, which seek to promote human social relations and human needs in the economy, are mainly sensual substances. It can also perhaps clarify why these goods are apparently most attractive to, and associated with, the better-off. These are people less constrained by 'value for money', who might be defined as living in a situation of 'post-scarcity' (Giddens 1996), and who can afford to take into consideration the social nature of objects and be reflexive in their shopping (Macnaghten and Urry 1998:25). It is this that gives credence to the idea that the consumption of fair-trade goods is a form of charitable giving.

Two things remain unanswered. The first is indicated by Baudrillard in a footnote to the discussion on the artisan mode of production, where he focuses upon the way exchange value collapses into use-value in the act of consumption:

In a certain way, the moment of consumption remains of the artisan type even in the system of our political economy. The user who consumes enters into personal relationship with the product and directly recovers its 'use-value', just as the process of artisan labour preserves the use-value of the labour power of the artisan. But this personal exchange in consumption is restricted for us to the level of the privatised individual. This also remains the only moment that seems to avoid exchange value, hence it is invested today with a very strong psychological and social charge (1975:97, note 2).

Baudrillard seems to suggest that consumption as an activity entails losing sight of exchange relations as we incorporate objects imbued with the energy of peasants and their environment into our bodies and daily lives. Here the attractions of the household and artisan production, in which producers and consumers are drawn closer, reaches its defining moment by way of a specific relationship to the self. Production and the exchange that ensues are obscured, and consumption itself becomes nothing less than the fetishised incorporation of use-value.[146]

So the question is the degree to which fair-trade goods, remaining in the world of private property as they do as consumer goods, really allow escape from alienation – or are they merely another form of fetishised object? There is probably no definitive answer to this question. In a recent article David Graeber has argued that all human creative activity involves the fetishisation of objects to some degree:

If fetishism is, at root, our tendency to see our own actions and creations as having power over us, how can we treat it as an intellectual mistake? Our actions and creations do have power over us. This is simply true. Even for a painter, every stroke one makes is a commitment of a sort (2005:431).

So the issue is not whether objects are fetishised to some extent but, as Graeber argues, whether one can occasionally avoid getting lost in the world of objects, stand back, and 'step into some overarching perspective from which the machinery is visible' (2005:431). What is this machinery? Graeber appears to mean creative activity as the basis upon which we apportion value to objects and relationships. To escape from what he elsewhere calls 'partial consciousness' we would need to understand and remain constantly aware of how our actions recreate the social system in which we live, and how through those actions we reflexively redefine and reshape ourselves as social beings (2001: 64). This is a feat he recognises as extraordinarily difficult to achieve. However, it is within that tradition, which has all sorts of cultural and political precedents, that I locate discourses on fair trade.

CONCLUSIONS

In recent years fair trade has been gathering momentum, and has achieved exceptional growth.[147] One consequence of this is fears of 'mainstreaming' and co-option by major retailers, arguments all too familiar to students concerned at the autonomy of new social movements (Hellman 1992). As in the case of organic agriculture, studied by Guthman (2002, 2004a), fair trade sets itself up as an alternative to mainstream practice which, when it finds success, throws up unresolved contradictions. To interrogate fair trade, to understand its attractions as well as some of the paradoxes it must negotiate, I have concentrated in this chapter upon what makes it possible. By what political and cultural criteria do we adjudge trade to be fair or unfair, and what moral ideas does it express?

The answer to that question depends upon where one stands. Fair trade works, at least in part, by evoking the closer, shorter circuits of petty commodity production and artisanship. For consumers, this answers a need to activate a more direct and substantive relationship with producers and their products. In this way fair trade provides an idealised solution to a problem some shoppers find in the modern depersonalised economy; it acts as a salve, mollifying the self-interested decisions made in relation to more generic products. The coffee growers and rural people in this study also use productive activity and goods to forge and maintain relationships, but they tend to do so in localised circuits. At the same time they often self-consciously limit engagement with the market, and by practising thrift in the household and producing and adapting the things they need from the world around them, create and recreate a moral, household economy. The evidence is that fair trade, to varying degrees, helps growers and rural coffee economies find stable prices, but its success depends upon the institutional framework within which it operates. There is a clue here to a contradiction; while fair trade gives iconic form to an economy based upon direct relations between producers and consumers, it still operates through inter-mediaries who appropriate value, even if their work only involves stable employment and a regular salary. For this reason there is some ambivalence among producers about the institutional structure of fair trade.

Despite such differences between the expectations, understand-ings and experiences of producers, 'middle-men' and consumers in relation to fair trade, there is also common ground. The concept feeds into popular concern about social and moral conduct in exchange, which has long been central to people's lives within Western culture. Admittedly, it has largely been abolished from retail trade, but the success of initiatives to reinject ethics into shopping should not surprise, since the multistranded cultural and political commitments that make it possible are already in place. The theme that brings all the strands together is the negative attitude to capitalist forms of organisation and practices. To order the issues and agendas I have drawn primarily on the writings of Marx and Mauss, and recent reappraisals of their work, particularly by David Graeber. The advantage of applying this to the case of fair trade is that it gives a context to the discussion that many readers would recognise.

The first theme is the most overtly political and economic, in as much as it focuses upon the way goods are distributed and value appropriated. From one perspective, of concern to producers and supported and reinforced by Christian theology, value comes from nature, from where it is appropriated by human labour. This view gives precedence to creative activity, particularly agricultural work, although it is easily applied to all kinds of manual labour by which raw materials are transformed. When value is understood to be instatiated in objects due to the labour that went into them, intermediaries are left isolated. Rather than creating value, intermediaries are judged to be merely appropriating it by exploiting the distance between producer and consumer. Fair trade does not always escape judgment on this score since it still utilises intermediaries who appropriate value, hence the ambivalence about its institutional workings. There are clear parallels between this stance and Marx's political economy. This analysis provides the frame for the more politicised trade-justice movement, which campaigns to redefine global trade relationships rather than appeal to shoppers' sensibilities through specific products.

The second theme is more cultural. It concerns the way people construe their relationship to each other, to productive activity, to objects and to themselves. The idea that modern life, and particularly capitalist forms of organisation, is an experience of rupture or alienation, sets the conditions for imagining alternatives. Firstly, there is the idea of unalienated social relations. While the economy separates the producer from the consumer, the idea that there should be a connection between them is a strong one. This is core to the fair-trade movement, which plays on the idea of direct connections in brand names such as Cafédirect, in publicity and in campaign work. For example, the manager of Coocafé explicitly states that he wants to reduce the distance between the producer and the consumer. As he says on the Fairtrade Foundation website: 'if we can look one another in the eyes, we can understand each other's needs'.[148] Formal economic relations in which the producer is cut off from the consumer suggest at the same time arenas in which this is not the case. In particular, certain kinds of production-consumption regimes; artisan modes, families, and local face-to-face economies all activate powerful historical and cultural associations.

Many products have long appealed in their packaging and marketing strategies to the desire of consumers to connect with producers. Fair trade takes this trend one step further by promoting a personal social relationship characterised by mutual responsibility; consumers are asked to pay an amount that will constitute a living wage and producers are expected to provide a certain kind of product in which they have invested specific qualities. So the second concept of alienation focuses attention on objects themselves as a means to establish and maintain relationships. In Western culture, the impersonality of the market is contested, or perhaps mitigated, by the ideology of the gift. In the market, entrepreneurs mediate between producer and consumer, and construe that as providing a service between people who are necessarily disconnected. In contrast to this formal view, there are arenas in which objects are used creatively to forge relationships. Part of this is the idea that giving should be selfless and involve sentiment and sacrifice; this easily elides with notions of charity.

But in a gift relationship, something can always be said to return, even if it is only of a spiritual nature. In the case of fair trade, which combines formal commodity exchange with a personalised relationship, it is fitting that what is exchanged are particular kinds of goods that stimulate the senses. If a shopper gives charity, symbolised by a price premium, they gain in return a moment of stimulation from the other side of the globe. As part of this reciprocal process producers sometimes reflect on the final destination of the beans they grow and pick, and they like to imagine that consumers care about their lives and conditions. For consumers, too, coffee reeks of exoticism and evokes connections with far-off lands. It is good to think, imagine and dream over a cup of coffee, and part of that experience is an identification with producers and their lives. This is a third avenue that allows us to hold up our guard against alienation as we realise ourselves as sentient beings. What better reminder that exchanges cannot be reduced to depersonalised 'value for money' than the exotic pleasures of coffee, tea and chocolate?

There are, then, two aspects to the broad appeal of fair trade. The first is the political reaction to capitalism as an exploitative and impersonal system, combined with a more cultural preoccupation with alienation and generic, fetishised commodities. The second is the perceived antidote to the first, expressed through the idea of drawing producers and consumers, production and consumption, closer to one another in order to realise the quality of objects and the value of labour embedded in goods, as imparted by growers in specific places. The power of such formulations lies in their capacity to resonate with radical ideas about the creation of value and exploitation, but combine them with more conservative agendas around tradition, community and the family. These common convictions, albeit expressed and pursued for different reasons and in different ways, by producers, cooperatives, alternative trade organisations and consumers, suggest fair trade will remain a broad and enduring feature of modern life.

TABLES

Table 1: Classification of Coocafé producers by coffee production in *fanegas* (1998–99)

Production in *fanegas**	Number of producers	% of producers	Total production	% of production
1–40	2,548	83.1	29,961	42
40–80	329	10.7	15,859	22
80–120	115	3.7	9,282	13
120–240	49	1.6	8,180	11
240–350	14	0.5	4,155	6
350–500	9	0.3	2,350	3
500–750	1	0.0	625	1
More than 750	3	0.1	1,500	2
Totals	3,068	100	71,912	100

Source: Coocafé R.L.
* 25 or 30 *fanegas* would be considered a reasonable but not exceptional return per hectare. Farmers producing less than 40 *fanegas* could therefore be expected to be farming less than two hectares.

Table 2: Prices paid to producers in *colones* per *fanega* of coffee by Coopeldos and Turín processing plants, including fair-trade premium (1987–98)

Year	Coopeldos price	Fair-trade premium	Coopeldos price plus premium	Turín price	% difference without premium	% difference with premium
1987–88	5,198	–	5,198	5,032	3.2	3.2
1988–89	6,077	–	6,077	5,748	5.4	5.4
1989–90	5,548	97*	5,645	4,897	11.9	13.4
1990–91	7,572	969*	8,541	6,477	14.5	24.2
1991–92	6,796	1,805*	8,646	6,003	11.7	30.6
1992–93	7,409	2,505*	9,914	5,965	19.5	39.8
1993–94	14,806	1,354*	16,160	13,944	5.8	13.7
1994–95	18,609	292*	18,901	18,846	–1.3	0.3
1995–96	17,184	1,112*	18,296	17,021	9.5	7.0
1996–97	24,599	430*	25,029	25,504	–3.7	–1.9
1997–98	28,113*	132*	28,245	25,652	8.8	9.2
Totals	141,911	8,696	150,652	135,089	–	–
Average	12,901	966	13,696	12,280	7.7	13.1

Source: 'Liquidación Final 1987–1988/1997–1998', *Icafe*: Costa Rica. Except *, supplied by Coopeldos R.L.

Table 3: Membership numbers of Coopeldos (1971–99)

Year	Number of members
1971–72	108
1972–73	140
1973–74	138
1974–75	130
1975–76	138
1976–77	153
1977–78	146
1978–79	212
1979–80	172
1980–81	161
1981–82	212
1982–83	247
1983–84	252
1984–85	268
1985–86	285
1986–87	280
1987–88	295
1988–89	305
1989–90	320
1990–91	332
1991–92	340
1992–93	348
1993–94	360
1994–95	363
1995–96	465
1996–97	460
1997–98	485
1998–99	521

Source: 'Coopeldos 25 Aniversario', *Agricultura & Ganaderia*, No. 6, 1996:27.

Table 4: Coffee Processed in *fanegas* by Coopeldos and Turín (1971–99)

Year	Coopeldos	Turín
1971–72	2,087	
1972–73	3,324	
1973–74	1,924	
1974–75	2,968	
1975–76	2,201	3,008
1976–77	2,257	3,166
1977–78	3,968	
1978–79	3,259	4,819
1979–80	3,260	5,920
1980–81	3,120	4,960
1981–82	2,930	3,774
1982–83	3,604	6,262
1983–84	3,529	5,484
1984–85	3,439	7,439
1985–86	2,761	4,152
1986–87	5,172	5,330
1987–88	4,798	6,144
1988–89	5,515	4,610
1989–90	8,505	1,556
1990–91	8,602	1,643
1991–92	12,185	2,718
1992–93	11,850	2,003
1993–94	13,333	1,288
1994–95	13,702	2,780
1995–96	14,580	2,503
1996–97	12,232	2,338
1997–98	14,055	2,701

Sources: 'Coopeldos Informa', April 1989:6.
'Coopeldos 25 Aniversario', *Agricultura & Ganaderia*, No. 6, 1996:27.
'Café Declarado por los Beneficiadores' (*cosechas* 1978–79/ 1997–1998), *Icafé*: Costa Rica.

Table 5: Agricultural activities by farm size: El Dos and Campos de Oro (1998)

Activity	El Dos		Campos de Oro	
	Total number of farms	Average land area (hectares)	Total number of farms	Average land area (hectares)
Coffee only	15	1.2	42	1.9
Dairy only	8	12	–	–
Beef only	3	45	1	–
Coffee and dairy	7	19	1	–
Coffee and beef	8	39	11	45*
Dairy and beef	7	59	–	–
Coffee, dairy and beef	1	30	4	223
Totals	49	29.3	59	26**
Landless households	32	–	7	–
Landowners not producing coffee, milk or beef for market	3	0.7	1	0.5
Total households	84		67	

Source: data compiled by author during fieldwork interviews.
*This figure is skewed by one landowner with 350 hectares. If we discount him the average figure drops to 14 hectares.
**Again, this result is distorted by two large landowners with more than 200 hectares each, and one owner who has more than 500 hectares.

Table 6: Annual coffee tasks (standard technical package)

Month	Task
February/March	Pruning (*la poda*)
March	Hoeing (*la raspa*)
May	1st application of fertiliser (*abonada*)
End of May	1st spraying (*atomizo*)
May/June	Pruning of shade (*descuaje*)
June	1st weeding (*chapea*)
June/July	1st removal of shoots (*deshija*)
August	2nd application of fertiliser
August	2nd spraying
August	2nd weeding
August	1st application of herbicide
September	2nd removal of shoots
October	3rd spraying
October/November	3rd weeding
November	2nd application of herbicide
December	3rd application of fertiliser
January	3rd removal of shoots
August–February	Harvest (*cosecha*)

Source: data compiled by the author during fieldwork interviews.

Table 7: Labour employed by coffee farmers in Campos de Oro (1997–98)

Labour	Harvesting (*cosecha*)	Remainder of year (*asistencia*)
Peón only	9	9
Family only	8	39
Peón and family	56	25
Total	73	73

Source: data compiled by the author during fieldwork interviews.

Table 8: Production trends in conversion from conventional to organic farming, *fanegas* per hectare

Initial production (*fanegas* per hectare)	Second year's harvest	Third year's harvest	Fourth year's harvest
60	40	45	50
50	35	40	45
40	30	37	42
30	25	28	32
20	20	25	28

Source: compiled from Coopemontes de Oro R.L. *Revista Anual* (1996:21).

Table 9: Production costs and profits: organic and conventional systems of coffee production, 1998

Technology	Yield (*fanega/ hectare*)	Price (*colones/ fanega*)	Total income	Costs (*colones/ fanega*)	Total costs	Net return per hectare	Net return (*colones/ fanega*)
Conventional	60	16,000	960,000	15,000	900,000	60,000	1,000
Organic	40	20,000	800,000	15,000	600,000	200,000	5,000

Source: Coopemontes de Oro R.L. *Revista Anual* (1996:20).
Fanega: 400 litres by volume
Costa Rican *colones*: 1998: 280 *colones* = $1

NOTES

1. See Terry Macalister, 'How Consumer Power Sparked a Revolution on our High Streets', *Guardian*, 8 March 2006, p. 27.
2. Both consumers' and producers' representatives have pointed out to me that these early fair-trade coffees were of extremely poor quality.
3. These NGOs were Oxfam, Traidcraft, Equal Exchange and Twin Trading.
4. A bar chart supplied by Daviron and Ponte (2005:205) shows that the value added in consumer countries has always been more than 50 per cent over the past 35 years, while the proportion of the average retail price paid to growers has hovered around the 20 per cent mark for the same period.
5. Witness, for example, the furore caused in late 2005 by the granting of fair-trade certification to Nescafé for its 'Partners Blend'.
6. We owe it to geographers in the main for pointing out and theorising these spatial aspects of fair trade. In their work they have explored issues around networks, commodity chains and the distribution of value (Bell and Valentine 1997; Daviron and Ponte 2005; Raynolds 2002; Renard 1999; Whatmore and Thorne 1997).
7. Barratt-Brown (1990), Coote (1992) and Grimes (2005) are examples of works that tend to reproduce popular ideas about fair trade promoting unmediated, unproblematic and wholly beneficial links between producers and consumers, constructed as a mirror image of mainstream commercial relations. More measured studies are provided by Auroi (2000), Conroy (2001), Lyon (2006) and Thompson (1999), who focus on fair-trade consumption, organisations, labelling, certification and quality norms as potential avenues for development. Alongside these contributions, Murray, Raynolds and Leigh Taylor (2003), Calo and Wise (2005) and Ronchi (2002) have produced useful case studies of coffee-producer groups. These accounts remain generally optimistic; experiences are seen to vary and certain obstacles and problems are identified, but the consensus is that cooperatives and coffee growers benefit from fair trade. Less optimistic contributions have either argued that the alternative commercial relationship is ineffectual in combating local, regional, national and international power relations, such that certification and participation become a form of governance (Fraser 2003; Mendoza and Bastiaensen 2003; Mutersbaugh 2002), or commentators identify contradictions between the ethical and business components of fair trade (Hughes 2005; Lewis 1998; Luetchford 2006; Renard 1999, 2003; Tallontire 2000). Probably the most comprehensive recent work on coffee that engages with the fair-trade phenomena to date is Daviron and Ponte's (2005) examination of the 'paradox' of the present crisis in production, combined with the renaissance in

consumption of speciality coffees sold at premium prices in coffee bars (Roseberry 1996). To account for the injustice of the higher value currently attached to coffee as a consumer item, corresponding with a squeeze on producers, the authors focus on how value is distributed down the chain, and on forms of governance that operate in the industry. To capture the ability of certain groups, particularly retailers, to appropriate the value generated by the chain and the constraints placed upon producers, Daviron and Ponte use the term 'upgrading'. While they remain sceptical about the transformative potential of organic coffees, they are more optimistic about the scope for producers to upgrade through fair trade.

8. We can usefully consider these diverse readings of fair trade in the light of recent commentaries on approaches to development (Lewis and Mosse 2006a; de Sardan 2005). The first type of engagement is ideologically driven and populist in intent. Whereas in development this takes the form of 'the unqualified valuation of indigenous knowledge and community tradition' (Lewis and Mosse 2006:3), in fair trade we might recognise ideological populism in the unproblematic valuation of production-consumption links. The second approach is critical and deconstructive. Because it analyses development as discourse, a totalising system circumscribed by power, it leaves little room for description of the strategies of different actors in the development process. Against ideological populism and deconstructivism is the approach termed methodological populism – 'taking a local point of view to discover the rationale of actions' (Lewis and Mosse 2006a:3). The advantage of methodological populism in understanding fair trade is that it recognises that different people are involved, and they have a range of commitments, motivations and agendas.

9. To give just one example of this tendency to homogenise producers, see Murray, Raynolds and Leigh Taylor (2003:3), who, following the work of Gresser and Tickle for Oxfam (2002:7), point out that '[s]eventy percent of the world's coffee is grown on farms of less than 25 acres, with the vast majority of these ranging between 2.5 and 12.5 acres'. Despite this huge range of landholdings and incomes that could be generated, this is then given as evidence of coffee production coinciding with a map of extreme poverty. While there is undoubted poverty in the coffee industry, it is unlikely to be felt by farmers with 25 acres, or 12.5 acres for that matter.

10. Convention theory should not be confused with the conventionalisation debate. Convention theory borrows from the work of Thévenot, and is an attempt to categorise norms (see Daviron and Ponte 2005:32–35; Murdoch and Miele 2004:108). The conventionalisation debate concerns itself with the tendency for capitalism to appropriate, industrialise and so conventionalise alternative forms of production and distribution (Guthman 2004b).

11. This is what Scott (1985) identifies as a process of 'euphemisation' – the process by which power relations between classes are represented as moral and social relationships.

12. On the history of Costa Rica, with specific reference to coffee see Cardoso 1977; Gudmundson 1995; Hall 1991; Pérez Brignoli 1994; Peters 1994; Peters and Samper 2001; Seligson 1980; Winson 1989.

For useful material that also adopts a more comparative perspective in the broader context of Latin America, see Paige 1997; Pérez Brignoli and Samper 1994; Roseberry, Gudmundson and Samper Kutschbach 1995; Williams R.G. 1994.

13. See for example the report by John Hale, who visited the country in 1825 (cited in Cardoso 1977:168).

14. Opinion is divided as to the date of the introduction of coffee in Costa Rica, although it probably entered the country at the turn of the nineteenth century, it remained for some years little more than a botanical curiosity (Cardoso 1977:168; Hall 1991:33–34).

15. See Deere (1990) for a summary of debates on the 'depeasantisation' thesis.

16. The closest English translation of *campesino* is 'peasant', although *campesinos* are generally thought of as rural people who work the land, and are not necessarily landowners.

17. Samper, in his study of the settlement of the northwestern edge of the *Meseta Central*, acknowledges this outwards migration from his own area of study into the Tilarán region (1990:117, 229).

18. Paige (1997), Williams, R.G. (1994) and Winson (1989) provide excellent accounts of the political and social history of Costa Rica with respect to coffee, while Williams, P. (1989) focuses upon the role of the church.

19. Good accounts of labour struggles by workers, and the political manoeuvring and intrigue of North American banana companies, most notably United Fruit, can be found in Moberg and Striffler (2003).

20. The key encyclicals are the *Rerum Novarum* of Pope Leo XIII (1891) and the *Quadragesimo Anno* by Pope Pius XI (1931). This was later followed by *Mater et Magistra* by Pope John XXIII (1961).

21. In Spanish the word *junta* does not generally have the negative connotations associated with it in English.

22. Figueres himself was head of state in 1948–49, 1953–1958 and 1974–1978 (Williams R.G. 1994:218).

23. These measures were introduced after a 10 per cent wealth tax failed to raise sufficient revenue.

24. For example, law 6437 makes the teaching of *cooperativismo* compulsory in all centres of education in the country.

25. In fact cooperatives often struggle to match prices offered by private companies. This can be because of factors such as the quality of the cherries they receive, inefficient machinery or marketing problems (see below).

26. See *Alianza Cooperativa Internacional* 1993; Edelman 1983, 1999; Masís 1989; Nelson 1989, 1990; Rosene 1990; Villasuso 1987; Zimbalist 1988.

27. Total production from 10 hectares should yield in excess of 200 *fanegas* (1 *fanega* = 400 litres by volume of unprocessed cherries); data from Coocafé shows that only about 10 per cent of cooperative members produce this amount (Table 1, p. 187), and the average production for all *asociados* is only about 23 *fanegas* per year, or one tenth of the quantity required to support a family. It should not be forgotten that the data hides anomalies, in particular that some producers are large landowners but grow only small quantities of coffee as one of their production strategies, and coffee is seldom the sole source of income.

Nevertheless, it is true that in the national context Coocafé is composed of marginal cooperatives, and members are small coffee producers.

28. 'Arabica coffee (the only type known until the end of the nineteenth century) grows best between 3,000 and 6,000 feet in areas with a mean annual temperature around 70°F., never straying below freezing, never going much above 80F. The high-grown coffee bean, developing slowly, is generally more dense and flavourful than lower growths' (Pendergrast 1999:26). The closer to the ideal conditions, the better the quality and the higher the price and demand that can be commanded.

29. In 1998, 280 *colones* were worth one dollar, by 2003 the exchange rate was 350 *colones* to the dollar.

30. Coocafé; *Asamblea General de Delegados* No. 11, December 1998.

31. References taken from *Coocafé Memoria, 1988–1999*, published by Coocafé to celebrate its 10th anniversary.

32. Translation from the words of the then manager of Coocafé, Sr. Francisco Zamora, reproduced on the occasion of the 10th anniversary of the organisation in *Coocafé Memoria 1988–1998*.

33. A cooperative supporter, or one who displays and supports cooperative values.

34. 'Cherry' refers to the coffee bean still in its fruit casing; it is a literal translation from Spanish for coffee *en cereza*. After the fruit has been removed, the coffee is known as 'green' or, rather more evocatively in Spanish, 'gold' (*café oro*).

35. Information on the origin of fair trade in Costa Rica comes from interviews with the manager of Coopecerroazul, Sr. William Zuñiga, as well as the collection of documents put together by that organisation: *Informe Sobre Relación S.O.S. y el Mercado Alternativo. Coopecerroazul, 1982–1990.*

36. Small amounts also go to an educational foundation (Hijos del Campo) and a campaign group.

37. Source: Coopeldos, Memoria Anual 2002, Asamblea Ordinaria No. 44, and Coopeldos Memoria Annual 2003, Asamblea Ordinaria No. 45.

38. During my original fieldwork in 1998–99 fair-trade markets were always referred to as an 'alternative market'. When I returned to the field in 2003 prices were disastrously low and, intriguingly, managers were readily referring to 'fair trade' (*comercio justo*).

39. In keeping with my discussions with informants, the data focus on connections with Europe; although expanding rapidly, North American alternative-trade markets were smaller at the time of fieldwork and were not mentioned in criticisms of the system.

40. Such exchanges are in any case ongoing, and are part of the regional forums, delegations and fact-finding missions in which the cooperatives engage.

41. Source: Coopeldos, Memoria Anual 2002, Asamblea Ordinaria No. 44, 1 March 2003.

42. This is contrary to influential strains in social thought, which claim that the growth and expansion of technical reason erodes human freedom. However, it is in tune with the aims and spirit of the Enlightenment: '[t]he idea was to use the accumulation of knowledge generated by many individuals working freely and creatively for the pursuit of human emancipation and the enrichment of daily life' (Harvey 1989:12). By

positing a radical disjuncture with tradition and putting progress in its place, the modernisers gathering under the Coocafé umbrella reflect a particular vision for the future. This is the optimism of the modern, 'a secular movement that sought the demystification and desacrilisation of knowledge and social organisation in order to liberate human beings from their chains' (Harvey 1989:13).

43. A good account of the wet and dry methods, and the differences between them, is given by Roseberry (1995:3).

44. One *fanega* is 400 litres by volume unprocessed coffee (*en cereza*). This is the measure used at the processing plant.

45. This certainly holds true up until the late 1990s. By 2003 the cooperative had begun to develop tourism by organising coffee tours.

46. The *cajuela* is the standard measure used during coffee harvesting, equivalent to 20 litres by volume (20 *cajuelas* therefore equals one *fanega*).

47. Coffee has now been superseded by tourism and information technology as principal industries.

48. Acuña Ortega tells us that taking 1924 as an index of 100, prices reached 150 points in 1928, descended to 102 in 1930, fell to 67 points in 1932, and reached a nadir of 61 in 1936 (1985:189–190).

49. For a detailed history of these events see Acuña Ortega (1985:190–192).

50. Although minimum prices were on the agenda, Winson gives no indication as to whether they were implemented (1989:48, note 14).

51. The main source for this section on the 1950s, up to 1961 and the introduction of law 2762, is González Ortega (1987), with some material drawn from Paige (1997) and Winson (1989).

52. The tax was initially set at 4 per cent, but according to the proposal would later be reduced to 2 per cent.

53. Optimistic and partisan reports at the time claimed up to 40,000 protestors attended the mobilisation. Winson himself suggests 'several thousands' (1989:80–81).

54. Peters and Samper (2001:128) document the decline in the number of *beneficios* in Costa Rica; there were more than 200 at the beginning of the twentieth century, 150 in the 1940s, 124 in the 1950s, just over 100 in the 1980s, and under 100 today. This trend is also noted by Paige (1997:79).

55. According to evidence presented to Congress, the cost of processing was 8 *colones* per fanega, while processors were charging 15 *colones* (González Ortega 1987:180).

56. González identifies this as a shift in the dominant discourse, away from a moral code towards a technical-rational one.

57. *Cooperativista* has no real equivalent in English; it roughly translates as someone who adheres to and demonstrates cooperative values.

58. For reasons of confidentiality I have not revealed the identity of critics of the cooperative and its policies. Despite this precaution criticism is often openly voiced, and was more than once forcefully expressed at public meetings I attended. Juan Carlos, the manager, is well aware that the organisation has its critics, but professes not to understand the basis of the complaints.

59. For example, in 2003, Nicaraguan coffee workers organised a 'hunger march' on Managua to publicise their plight, an event that tragically lived up to its name as deaths from starvation occurred en route.

60. In one tradition in economic anthropology farming was understood through the lens of rational decision-making. The point that rural producers make choices and decisions as they proceed in agriculture, but within certain parameters, conceptualised as risks or uncertainties, was central to influential work by authors such as Cancian (1972), Ortiz (1967, 1973) and, for Costa Rica, Barlett (1977, 1982). Bourdieu's (1977) concept of 'practice' arguably better captures the complex interplay between agency and structure, freedom and constraint in social life. In any case, both approaches focus attention on strategies in uncertain conditions. More recently, the observation that human activity itself creates uncertainty has inspired the literature on 'reflexive risk', most usually associated with Beck (1992).

61. Primarily the bulletin produced by Coopeldos four times a year, and the document published to accompany the annual assembly.

62. To this extent the kinship system conforms to the 'closed corporate peasant communities' classically documented by Wolf (1957).

63. Cooperative records show that in 1999 approximately 20 per cent of members were women. Yet during more than a year in El Dos I met only one woman who claimed to work in commercial agriculture and never came across women working in the fields, unless they were picking coffee. I therefore disagree with Ronchi who claims that in half of all households women and men share agricultural tasks (2002:21). Women are either members of the cooperative because they own a *cafetal*, in which case a male relation or paid male labourers work the land or, more commonly, they join to allow their husbands to disassociate themselves, and hence withdraw the social capital they have built up in the organisation.

64. During fieldwork I attempted to quantify inputs and calculate profits from agriculture. Data were produced with the help of half a dozen informants, considered specialists in the various activities, yet farmers were not convinced of the benefits of the exercise. Some appeared distracted and provided vague answers to my questions, although I knew them well and had had fruitful discussions with them on other topics. Others professed curiosity in the results obtained, but always qualified the figures, insisting 'it is very variable'. Eventually, I understood that a desire to quantify was my own preoccupation and that for farmers each piece of land has its own particular requirements, every agricultural year is different, and each producer has their own preference when it comes to working practices. Particular activities may have certain characteristics and make specific demands, but the huge range of approaches and possible outcomes mean that farmers do not consider rational calculation and formal accounting procedures applicable to agriculture. Rather it requires experimentation and depends on chance. Nevertheless, through these discussions I gained more general information on farming systems, an insight into how farmers approach agriculture, and an appreciation of the endless array of practices and possible outcomes.

65. The milk producer must pay nearly $1,000 for each 60-litre churn registered with the factory.

66. The *manzana* is the most common way to measure land area; it is 7,000 square metres, or 0.7 hectares.

67. Pete Stewart, personal communication. For a discussion of coffee markets and their history see Daviron and Ponte (2005:70–73).

68. Pelupessy, for example, states that a coffee plantation takes between six and eight years to produce a maximum crop, and that as a result 'the capacity to respond to demand is much less in the short, than in the long term' (1993:25, my translation). Roseberry, in his discussion of different production systems in a different epoch, gives a slightly lower figure of five years (1995:11–12).

69. Coopeldos was paying 10,000 *colones* per *fanega*, from which 4 per cent is subtracted as social capital, giving a final figure of 9,600 *colones*. By contrast Turín was offering 15,000 *colones*.

70. Describing *tanteando los precios* as an act of resistance borrows from James Scott's work (1985) on everyday forms of resistance, associated with foot-dragging, sabotage and the like. The above case, characterised by the producers themselves as a protest against cooperative policy, points to an intermediate situation. It is neither a subtle form of sabotage, nor outright revolution (Fox and Starn 1997; Turton 1986). The protest against payment of the 4 per cent social capital by a minority of producers demonstrates that resistance need not always be directed solely against the state, but can also engage with and contest dominant modes for development at a local level. As Pelzer White (1986:60) has demonstrated, acts of resistance involve different 'levels': the state and the local elite, on the one hand, and peasant households and individuals within households, on the other. Each of these may have different capacities to influence proceedings, and propensities to resist or comply with dominant orders and representations; what is more, the desire to resist and contest, and the justification for such acts, will not be agreed upon by different parties in ostensibly the same position with respect to the cooperative. Many producers regard selling to the competition under the guise of protest against cooperative policy as little more than thinly veiled self-interest. Maintaining a distinction between what counts as resistance and what is self-interest is problematic. Part of the appeal of the concept of resistance may be its ability to combine notions of Marxist class struggle with the rational choice approach of neoclassical economics (Pelzer White 1986:49).

71. By one estimate coffee production requires 130 days' labour per hectare per year, while cattle require only six (Evans 1999:47).

72. The notable exception is Ortiz (1999). Many of the arguments central to this chapter, such as attitudes to migrants, surveillance and quality control, and power differentials in bargaining over wages and conditions, are to be found in her detailed work on rural labour markets and the coffee industry in Colombia.

73. The peaking of the harvest in different areas at different times around Coopeldos was initially explained by growers, but was later checked against Cooperative records of coffee received from different areas over the season. (See 'Coopeldos R.L. Departamento de Contabilidad.

Sistema de Control de Recibo de Café; medidas y remedidas por fecha, 1999').

74. The harvest pattern is revealed by the cooperative's records for coffee delivered to reception points (*recibidores*) in each zone of production (*Sistema de control de recibo de café, medidas y remedidas por fecha, Departamento de Contabilidad, Coopeldos R.L*).

75. Estimates of the number of Nicaraguans in Costa Rica vary, but most put the number at around 500,000, about half of whom are classified as illegal (see *Tico Times*, 9 October 1998, p. 4).

76. This figure will include some members who no longer produce coffee, and, more importantly, families with more than one member inscribed in the cooperative.

77. The term *nica* is not necessarily pejorative; it may be compared to the equivalent term *tico*, which Costa Ricans use as a form of self-identification. The name *paisa*, which is also used with reference to Nicaraguans, has more negative connotations.

78. A useful review of the literature on sharecropping can be found in an edition dedicated to the subject by the *Journal of Peasant Studies*, vol. 10, nos 2 and 3 (1983). Whereas earlier analyses focused upon the efficiency or otherwise of sharecropping arrangements, more recent attention has fallen upon sharecropping as an exercise in power, particularly the extraction of labour and the appropriation of surplus (Martinez-Alier 1983; Pearse 1983). In the case of the *mezzadria* in Tuscany, for example, sharecropping allowed the continued exploitation of impoverished rural peasants by absentee urban landlords, until the system was effectively challenged by political agitation and the affiliation of sharecroppers to the Communist party (Pratt 1994). Conversely, Martinez-Alier (1971) shows how landlords in Southern Spain resisted sharecropping on social rather than economic grounds, since they feared it would provide the tenant with leverage in demands to redistribute land. The situation in El Dos is different yet again, not least because it involves neighbours and near neighbours rather than absentee landlords, and although the contributions of each participant are ostensibly fixed, the evidence shows that this is open to negotiation, a point that is appreciated by Stolcke. 'The crucial point of contention between labour and capital in sharecropping is the setting of the "share" level, which depends on the bargaining power of both parties. Interests are opposed. When profits are low landowners prefer sharecropping to labour earning a fixed wage, whereas the workers prefer the latter, and vice-versa' (1995:79). The inference from the cases above, and Stolcke's more general point, is that sharecropping, the way it is viewed and its operation on the ground are embedded in social relationships and power relations.

79. The element of constraint, at the expense of formal freedom, which may be seen as an unintended consequence, is one legacy of Marx's thought. As Giddens explains: '[t]he escape of human history from human intentions, and the return of the consequences as causal influences on human action, is a chronic feature of social life' (Giddens 1979:7). This can be seen as a problem of risk and danger, since the unintended consequences, here taken as extreme fluctuations in labour requirements, fall squarely upon the shoulders of the landless and

migrant labourers; as Beck points out, 'poverty attracts an unfortunate abundance of risks' (1992:35).

80. The separation between goal-oriented, maximising strategies and social and cultural ideas on the economy corresponds to the controversy between the formalists and substantivists in economic anthropology, originally sparked by Karl Polanyi (1957). It is now commonly accepted, at least in anthropology, that people are self-interested maximisers, but that their actions are also influenced by moral, social and cultural commitments. For a balanced recent summary of the extended arguments see Wilk (1996).

81. Farmers ensure that weeds are kept down or removed with herbicide, for more efficient gathering, or *juntando*, of the coffee from the floor of the *cafetal*.

82. Heavy rain is also said to 'burn' plants, so perhaps a better translation here of the Spanish word *quemar* would be 'raze'.

83. This section is influenced by the ideas of Beck (1992, 1994) and Giddens (1990), who have coined the term 'reflexive modernisation' to indicate the unintended consequences of modernity. Hence Beck famously argues that in applying solutions by attempting to control risks and subdue dangers, new hazards are reflexively produced: 'the more we try to colonise the future, the more it is likely to spring surprises on us' (Beck 1998:12). Farmers, too, are aware of such reflexively produced risks, which emerge in the wake of the modern techniques they apply to crop production.

84. Carlos estimated the cost of a barrel of his mixture at 300 *colones*, compared to the cost of 12,000 *colones* for the commercial brand (Artemí).

85. An epidemiological study showed 429 deaths and 3,330 people hospitalised between 1980 and 1986 in Costa Rica as a result of intoxication by agrochemicals. Imports of pesticides, meanwhile, have grown at an alarming rate. Some studies cite an increase in this respect of 1,000 per cent between 1991 and 1996 (*El Día*, 18 November 1998).

86. My translation from the original funding proposal submitted by Coopeldos.

87. Mutersbaugh (2002) records a similar violent reaction to organic coffee, with particular reference to the demands of certification, in Mexico.

88. From this it might be possible to argue from a 'green perspective' that higher prices for smaller volumes could counteract the market instability caused by world overproduction, and still provide sustainable livelihoods. Rice (1997:256), for example, presents this kind of argument. This vision is undone, however, by the limited size of the organic coffee market; by 2003 the cooperative manager was predicting a fall in organic coffee prices as more farmers accessed the niche market, and supply came to match demand.

89. To comply with technical recommendations coffee trees should be pruned hard every five or six years.

90. Similar observations are made by Redfield and Villa Rojas (1964:207).

91. This tradition of liberal and possessive individualism can be traced back to the philosophies of John Locke, who argued that people have a right to appropriate property as the means to self-preservation (Tully

1993:27). For Locke this is the origin of both society and state: '[t]he great and chief end of men uniting into commonwealths and putting themselves under government is the preservation of their property' (Locke, *Two Treatises of Government*, cited in Tawney 1938 [1926]:20).

92. Ironically, a similar, though secular model appears in the Marxist tradition of the 'domestic community' (Meillassoux 1981:3; Taussig 1982). By practising self-sustaining agriculture, with individuals linked by unequal ties of personal dependence, and producing and consuming together on common land, this domestic community aims to reproduce itself both socially and physically. In this way the domestic space is separated from capitalist rationality and profit accumulation, although through reproductive activities it produces, sustains and subsidises underpaid waged workers.

93. The moral commitment to household self-sufficiency as the basis of a critique capitalism is highlighted by Gudeman (1986), Parry (1989) and Taussig (1980).

94. Gudeman and Rivera describe the house and the corporate model as exclusive, and in opposition to one another. This allows a clear description of each model, but the polarised opposition contradicts the data presented here. Pratt (1994) provides a useful discussion on this theme.

95. We owe to Marshall Sahlins's work 'On the Sociology of Primitive Exchange' (Sahlins 1974) the more systematic analysis of reciprocal relations, and the distinction between redistribution or pooling *within* groups, and types of reciprocity (general, balanced or negative) *between* groups. However, he himself sees these as generalisations, and 'a plea to ethnography', since in any context, as here, people will practise a combination of these forms of reciprocity and pooling. In this book I focus on 'the gift' since it speaks more to the issue of fair trade, and because of the influence of the work of David Graeber.

96. There are also some written accounts, such as those in *Agricultura & Ganadería*, No. 6, 1996:27, a special edition published to commemorate the 25th anniversary of Coopeldos.

97. In the feminist interpretation this wilderness, being pure nature, is associated with the feminine and is subject to the domination of (masculine) culture (Barnes 1973; Ortner 1974; MacCormack and Strathern 1980). In the yet more radical critique of the 'rape script', the virgin territory is rendered an empty 'female' space waiting to be lent form, which it gains by acts of penetration and colonisation (Gibson-Graham 1996).

98. Of the several species of big cat, none remain in the El Dos area, the tapirs have retreated into deeper forest and only one of the three species of monkey is now common. One can still find sloths, armadillos, the pig-like *tepesquintle*, which are also prized for their meat, and coyote, but all are relatively uncommon. Bird life remains prolific, and includes toucans and hummingbirds as well as less colourful species. The scarlet macaw, which was prized as a food, has now disappeared, and residents recalled other notable and possibly undocumented species that are no longer seen. A wide range of reptiles, particularly snakes, were spoken about, and insect life is almost incomprehensibly diverse for visitors from Northern regions.

99. This discussion is heavily indebted to the lead set by the exemplary work of Gudeman and Rivera (1990).
100. There are clear parallels between the formulation of nature as a life-giving force, and of humans taking up an ordained place in a providential divine order, and ideas associated with 'pre-modern' cosmology (Macnaghten and Urry 1998:9–11).
101. Gudeman also notes different bases for claiming rights to land, primarily through work and by surveying (1978:27).
102. This text by Hernán Elizondo Arce was taken from a calendar published by a financial cooperative, and prominently displayed throughout the town of Tilarán.
103. Reference to work is reproduced in national discourse: Costa Ricans, it is said, are a nation of 'workers' (*trabajadores*) or 'labourers' (*labriegos*) (Rodriguez 1993).
104. In this sense *la lucha* can be said to be part of the dominant ideology identified by Marx in 'The German Ideology' (Marx 2000:192), later developed by Gramsci through the concept of hegemony, and since then much commented upon and discussed in social science. For useful discussions on ideology and hegemony see Abercrombie, Hill and Turner (1980); Asad (1979); Scott (1985); Walsh (1993).
105. Gudeman, in his study of Los Boquerones, Panama, records the evocative proverb that captures this gendered division of labour: 'the man is in the fields, the woman is at home' (1978:35), and a similar division is noted by Tucker in Victorian England (1998:185). The active and sometimes dominant part played by women in Costa Rican political life seems to be a middle class, and certainly urban, phenomenon (Palmer and Rojas 1998).
106. Of the 100-plus families I visited, only in two did women claim to work their coffee themselves, and both admitted using male labour for heavy tasks.
107. Strathern (1992) sees the creation of diversity, after individualism, as a core principle of English kinship.
108. There is a correspondence here with the mechanical form of solidarity outlined by Durkheim in *The Division of Labour in Society* (1984 [1893]), in which social reproduction and collective consciousness is based upon a succession of structurally similar yet independent units. In Durkheim's work this form makes sense as a contrast, and in the transition to organic solidarity, characterised by economic interdependence between specialists.
109. Edelman (1999:124) tells us that the 'culture of maize' is more developed in Guanacaste than any other province of Costa Rica, and that the culture of Guanacaste, at least in Nicoya where he worked, has more in common with more northerly regions of Mesoamerica.
110. Annis highlights the symbolic aspect of maize production and points to what he terms '*milpa* logic'. In Guatemala the *milpa* embodies the culture and ideology of the Indians of the highlands (1987:39). Annis suggests '*milpa* logic' is 'Catholic' and Protestantism is symptomatic of 'anti-*milpa* forces', and he provides compelling evidence for a Weberian Protestant work ethic. However, in El Dos, which is almost equally divided between Catholicism and evangelical Protestantism, neither group was exclusively associated with the *milpa*.

111. A similar theme is developed by Yapa, who argues that development causes 'socially constructed scarcity' (1996:69).

112. Values that were also central to the classical Greek household, or *oikos*. See Booth (1993).

113. Redfield and Villa Rojas also document the values of independence and self-sufficiency in the founding of Chan Kom, Mexico (1964:213).

114. This definition follows the lead of Cohen and Arato (1992), and their tripartite scheme of state, market and civil society (see Anderson 1996:112).

115. Láscaris (2004 [1994]) documents the importance of the local store in Costa Rican social life generally, and, of especial importance here, he documents the opening up of the forests by yeoman-style farmers, and the role of the *pulpería* in providing a service, a forum and a meeting point for isolated homesteaders (2004:193).

116. A cautiously optimistic assessment of the effects of neoliberal reforms, at least in comparison to other parts of Latin America, is given by Mesa Lago (2000).

117. At the time of writing, the ex-president, Miguel-Angel Rodriguez, who was in office during fieldwork, is under investigation for corruption.

118. The word *pueblo* has no direct correspondence in English. It can refer to a group of people with shared characteristics, a village or a town. I have tried to avoid using the term 'community' because of the consensus it often implies, and because of its association with the 'communitarian thesis' (Etzioni 1993). I use it here since it best captures the intended spirit of the message.

119. In this respect they have much in common with Scott's informants in Sedaka, including furtive and overt acts of resistance – for example, as we saw in Chapter 4, in shifting allegiance and manipulating the labour shortage in the coffee season to some advantage (Scott 1985).

120. See Gudeman (1978:40) for a similar discussion on the opposition between 'luxury' and 'vice', on the one hand, and 'necessities', on the other.

121. Although anthropologists have noted an ambivalent attitude to wealth in many societies and traditions, including Muslim and Christian, attitudes to wealth are best seen as specific to cultural context, rather than universal (Parry and Bloch 1989).

122. Movements against consumerism in Latin America have also taken a more overtly politicised form. For example, see Richard Wilson's (1995) account of the Qawa Quk'a movement in Guatemala.

123. In a similar vein see Maurice Bloch's (1989) account of the disquiet he felt on being given a cash gift on his departure from the field, a situation he uses to explore the variation in cultural meaning attached to money.

124. Similar attitudes and ideas among peasants are discussed by Foster (1965) and his 'image of the limited good', and by James Scott in *The Moral Economy of the Peasant* (1976).

125. Even if we accept the postmodern deconstruction of universals, whereby 'justice is consigned to the grand narrative in the same way as truth' (Lyotard 1984:xxiv), we can still document discourses and political struggles that pursue a concept of justice 'on the ground' (Wilson 1997).

126. The contestation of the value of different occupations is a recurring theme in the literature; see, for example Young and Wilmott's observations on working-class evaluations of business managers in East London (1962:9), E.P. Thompson's analysis of the moral precepts informing class consciousness (1980:848–849, 856) and Pratt's (1994:116) discussion on the shifts in meaning in the concept of *lavoro*.

127. A classic case of circuits, or spheres, of exchange is the Tiv, discussed by Bohannan and Bohannan (1968).

128. A similar view of nature might be said to inform the delight taken in the West in picking berries, the tolerance of scrumping apples from orchards, and the often romantic figure of the poacher, who challenges the exclusive rights to what nature 'automatically' produces, as claimed by the landowner.

129. There are a number of case studies from Africa, Asia and Latin America that show how fair trade is incorporated into local power relations and the strategies of different actors. See for example Fraser (2003); Lewis (1998); Luetchford (2006); Renard (1999, 2003); Tallontire (2000).

130. As we shall see, Marcel Mauss was particularly driven by the search for a common basis for human moral commitments. For the specific case of Islamic economic morality see Kahn (1997).

131. In philosophy these two positions are defended by libertarians such as Robert Nozick (1974) and liberals, most notably John Rawls (1971), respectively. Libertarianism promotes the standard of individual rights, chiefly the freedom to exercise one's capabilities, and the entitlement to the minimum protection of the state to secure that right. Liberals, on the other hand, worry that where the aim is to protect choice and ensure efficiency, contingent factors (such as inherited wealth, natural talents and good fortune) determine life chances, and such contingency is no basis for a just society. For Rawls, 'the basic structure of societies incorporates the arbitrariness found in nature. But there is no necessity for men to resign themselves to these contingencies. The social system is not an unchangeable order beyond human control but a pattern of human action' (1971:102). Ethics in this branch of liberal philosophy then becomes a search for maxims that all rational people will agree to and which establish palliative measures to counteract contingency.

132. In the agro-food literature the importance of place is commonly discussed under the French term *terroir* (see for example Barham 2003).

133. For a discussion of the place of the labour theory of value in Smith, Ricardo and Marx, particularly in relation to surplus, see Bradley and Howard (1982).

134. Marx realised that 'man…can work only as Nature does, that is by changing the form of matter and in changing this form he is constantly helped by natural forces' (2000:464; see Ingold (1992) for a parallel argument).

135. This outline of capitalist commodity production follows Fine (1975).

136. In addition to the original text, see D. Miller (1987, especially chapter 3) for a fuller exposition of Marx's ideas on alienation.

137. Derrida points out that the ideology of the gift, given without interest or expectation of return, constitutes a paradox for the economy, based as it is upon exchange, and hence circulation. Derrida characterises the

gift as 'the impossible'; it attempts to break the circle and deny the idea of return, which is the essence of the 'law' of economy (1992:6–7; see also Graeber 2001:161 for commentary).

138. For extended discussion of this point see Graeber (2001:30–33).

139. Gudeman has recently suggested that reciprocity is a means to explore, expand and presumably define the boundaries of community (2001:80), an idea that resonates with the fair-trade notion of extending trade relations based on social concern for Southern producers.

140. Bourdieu describes as the 'two antagonistic principles of gift exchange: the gift as experienced, or, at least, meant to be experienced, and the gift as seen from the outside' (1977:5). Whereas we may think the gift is freely given, objectivism shows us that reciprocal laws are based upon obligations to give, to receive and to return the gift, albeit in a different guise.

141. The voluntary nature of participation in fair-trade consumption is made explicit in a recent poster campaign, with the headline: 'Trust your Taste: Choose Fair Trade'.

142. These themes are also explored by Georges Bataille (1989 [1967]); for commentary see Luetchford (2005) and Yang (2000).

143. My evidence for this is largely circumstantial, based upon observation and informal discussions with middle-class shoppers.

144. Linking consumption to distinction is, of course, the approach developed by Bourdieu (1984), whose work in turn reflected Veblen's *Theory of the Leisure Class* (1994 [1899]).

145. The Fair Trade Foundation website lists the following products: fresh fruit, cocoa and chocolate, coffee, cotton, sugar and sweets, tea, honey, nuts and snacks, fruit juice and yoghurt, and preserves. Figures show that of the £195 million worth of fair-trade products sold in 2005, over £150 million was accounted for by four products (coffee, bananas, chocolate and tea).

146. For further commentary on the fetishisation of use-value in Marx see the extract from 'For a Political Economy of the Sign' in Mark Poster (ed.) *Jean Baudrillard: Selected Writings* (1988:64–75).

147. In 2005, sales are reported to have increased in the UK by 40 per cent (Terry Macalister, 'How Consumer Power Sparked a Fairtrade Revolution on our High Streets', *Guardian*, 8 March 2006).

148. www.fairtrade.org.uk/suppliers_growers_coffee_guillermo.htm

BIBLIOGRAPHY

Abercrombie, N., Hill, S. and Turner, B. (1980) *The Dominant Ideology Thesis* (Allen and Unwin: London).

Acuña Ortega, V.H. (1985) 'Clases Sociales y Conflicto Social en la Economía Cafetelera Costarricense: Productores contra Beneficiadores 1921–1936', *Revista de Historia*, Numero Especial: Historia, Problemas y Perspectivas Agrarias en Costa Rica. 1985:181–206 (EUNA: Heredia, Costa Rica).

—— (1987) 'La Ideología de los Pequeños y Medianos Productores Cafateleros Costarricenses, 1900–1961', *Revista de Historia*, 16:137–159.

Agricultura y Ganaderia (1996) No. 6 (commemorative edition, published to celebrate the 25th anniversary of Coopeldos).

Alianza Cooperativa Internacional (1993) *El Estado de las Cooperativas en Costa Rica* (San José, Costa Rica).

Anderson, D. (1996) 'Bringing Civil Society to an Uncivilised Place: Citizenship Regimes in Russia's Arctic Frontier', in C. Hann and E. Dunn (eds) *Civil Society: Challenging Western Models* (Routledge: London and New York).

Annis, S. (1987) *God and Production in a Guatemalan Town* (University of Texas Press: Austin).

Apffel Marglin, F. and Marglin, S. (1990) *Dominating Knowledge: Development, Culture and Resistance* (Clarendon Press: Oxford).

Appadurai, A. (1986) 'Introduction: Commodities and the Politics of Value', in A. Appadurai (ed.) *The Social Life of Things: Commodities in Cultural Perspective* (Cambridge University Press).

—— (1990) 'Disjuncture and Difference in the Global Cultural Economy', *Theory, Culture and Society* 7:295–310.

Aristotle (1962) *The Politics* (Penguin Books: London).

Arrivillaga, J. (1997) 'Sustainable Coffee Production: Guatemala's Approach and Beyond', in R. Rice, A.M. Harris and J. McLean (eds) *Proceedings of the First Sustainable Coffee Conference* (Smithsonian Migratory Bird Center: Washington DC).

Arthur, C. (1986) *The Dialectics of Labour: Marx and His Relation to Hegel* (Blackwell: Oxford).

Asad, T. (1979) 'Anthropology and the Analysis of Ideology', *Man* 14:607–627.

Auroi, C. (2000) 'Le Commerce "Équitable", un Créneau Potentiel pour les Petits Producteurs des Pas en Voie de Développement', *Économies et Sociétés*, série 'Systemes Agrolimentaires', *AG* No. 24:199–211.

Barahona Jiménez, L. (1975) *El Gran Incógnito* (Editorial Costa Rica: San José).

Barham, E. (2003) 'Translating "Terroir": The Global Challenge of French AOC Labelling', *Journal of Rural Studies* 19:127–138.

Barlett, P. (1977) 'The Structure of Decision Making in Paso', *American Anthropologist* Vol. 4, No. 2:285–307.

—— (1982) *Agricultural Choice and Change: Decision-making in a Costa Rican Community* (Rutgers University Press: New Brunswick).

Barnes, J. (1973) 'Genetrix: Genitor :: Nature: Culture', in J. Goody (ed) *The Character of Kinship* (Cambridge University Press).

Barratt-Brown, M. (1990) *Fair Trade: Reform and Realities in the International Trading System* (Zed Books: London and New Jersey).

Barth, F. (1997) 'Economy, Agency and Ordinary Lives', *Social Anthropology* (Journal of the European Association of Social Anthropologists) Vol. 5, No. 3:233–242.

Bataille, G. (1989 [1967]) *The Accursed Share: Volume I* (Zone Books: New York).

Baudrillard, J. (1975) *The Mirror of Production* (Telos Press: St Louis).

—— (1981) *For a Critique of the Political Economy of the Sign* (Telos Press: St Louis).

Beck, U. (1992) *Risk Society* (Sage Publications: London, Thousand Oaks, New Delhi).

—— (1994) 'The Reinvention of Politics: Towards a Theory of Reflexive Modernisation', in *Reflexive Modernisation: Politics, Tradition and Aesthetics in the Modern Social Order* (Polity Press: Cambridge).

—— (1998) 'The Politics of Risk Society', in J. Franklin (ed.) *The Politics of Risk Society* (Polity Press: Cambridge).

Bell, D. and Valentine, G. (1997) *Consuming Geographies: We Are Where We Eat* (Routledge: London and New York).

Berger, J. (1979) *Pig Earth* (Bloomsbury: London).

Bernstein, H. and Campling, L. (2006) 'Commodity Studies and Commodity Fetishism II: 'Profits with Principles', unpublished ms, School of Oriental and African Studies, University of London.

Bhabha, H. (1994) *The Location of Culture* (Routledge: New York).

Bloch, M. (1989) 'The Symbolism of Money in Imerina', in J. Parry and M. Bloch (eds) *Money and the Morality of Exchange* (Cambridge University Press).

Bloch, M. and J. Parry (1989), 'Introduction: Money and the Morality of Exchange', in J. Parry and M. Bloch (eds) *Money and the Morality of Exchange* (Cambridge University Press).

Bohannan, P. and Bohannan, L. (1968) *Tiv Economy* (Northwestern University Press: Evanston).

Booth, W. (1993) *Households: On the Moral Architecture of the Household* (Cornell University Press: Ithaca).

Bourdieu, P. (1977) *Outline of a Theory of Practice* (Cambridge University Press).

—— (1984) *Distinction: A Social Critique of the Judgement of Taste* (Routledge: London).

Bowman, K. (2004) 'Democracy on the Brink: The First Figueras Presidency', in S. Palmer and I. Molina. (eds) *The Costa Rica Reader: History, Culture, Politics* (Duke University Press: Durham NC and London).

Bradley, I. and Howard, M. (eds) (1982) *Classical and Marxian Political Economy: Essays in Honour of Ronald L. Meek* (Macmillan: London).

Burdick, J. (1992) 'Rethinking the Study of Social Movements: The Case of Christian Base Communities in Urban Brazil', in A. Escobar and S. Alvarez (eds) *The Making of Movements in Latin America: Identity, Strategy and Democracy* (Westview Press: Boulder).

Calderón Guardia, R. (2004 [1942]) 'A Governor and a Man Faces the Social Problem', in S. Palmer and I. Molina. (eds) *The Costa Rica Reader: History, Culture, Politics* (Duke University Press: Durham NC and London).

Calo, M. and Wise, T. (2005) 'Revaluing Peasant Coffee Production: Organic and Fair-trade Markets in Mexico' (Global Development and Environment Institute: Tufts University, Medford).

Campbell, L. (2002) 'Conservation Narratives in Costa Rica: Conflict and Co-existence', *Development and Change* 33:29–56.

Cancian, F. (1972) *Change and Uncertainty in a Peasant Community: the Maya Corn Farmers of Zinacantan* (Stanford University Press: Stanford).

Cardoso, C. (1977) 'The Formation of the Coffee Estate in Nineteenth-Century Costa Rica', in K. Duncan. and I. Routledge (eds) *Land and Labour in Latin America* (Cambridge University Press).

Carrier, J. (1995) *Gifts and Commodities: Exchange and Western Capitalism since 1700* (Routledge: London).

Carrier, J. and Miller, D. (1999) 'From Private Virtue to Public Vice', in H. Moore (ed.) *Anthropological Theory Today* (Polity Press: Cambridge and Oxford).

Carriere, J. (1991) 'The Crisis in Costa Rica: An Ecological Perspective', in D. Goodman and M. Redclift (eds) *Environment and Development in Latin America: The Politics of Sustainability* (Manchester University Press).

Cazanga, J. (1987) *Las Cooperativas de Cafeculturas en Costa Rica* (Editorial Alma Mater: Universidad de Costa Rica, San José).

Cifuentes, L. (1997) 'The Option of Sustainable Organic Coffee Farming in Colombia', in R. Rice, A.M. Harris and J. McLean (eds) *Proceedings of the First Sustainable Coffee Conference* (Smithsonian Migratory Bird Center: Washington DC).

Cohen, A. (1985) 'Symbolism and Social Change: Matters of Life and Death in Whalsay, Shetland', *Man* 20:307–324.

Cohen, J. and Arato, A. (1992) *Civil Society and Political Theory* (MIT Press: Cambridge, Mass. and London).

Collier, A. (2001) *Christianity and Marxism: A Philosophical Guide to their Reconciliation* (Routledge: London).

Conford, P. (2001) *The Origins of the Organic Movement* (Floris Books: Edinburgh).

Conroy, M. (2001) 'Can Advocacy-Led Certification Systems Transform Global Corporate Practices? Evidence and Some Theory', Paper 21 (Natural Assets Project, PERI, University of Massachusetts: Amherst).

Coote, B. (1992) *The Trade Trap: Poverty and the Global Commodity Markets* (Oxfam Publications: York).

Crowley, J.E. (1974) *This Sheba, Self: The Conceptualization of Economic Life in 18th-century America* (Johns Hopkins University Press: Baltimore).

Cubero, G. (1998) *Modelo de Costos de Producción de Café* (Icafé: San José, Costa Rica).

Daviron, B. and Ponte, S. (2005) *The Coffee Paradox: Global Markets, Commodity Trade and the Elusive Promise of Development* (Zed Books: London and New York).

Davis, J. (1992) *Exchange* (Open University Press: Buckingham).

Deere, C.D. (1990) *Household and Class Relations: Peasants and Landlords in Northern Peru* (University of California Press: Berkeley).

de Vries, P. (1995) 'Squatters Becoming Beneficiaries: The Trajectory of an Integrated Rural Development Programme', *European Review of Latin American and Caribbean Studies* 58:45–70.

Dumont, L. (1977) *From Mandeville to Marx: The Genesis and Triumph of Economic Ideology* (University of Chicago Press: Chicago and London).

Durkheim, E. (1984 [1893]) *The Division of Labour in Society* (Macmillan: London).

Edelman, M. (1990) 'When They Took the "Muni": Political Culture and Anti-austerity Protest in Rural Northwestern Costa Rica', *American Ethnologist* Vol. 17, No. 4:736–757.

—— (1995), 'Rethinking the Hamburger Thesis: Deforestation and the Crisis of Central America's Beef Exports', in M. Painter and W. Durham (eds) *The Social Causes of Environmental Destruction in Latin America* (University of Michigan Press: Ann Arbor).

—— (1999) *Peasants Against Globalization: Rural Social Movements in Costa Rica* (Stanford University Press: Stanford).

El Cooperador (1998) 'Nuestro Movimiento Cooperativo Crece con Fuerza y se Diversifica', *Epoca* II, No. LVIII (October).

Escobar, A. (1995) *Encountering Development: The Making and Unmaking of the Third World* (Princeton University Press: Princeton).

Etzioni, A. (1993) *The Spirit of Community: Rights, Responsibilities, and the Communitarian Agenda* (Crown: New York).

Evans, S. (1999) *The Green Republic: A Conservation History of Costa Rica* (University of Texas Press: Austin).

Evers, H-D. (1994) 'The Trader's Dilemma: A Theory of the Social Transformation of Markets and Society', in H-D. Evers and H. Schrader (eds) *The Moral Economy of Trade: Ethnicity and Developing Markets* (Routledge: London and New York).

Fairhead, J. and Leach, M. (1997) 'Webs of Power and the Construction of Environmental Policy Problems: Forest Loss in Guinea', in R.D. Grillo and R.L. Stirrat (eds) *Discourses of Development: Anthropological Perspectives* (Berg: Oxford and New York).

Ferguson, J. (1990) *The Anti-politics Machine: Development, Depoliticization and Bureaucratic Power in Lesotho* (Cambridge University Press).

Fine, B. (1975) *Marx's 'Capital'* (Macmillan: London).

Fold, N. and Pritchard, W. (eds) (2004) *Cross-continental Food Chains* (Routledge: London and New York).

Foster, G. (1965) 'Peasant Society and the Image of the Limited Good', *American Anthropologist* 67:293–315.

Fox, R. and Starn, O. (1997) *Between Resistance and Revolution: Cultural Politics and Social Protest* (Rutgers University Press: New Brunswick and London).

Fraser, J. (2003) 'The Coffee Crisis and Fair Trade in Nicaragua: Practices of Livelihood and Survival in Rural Jinotega', unpublished MSc dissertation, Waningen University, the Netherlands.

Friedman, J. (1989) 'The Consumption of Modernity', *Culture and History* 4:117–130.

Friedmann, H. (1999) 'Remaking "Traditions": How We Eat, What We Eat and the Changing Political Economy of Food', in D. Brandt (ed.) *Women Working the NAFTA Food Chain: Women, Food and Globalization* (Second Story Press: Toronto).

Gell, A. (1992) 'Inter-tribal Commodity Barter and Reproductive Gift Exchange in Old Melanesia', in C. Humphries and S. Hugh-Jones. (eds) *Barter, Exchange and Value: An Anthropological Approach* (Cambridge University Press).

Gibson-Graham, J.K. (1996) *The End of Capitalism (As We Knew It): A Feminist Critique of Political Economy* (Blackwell: Oxford).

Giddens, A. (1979) *Central Problems in Social Theory: Action, Structure and Contradiction in Social Analysis* (Macmillan: London and Basingstoke).

—— (1990) *The Consequences of Modernity* (Polity Press: London).

—— (1996) 'Affluence, Poverty and the Idea of a Post-scarcity Society', *Development and Change* Vol. 27, No. 2:365–377.

Godelier, M. (1972) *Rationality and Irrationality in Economics* (Monthly Review Press: New York).

González Ortega, A. (1987) 'El Discurso Oficial de los Pequeños y Medianos Cafetaleros (1920–1940, 1950–1961)', *Revista de Historia* 16:161–191.

González, A. and Solís, M. (2004) 'Corruption', in S. Palmer and I. Molina (eds) *The Costa Rica Reader: History, Culture, Politics* (Duke University Press: Durham NC and London).

Graeber, D. (2001) *Toward an Anthropological Theory of Value: The False Coin of Our Own Dreams* (Palgrave: New York).

—— (2004) *Fragments of an Anarchist Anthropology* (Prickly Paradigm Press: Chicago).

—— (2005) 'Fetishism as Social Creativity: Or, Fetishes are Gods in the Process of Construction', *Anthropological Theory* Vol. 5, No.4:407–438.

Greenberg, R. (1997) 'Why Birds Like Traditionally Grown Coffee and Why You Should Care', in R. Rice, A.M. Harris and J. McLean (eds) *Proceedings of the First Sustainable Coffee Conference* (Smithsonian Migratory Bird Center: Washington DC).

Gresser, C. and Tickle, S. (2002) *Mugged: Poverty in Your Coffee Cup* (Oxfam UK).

Grillo, R.D. (1997) 'Discourses of Development: The View from Anthropology', in R.D. Grillo and R.L. Stirrat (eds) *Discourses of Development: Anthropological Perspectives* (Berg: Oxford).

Grimes, K. (2005) 'Changing the Rules of Trade with Global Partnerships: The Fair-trade Movement', in J.Nash (ed) *Social Movements: An Anthropological Reader* (Blackwell: Oxford).

Gudeman, S. (1978) *The Demise of a Rural Economy: From Subsistence to Capitalism in a Latin American Village* (Routledge: London).

—— (1986) *Economics as Culture: Models and Metaphors of Livelihood* (Routledge: London).

—— (2001) *The Anthropology of Economy: Community, Market and Culture* (Blackwell: Oxford).

Gudeman, S. and Rivera, A. (1990) *Conversations in Colombia: The Domestic Economy in Life and Text* (Cambridge University Press).

Gudmundson, L. (1983) 'Peasant Movements and the Transition to Agrarian Capitalism: Freeholding versus Hacienda Peasantries and Agrarian Reform in Guanacaste, Costa Rica, 1880–1935', *Peasant Studies* Vol. 3, No. 3:145–162.

—— (1995) 'Peasant, Farmer, Proletarian: Class Formation in a Smallholder Coffee Economy' in W. Roseberry, L. Gudmundson and M. Samper Kutschbach (eds) *Coffee, Society and Power in Latin America* (Johns Hopkins University Press: Baltimore).

Guthman, J. (2002) 'Commodified Meanings, Meaningful Commodities: Rethinking Production-Consumption Links through the Organic System of Provision', *Sociologia Ruralis* Vol. 42, No. 4:295–311.

—— (2004a) *Agrarian Dreams: The Paradox of Organic Farming in California* (University of California Press: Berkeley)

—— (2004b) 'The Trouble with "Organic Lite" in California: A Rejoinder to the Conventionalisation Debate', *Sociologia Ruralis* Vol. 44, No. 3:301–316.

Hall, C. (1991) *El Café y el Desarrollo Histórico-Geográfico de Costa Rica* (Editorial Costa Rica, San José).

Hann, C. (1996) 'Introduction: Political Society and Civil Anthropology', in C. Hann and E. Dunn (eds) *Civil Society: Challenging Western Models* (Routledge: London and New York).

Harris, O. (1984) 'Households as Natural Units', in K. Young, C. Wolkowitz and R. McCullogh, *Of Marriage and the Market: Women's Subordination Internationally and Its Lesson* (Routledge and Kegan Paul: London).

Harvey, D. (1989) *The Condition of Postmodernity: An Enquiry into the Origins of Cultural Change* (Blackwell: Oxford).

—— (1993) 'Class Relations, Social Justice and the Politics of Difference', in M. Keith and K. Pile (eds) *Place and the Politics of Identity* (Routledge: London).

—— (2001) *Spaces of Capital: Towards a Critical Geography* (Routledge: New York).

Hellman, J. (1992) 'The Study of Social Movements in Latin America and the Question of Autonomy', in A. Escobar and S. Alvarez (eds) *The Making of Social Movements in Latin America: Identity, Strategy and Democracy* (Westview Press: Boulder).

Hernández Castillo, R. and Nigh, R. (1998) 'Global Processes and Local Identity among Mayan Coffee Growers in Chiapas, Mexico', *American Anthropologist* Vol. 100, No. 1:136–147.

Hirsch, E. (2004) 'Environment and Economy', *Anthropological Theory* 4:435–453.

Hudson, I. and Hudson, M. (2003) 'Removing the Veil? Commodity Fetishism, Fair Trade and the Environment', *Organisation and Environment*, Vol. 16, No. 4:413–430.

Hughes, A. (2005) 'Responsible Retailers? Ethical Trade and the Strategic Re-regulation of Cross-continental Food Chains', in N. Fold and B. Pritchard (eds) *Cross-continental Food Chains* (Routledge: London and New York).

Hughes, A and Reimer, S. (2004) *Geographies of Commodity Chains* (Routledge: London and New York).

Ingold, T. (1993) 'The Temporality of the Landscape', *World Archeology* 25: 125–174.

—— (1992) 'Culture and the Perception of the Environment', in E. Croll and D. Parkin (eds) *Bush Base, Forest Farm: Culture, Environment and Development* (Routledge: London).

—— (2000) *The Perception of the Environment: Essays on Livelihood, Dwelling and Skill* (Routledge: London).

Jay, E. and Jay, R. (1986) *Critics of Capitalism: Victorian Reactions to Political Economy* (Cambridge University Press).

Jiménez, M. (1995) 'From Plantation to Cup: Coffee and Capitalism in the United States, 1830–1930', in W. Roseberry, L. Gudmundson and M. Samper

Kutschbach (eds) *Coffee, Society and Power in Latin America* (Johns Hopkins University Press: Baltimore).

Kahn, J. (1995) *Culture, Multiculture, Postculture* (Sage Publications: London, Thousand Oaks, New Delhi).

—— (1997) 'Demons, Commodities and the History of Anthropology', in J. Carrier (ed.) *Meanings of the Market: The Free Market in Western Culture* (Berg: Oxford and New York).

Kaplinsky, R. (2000) 'Spreading the Gains from Globalisation: What Can Be Learned from Value-chain Analysis?', *Journal of Development Studies* Vol. 37, No. 2:117–46.

Kearney, M. (1996) *Reconceptualizing the Peasantry: Anthropology in Global Perspective* (Westview Press: Boulder).

Kopytoff, I. (1986) 'The Cultural Biography of Things: Commoditisation as Process', in A. Appadurai (ed.) *The Social Life of Things: Commodities in Cultural Perspective* (Cambridge University Press).

Láscaris, C. (2004) 'In Defence of the Corner Store', in S. Palmer and I Molina (eds) *The Costa Rica Reader: History, Culture, Politics* (Duke University Press: Durham NC and London).

Latour, B. (1993) *We Have Never Been Modern* (Harvard University Press: Cambridge, Mass).

Lehmann, D. (ed) (1982) *Ecology and Exchange in the Andes* (Cambridge University Press).

Lewis, D. (1998) 'Non-governmental Organizations, Business and the Management of Ambiguity: Case Studies of "Fair Trade" from Nepal and Bangladesh', *Nonprofit Management and Leadership* Vol. 9, No. 2:135–151.

Lewis, D. and Mosse D. (eds) (2006a) *Development Brokers and Translators: The Ethnography of Aid and Agencies* (Kumarian Press: Bloomfield).

—— (2006b) 'Theoretical Approaches to Brokerage and Translation in Development', in D. Lewis and D. Mosse (eds) *Development Brokers and Translators: The Ethnography of Aid and Agencies* (Kumarian Press: Bloomfield).

Li, T. (1996) 'Images of Community: Discourse and Strategy in Property Relations', *Development and Change* 27:501–527.

—— (1999) 'Compromising Power: Development, Culture, and Rule in Indonesia', *Cultural Anthropology* Vol. 14, No. 3:295–322.

Lind, D. and Barham, E. (2004) 'The Social Life of the Tortilla: Food, Politics and Contested Commodification', *Agriculture and Human Values* 21:47–60.

Lowe, P., Marsden, T. and Whatmore, S. (1994) *Regulating Agriculture* (Fulton: London).

Luetchford, P. (2005) 'Economic Anthropology and Ethics' in J. Carrier (ed.) *A Handbook of Economic Anthropology* (Edward Elgar: Cheltenham).

—— (2006) 'Brokering Fair Trade: Relations Between Coffee Cooperatives and Fair-trade Organisations: A View from Costa Rica', in D. Lewis and D. Mosse (eds) *Development Brokers and Translators: The Ethnography of Aid and Agencies* (Kumarian Press: Bloomfield).

Lyon, S. (2006) 'Evaluating Fair-trade Consumption: Politics, Defetishisation and Producer Participation', *International Journal of Consumer Studies* 30:452–464.

Lyotard, J-F. (1984) *The Postmodern Condition: A Report on Knowledge* (Manchester University Press).

MacCormack, C. and Strathern, M. (eds) (1980) *Nature, Culture and Gender* (Cambridge University Press).

Mackintosh, M. (1984) 'Gender and Economics: The Sexual Division of Labour and the Subordination of Women', in K. Young, C. Wolkowitz and R. McCullagh (eds) *Of Marriage and the Market: Women's Subordination Internationally and Its Lessons* (Routledge and Kegan Paul: London).

Macnaghten, P. and Urry, J. (1998) *Contested Natures* (Sage: London).

Malinowski, B. (1922) *Argonauts of the Western Pacific: An Account of Native Enterprise and Adventure in the Archipelagoes of Melanesian New Guinea* (Routledge and Kegan Paul: London).

Martinez-Alier, J. (1983) 'Sharecropping: Some Illustrations' *Journal of Peasant Studies* 10 (nos. 2 and 3):94–106.

Martinez-Torres, E. (1997) 'Outlook on Ecological Coffee Farming: A New Production Alternative in Mexico', in R. Rice, A.M. Harris and J. McLean (eds) *Proceedings of the First Sustainable Coffee Conference* (Smithsonian Migratory Bird Centre: Washington DC).

Marx, K. (2000) *Selected Writings* (D. McLellan ed) (Oxford University Press).

Masís, G. (1989) 'Cooperativismo Agrario en Costa Rica', *Aportes* 11:20–22. (San José, Costa Rica).

Mauss, M. (2002) [1925] *The Gift: The Form and Reason for Exchange in Archaic Societies* (Routledge: London and New York).

May, R. (1993) *Tierra: Herencia ó Mercancia?* (Editorial DEI: San José, Costa Rica).

McMichael, P. (2000) 'The Power of Food', *Agriculture and Human Values* 17:21–33.

Meillassoux, C. (1981) *Maidens, Meal and Money: Capitalism and the Domestic Community* (Cambridge University Press).

Mendoza, R. and Bastiensen, J. (2003) 'Fair Trade and the Coffee Crisis in the Nicaraguan Segovias', *Small Enterprise Development* Vol. 14, No. 2:36–46.

Mesa Lago (2004) 'Social Development with Limited Resources', in S. Palmer and I. Molina (eds) *The Costa Rica Reader: History, Culture, Politics* (Duke University Press: Durham NC and London).

Miller, D. (1987) *Material Culture and Mass Consumption* (Blackwell: Oxford).

—— (1994) *Modernity, an Ethnographic Approach: Dualism and Mass Consumption in Trinidad* (Berg: Oxford).

—— (1995a) 'Introduction: Anthropology, Modernity and Consumption', in D. Miller (ed.) *Worlds Apart: Modernity through the Prism of the Local* (Routledge: London and New York).

—— (1995b) 'Consumption as the Vanguard of History: A Polemic by Way of an Introduction', in D. Miller (ed.) *Acknowledging Consumption: A Review of New Studies* (Routledge: London).

—— (1995c) 'Consumption Studies as the Transformation of Anthropology', in D. Miller (ed.) *Acknowledging Consumption: A Review of New Studies* (Routledge: London).

——(1995d) 'Consumption and Commodities' *Annual Review of Anthropology* 24:141–161.

—— (2001) 'Alienable Gifts and Inalienable Commodities', in F. Myers (ed.) *The Empire of Things: Regimes of Value and Material Culture* (James Currey: Oxford).

Miller, E. (1996) *A Holy Alliance? Church, Labour and the Communist Party in Costa Rica (1932–1948)* (M.E. Sharpe: New York).

Mills, M. (1997) 'Contesting the Margins of Modernity: Women, Migration, and Consumption in Thailand', *American Ethnologist* Vol. 24, No. 1:37–61.

Mintz, S. (1985) *Sweetness and Power: The Place of Sugar in Modern History* (Viking: New York).

—— (1996) *Tasting Food, Tasting Freedom: Excursions into Eating, Culture and the Past* (Beacon Press: Boston).

Moberg, M. and Striffler, S. (eds) (2003) *Banana Wars: Power, Production and History in the Americas* (Duke University Press: Durham NC and London).

Montero Zeledón, R. (1997) 'Environmentally Sound Production on a Large Scale', in R. Rice, A.M. Harris and J. McLean (eds) *Proceedings of the First Sustainable Coffee Conference* (Smithsonian Migratory Bird Center: Washington DC).

Moore, H. (1988) *Feminism and Anthropology* (Polity Press: Cambridge).

Murdoch, J. and Miele, M. (2004) 'Culinary Networks and Cultural Connections: A Conventions Perspective', in A. Hughes and S. Reimer, *Geographies of Commodity Chains* (Routledge: London and New York).

Murphy, J. (1993) *The Moral Economy of Labour: Aristotelian Themes in Economic Theory* (Yale University Press: New Haven).

Murray, D., Raynolds, L. and Leigh Taylor, P. (2003) *One Cup at a Time: Poverty Alleviation and Fair Trade in Latin America* (Fair Trade Research Group: Colorado State University).

Mutersbaugh, T. (2002) 'The Number is the Beast: A Political Economy of Organic-Coffee Certification and Producer Unionism' *Environment and Planning A* 34:1165–1184.

National Association of Coffee Producers (2004) [1922] 'Prospectus', in S. Palmer and I. Molina (eds) *The Costa Rica Reader: History, Culture, Politics* (Duke University Press: Durham NC and London).

Neilson, J. (2004) 'The Politics of Place: Geographical Identities along the Coffee Supply Chain from Toraja to Tokyo', in N. Fold and W. Pritchard (eds) *Cross-continental Food Chains* (Routledge: London and New York).

Nelson, J. (1989) 'Crisis Management, Economic Reform and Costa Rican Democracy', in B. Stallings and R. Kaufman (eds) *Debt and Democracy in Latin America* (Westview Press: Boulder).

—— (1990) 'The Politics of Adjustment in Small Democracies: Costa Rica, the Dominican Republic, Jamaica', in J. Nelson (ed) *Economic Crisis and Policy Choice: The Politics of Adjustment in the Third World* (Princeton University Press: Princeton).

Nozick, R. (1974) *Anarchy, State and Utopia* (Basic Books: New York).

Nygren, A. (1998) 'Environment as Discourse: Searching for Sustainable Development in Costa Rica', *Environmental Values* 7: 210–222.

Orozco, J. (1992) 'La Consultoría Agro-Económica: Un Proyecto de la Fes', in J. Martinez (ed.) *Siete Años ... por el Desarrollo Campesino* (Consultoría Agro-Económica: Cañas, Guanacaste, Costa Rica).

Ortiz, S. (1967) 'The Structure of Decision Making among the Indians of Colombia', in R. Firth (ed.) *Themes in Economic Anthropology* (Association of Social Anthropologists of the Commonwealth, 6: Tavistock, London).

—— (1973) *Uncertainties in Peasant Farming: A Colombian Case* (Athlone Press: London).

—— (1979) 'The Estimation of Work: Labour and Value among Paez Farmers', in S. Wallman (ed.) *Social Anthropology of Work* (Academic Press: London).

—— (1999) *Harvesting Coffee, Bargaining Wages: Rural Labour Markets in Colombia* (University of Michigan Press: Ann Arbor).

Ortner, S. (1974) 'Is Female to Male as Nature is to Culture?', in M. Rosaldo and L. Lamphere (eds) *Women, Culture and Society* (Stanford University Press: Stanford).

Paige, J. (1997) *Coffee and Power. Revolution and the Rise of Democracy in Central America* (Harvard University Press: Cambridge, Mass.).

Palmer, S. and Molina, I. (eds) (2004) *The Costa Rica Reader: History, Culture, Politics* (Duke University Press: Durham NC and London).

Palmer, S. and Rojas, G. (2004) 'Democrats and Feminists', in S. Palmer and I. Molina (eds) *The Costa Rica Reader: History, Culture, Politics* (Duke University Press: Durham NC and London).

Parry, J. (1986) 'The Gift, the Indian Gift, and the "Indian Gift"', *Man* 21:453–473.

—— (1989) 'On the Moral Perils of Exchange', in J. Parry and M. Bloch (eds) *Money and the Morality of Exchange* (Cambridge University Press).

Parry, J. and Bloch, M. (eds) (1989) *Money and the Morality of Exchange* (Cambridge University Press).

Pearse, R. (1983) 'Sharecropping: Towards a Marxist View', *Journal of Peasant Studies* 10 (nos 2 and 3):42–70.

Peet, R. and Watts, M. (1996a) 'Liberation Ecology: Development, Sustainability and Environment in an Age of Market Triumphalism', in R. Peet and M. Watts (eds) *Liberation Ecologies: Environment, Development and Social Movements* (Routledge: London and New York).

—— (1996b) 'Conclusion: Towards a Theory of Liberation Ecology', in R. Peet and M. Watts (eds) *Liberation Ecologies: Environment, Development and Social Movements* (Routledge: London and New York).

Pelupessy, W. (1993) *El Mercado Mundial del Café* (Editorial DEI: San José, Costa Rica).

Pelzer White, C. (1986) 'Everyday Resistance, Socialist Revolution and Rural Development: the Vietnamese Case', in J. Scott and B. Tria Kerkvliet (eds) *Everyday Forms of Peasant Resistance in Southeast Asia* (Frank Cass: London).

Pendergrast, M. (1999) *Uncommon Grounds: The History of Coffee and How it Transformed the World* (Basic Books: New York).

Pérez Brignoli, H. (1994) 'Economía Política del Café en Costa Rica (1850–1950)', in H. Pérez Brignoli and M. Samper (eds) *Tierra, Café y Sociedad* (Flacso: Costa Rica).

Pérez Brignoli, H. and Samper, M. (eds) (1994) *Tierra, Café y Sociedad* (Flacso: Costa Rica).

Perfecto, I. (1997) 'Loss of Insect Diversity in a Changing Agroecosystem: The Case of Coffee Technification', in R. Rice, A.M. Harris and J. McLean (eds) *Proceedings of the First Sustainable Coffee Conference* (Smithsonian Migratory Bird Center: Washington DC).

Peters, G. (1994) 'Empresarios e Historia del Café en Costa Rica, 1930–1950', in H. Pérez Brignoli and M. Samper (eds) *Tierra, Café y Sociedad* (Flacso: Costa Rica).

Peters, G. and M. Samper (2001) *Café de Costa Rica: Un Viaje a lo Largo de su Historia* (Icafé: San José, Costa Rica).

Polanyi, K. (1944) *The Great Transformation* (Farrar & Rinehart: New York).

Poster, M. (ed.) (1988) *Jean Baudrillard: Selected Writings* (Polity Press: Cambridge).

Pratt, J. (1994) *The Rationality of Rural Life: Economic and Cultural Change in Tuscany* (Harwood Academic Press: Chur, Switzerland).

—— (2003) *Class, Nation and Identity: The Anthropology of Political Movements* (Pluto Press: London).

—— (2006), 'Food: The Local and the Authentic', unpublished ms, University of Sussex.

Preston, P. (1994) 'The Political Economy of Trade', in H-D. Evers and H. Schrader (eds) *The Moral Economy of Trade. Ethnicity and Developing Markets* (Routledge: London and New York).

Rawls, J. (1971) *A Theory of Justice* (Harvard University Press: Cambridge, Mass).

Raynolds, L. (2002) 'Producer Consumer Links in Fair-trade Coffee Networks', *Sociologia Ruralis* Vol. 42, No. 4:404–424.

—— (2003) 'The Global Banana Trade', in S. Striffler and M. Moberg (eds) *Banana Wars: Power, Production and History in the Americas* (Duke University Press: Durham NC and London).

Redfield, R and Villa Rojas, A. (1964) *Chan Kom: A Maya Village* (University of Chicago Press).

Renard, M-C. (1999) 'The Interstices of Globalisation: The Example of Fair-trade Coffee', *Sociologia Ruralis* Vol. 39, No. 4:484–500.

—— (2003) 'Fair Trade: Quality, Market and Conventions', *Journal of Rural Studies* 19:87–96.

Rerum Novarum (1960) [1891] *The Workers' Charter: Encyclical Letter of Pope Leo XIII* (Catholic Truth Society: London).

Rice, R., Harris, A.M. and McLean, J. (eds) (1997) *Proceedings of the First Sustainable Coffee Conference* (Smithsonian Migratory Bird Center: Washington DC).

Rodríguez, C. (1993) *Tierra de Labriegos: Los Campesinos en Costa Rica desde 1950* (Flacso: Costa Rica).

Ronchi, L. (2002) 'The Impact of Fair Trade on Producers and their Organisations: A Case Study with Coocafé in Costa Rica', *PRUS Working Paper* No. 11 (University of Sussex).

Roseberry, W. (1989) *Anthropologies and Histories* (Rutgers University Press: New Brunswick).

—— (1995) 'Introduction', in W. Roseberry, L.Gudmundson and M. Samper Kutschbach (eds), *Coffee, Society and Power in Latin America* (Johns Hopkins University Press: Baltimore).

—— (1996) 'The Rise of Yuppie Coffees and the Reimagination of Class in the United States', *American Anthropologist* Vol. 98 No. 4:762–775.

Roseberry, W., Gudmundson, L. and Samper Kutschbach, M. (eds) (1995) *Coffee, Society and Power in Latin America* (Johns Hopkins University Press: Baltimore).

Rosene, C. (1990) 'Modernisation and Rural Development in Costa Rica: A Critical Perspective', *Canadian Journal of Development Studies* Vol. XI, No. 2: 367–374.

Rovira Mas, J. (2004) 'The Crisis: 1980–1982', in S. Palmer and I. Molina. (eds) *The Costa Rica Reader: History, Culture, Politics* (Duke University Press: Durham NC and London).

Sahlins, M. (1974) *Stone Age Economics* (Tavistock Publications: London).

—— (1976) *Culture and Practical Reason* (University of Chicago Press: London and Chicago).

Samper, M. (1990) *Generations of Settlers: Rural Households and Markets on the Costa Rican Frontier, 1850–1935* (Westview Press: Boulder, San Francisco, Oxford).

Samper Kutschbach, M. (1995) 'In Difficult Times: Colombian and Costa Rican Coffee Growers from Prosperity to Crisis, 1920–1936', in W. Roseberry, L. Gudmundson and M. Samper Kutschbach (eds) *Coffee, Society and Power in Latin America* (Johns Hopkins University Press: Baltimore).

de Sardan, O. (2005) *Anthropology and Development: Understanding Contemporary Social Change* (Zed Books: London)

Scott, J. (1976) *The Moral Economy of the Peasant: Rebellion and Subsistence in Southeast Asia* (Yale University Press: New Haven).

—— (1985) *Weapons of the Weak: Everyday Forms of Peasant Resistance* (Yale University Press: New Haven).

—— (1992) *Domination and the Arts of Resistance: Hidden Transcripts* (Yale University Press: London and New Haven).

Seligson, M. (1980) *Peasants of Costa Rica and the Development of Agrarian Capitalism* (University of Wisconsin Press: Madison).

Sick, D. (1999) *Farmers of the Golden Bean: Costa Rican Households and the Global Coffee Economy* (North Illinois University Press: DeKalb).

Sklair, L. (1995) 'Social Movements and Global Capitalism', *Sociology* Vol. 29, No. 3:495–512.

Slater, D. (1997) *Consumer Culture and Modernity* (Polity Press: Cambridge).

Stewart, S. (2005) 'Remembering the Senses', in D. Howes (ed.) *Empire of the Senses: The Sensual Culture Reader* (Berg: Oxford and New York).

Stirrat, R. (1989) 'Money, Men and Women', in J. Parry and M. Bloch (eds) *Money and the Morality of Exchange* (Cambridge University Press).

Stirrat, R.L. and Henkel, H. (1997) 'The Development Gift: The Problem of Reciprocity in the NGO World', *Annals of the American Academy of Political and Social Science* 554:66–80.

Stolcke, V. (1995) 'The Labors of Coffee in Latin America: The Hidden Charm of Family Labor and Self-Provisioning', in W. Roseberry, L. Gudmundson and M. Samper Kutschbach (eds) *Coffee, Society and Power in Latin America* (Johns Hopkins University Press: Baltimore).

Stone, P., Haugerud A. and Little, P. (2000) 'Commodities and Globalisation: Anthropological Perspectives', in A. Haugerud, P. Stone and P. Little (eds) *Commodities and Globalisation: Anthropological Perspectives* (Rowman and Littlefield: Lanham MD).

Strathern, M. (1992) *After Nature: English Kinship in the Late Twentieth Century* (Cambridge University Press).

Tallontire, A. (2000) 'Partnerships in Fair Trade: Reflections from a Case Study of Cafédirect', *Development and Practice* Vol. 10, No. 2:166–177.

Taussig, M. (1980) *The Devil and Commodity Fetishism in South America* (University of North Carolina Press: Chapel Hill).

—— (1982) 'Peasant Economics and the Development of Capitalist Agriculture in the Cauca Valley, Colombia', in J. Harriss (ed.) *Rural Development: Theories of Peasant Economy and Agrarian Change* (Hutchinson: London).

Tawney, R.H. (1938) [1926] *Religion and the Rise of Capitalism* (Penguin Books: West Drayton).

Thompson, B. (1999) 'Lessons for Fair Trade', *Small Enterprise Development* Vol. 10, No. 4:56–60.

Thompson, E.P. (1980) *The Making of the English Working Class* (Penguin Books: Harmondsworth).

Toledo, V. and Moguel, P. (1997) 'Searching for Sustainable Coffee in Mexico: The Importance of Biological and Cultural Diversity', in R. Rice, A.M. Harris and J. McLean (eds) *Proceedings of the First Sustainable Coffee Conference* (Smithsonian Migratory Bird Center: Washington DC).

Tully, J. (1993) *An Approach to Political Philosophy: Locke in Context* (Cambridge University Press).

Turton, A. (1986) 'Patrolling the Middle Ground: Methodological Perspectives on Everyday Peasant Resistance', in J. Scott and B. Tria Kerkvliet (eds) *Everyday Forms of Peasant Resistance in Southeast Asia* (Frank Cass: London).

Veblen, T. (1994) [1899] *The Theory of the Leisure Class* (Dover Publications: New York).

Villasuso, J. (1987) 'Costa Rica: Crisis, Adjustment Policies and Rural Development', *CEPAL Review* No. 33, December (United Nations: Santiago, Chile).

Vunderink, G. (1990) 'Peasant Participation and Mobilisation during Economic Crisis: The Case of Costa Rica', *Studies in Comparative Economic Development* Vol. 25, No. 4:3–34.

Walsh, D. (1993) 'The Role of Ideology in Cultural Reproduction', in C. Jenks (ed.) *Cultural Reproduction* (Routledge: London).

Weiner, A. (1992) *Inalienable Possession: The Paradox of Keeping While Giving* (University of California Press: Berkeley).

Whatmore, S. and Thorne L. (1997) 'Nourishing Networks: Alternative Geographies of Food', in M. Watts and D. Goodman (eds) *Globalising Food: Agrarian Questions and Global Restructuring* (Routledge: London and New York).

Wilk, R. (1996) *Economies and Cultures* (Westview Press: Boulder).

Williams, P. (1989) *The Catholic Church and Politics in Nicaragua and Costa Rica* (Macmillan: Basingstoke).

Williams, R. (1988) *Keywords: A Vocabulary of Culture and Society* (Fontana Press: London).

Williams, R.G. (1994) *States and Social Evolution: Coffee and the Rise of National Governments in Central America* (University of North Carolina Press: Chapel Hill).

Wilson, R. (1995) *Maya Resurgence in Guatemala: Q'eqchi' Experiences* (University of Oklahoma Press: Norman).

—— (1997) 'Human Rights, Culture and Context: An Introduction' in R. Wilson (ed.) *Human Rights, Culture and Context: Anthropological Perspectives* (Pluto Press: London).

Winson, A. (1989) *Coffee and Democracy in Modern Costa Rica* (Macmillan Press: Basingstoke).

Wolf, E. (1957) 'Closed Corporate Peasant Communities in Mesoamerica and Central Java', *Southwestern Journal of Anthropology* Vol. 13, No. 1:1–18.

—— (1969) *Peasant Wars of the Twentieth Century* (Harper & Row: New York).

Yang, M. (2000) 'Putting Global Capitalism in Its Place', *Current Anthropology* 41:477–509.

Yapa, L. (1996) 'Improved Seeds and Constructed Scarcity' in R. Peet. and M. Watts (eds) *Liberation Ecologies: Environment, Development and Social Movements* (Routledge: London and New York).

Young, M. and Wilmott, P. (1962) *Family and Kinship in East London* (Penguin Books: Harmondsworth).

Zimbalist, A. (1988) 'Costa Rica', in E. Paus (ed.) *Struggle Against Dependence: Non-traditional Export Growth in Central America and the Caribbean* (Westview Press: Boulder).

INDEX

Compiled by Sue Carlton